COUNTRY TOYS AND CHILDREN'S FURNITURE

COUNTRY TOYS AND CHILDREN'S FURNITURE

Antique Designs with Complete Plans and Instructions

KEN FOLK

STACKPOLE
BOOKS

Published by
STACKPOLE BOOKS
5067 Ritter Road
Mechanicsburg, PA 17055

Printed in the United States of America

10 9 8 7 6 5 4 3 2 1

FIRST EDITION

Cover design by Tina Marie Hill
Cover photograph by Douglas J. Nicotera
Rag doll in cover photograph by Eugenia French
Interior photographs and designs by Ken Folk
Eagle & Flag decal on page 139 used with permission of Decorcal Inc.

Although every effort has been made to design the items in this book for safety, the author and publisher disclaim any and all liability for the safety and design of the various items as ultimately crafted and built.

Library of Congress Cataloging-in-Publication Data

Folk, Ken.
  Country toys and children's furniture : antique designs with complete plans and instructions / Ken Folk.—1st ed.
    p.   cm.
  ISBN 0-8117-2428-X
  1. Wooden toy making—United States—History. 2. Children's furniture—United States—History. 3. Wooden toys—United States—History. I. Title.
TT174.5.W6F65   1996
684.104'083—dc20   96-12880
                                                 CIP

Contents

EARLY AMERICAN TOYS
FOR THE WOODWORKER

Although evidence of toys can be found in ancient civilizations, they were scarce and for the most part limited to affluent families. In colonial America the Puritan lifestyle was difficult and everyone had to contribute to the survival of the family, which left little time for child's play. By age six children were expected to do meaningful work, and by age twelve boys were fully employed or entered into an apprenticeship for a trade. But even with these demands on their lives, children still found time to play and had toys, no matter how crude.

The country roared into the nineteenth century with Yankee ingenuity in one hand and a desire for a better life in the other. Entrepreneurship flourished, and out of it came the industrial revolution and a new age of prosperity. Seemingly overnight, new and less expensive goods became available for the average home. And as the wealth of the family grew, parents were willing to share their good fortune with their children by buying them more toys. By the 1850s this new demand quickly pushed the toy business from a cottage industry to an industrial giant. Toy inventors quickly seized the opportunity and created a wide variety of new toys, conceived not only to amuse but also to educate, exercise, and fortify the values of the period. Doll furniture, rock-ing horses, wagons and games of all description were offered by hundreds of manufacturers across the country. By the turn of the twentieth century these businesses would grow into a $20 million industry.

Early American craftsman relied on wood for their products because it was strong, easy to work with, abundant, and inexpensive. It was used to make kitchenware, farm implements, horse-drawn vehicles, and yes, toys. This period offers the contemporary woodworker a bountiful source of project ideas for children's furniture and toys. The projects in this book are very close representations of choice eighteenth-, nineteenth-, and early twentieth-century pieces. Drawings accompanying many of the projects illustrate simplified joinery for those interested in achieving the look of the piece within a reasonable amount of time, and for the traditionalist, the original joinery is always included.

Occasionally a toy comes along that has the ability to challenge participants so intensely that they become ardent players for life. Projects in this book like Diabolo, Marble Solitaire, and Nine Men's Morris are examples of "classic" games that have entertained children and adults alike for centuries and will no doubt continue to do so for many more.

This book offers just a sampling of the treasures from this era.

Tools and Techniques, Past and Present

In woodworking, learning a new (or old) technique can improve the quality of your work or open the door to a project you felt was beyond your reach. Exciting new methods and tools are being introduced every year. One of the most rewarding resources lies within the crafts of our forefathers. Early tradesmen created elegant products using simple hand tools and techniques that are as useful today as they were in the eighteenth and nineteenth centuries. To cover this subject properly would take a book in itself, but this chapter gives the basics that you'll need to construct the projects that follow.

Buying Materials

The most expensive part of a project is almost always the lumber, so it's important to understand the terms of what's being sold and to know how to calculate what you'll need. All of the projects have a bill of materials that lists just what you need to complete the project and a stock plan that gives the actual size of the surfaced boards and illustrates the most efficient way to use the lumber. With this chore out of the way, you can concentrate on picking the best quality lumber for the dollar.

Board Feet. Most supply sources, except home-improvement centers, price their lumber by the board foot (BF), which is a board 12 inches square by 1 inch thick. This unit of measurement is very useful for estimating the cost of projects. When doing the calculations, the rough-sawn dimensions are always used, and any board thickness less than 1 inch is calculated as 1 inch. The term "rough-sawn means the size of the board as it's cut from the log and prior to surface planing. Lumber is always

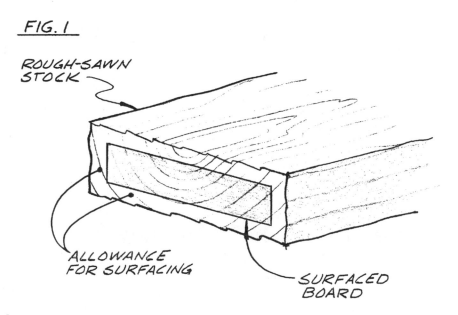

FIG. 1

ROUGH-SAWN STOCK

ALLOWANCE FOR SURFACING

SURFACED BOARD

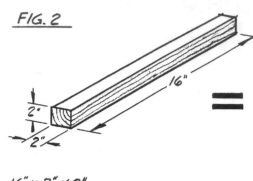

FIG. 2

16″ × 2″ × 2″ / 144 = .44 BD. FT.

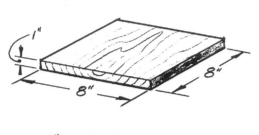

8″ × 8″ × 1″ / 144 = .44 BD. FT.

advertised in its rough dimensions even though it's been surfaced; a 1-by-12 inch pine board, for example, will actually be ¾ by 11¼ inches.

Boards can be converted into board feet by applying the following formula:

$$\frac{\text{length (in.)} \times \text{width (in.)} \times \text{thickness (in.)}}{144} = \frac{\text{board}}{\text{feet}}$$

Using this formula, it's clear that the two pieces illustrated have the same number of board feet.

Before you head to the lumberyard, get out the stock plan for your project and determine the number of board feet for each board and the total. Be sure to add material for the rough-sawn dimensions. With this information at your fingertips, you can quickly determine the project cost for different woods, grades, and sources.

Lumber Grades and Sizing of Hardwood. The safest way to buy lumber is to pick the boards yourself. But you may find it handy to understand some of the basic terms if you plan to buy mail-order stock or discuss a dealer's stock over the phone. For hardwoods, such as oak, cherry, or maple, the best quality, or grade, is first, followed by second, select, then #1 common. Firsts and seconds are usually combined and referred to as FAS. This grade is almost free of defects and is a good choice if you plan to buy only what's needed for the project. If you don't mind stocking leftover material, overorder on the select grade to get a lower price, and make your cuts around the defects.

Hardwood lumber is generally sold in random lengths and widths. Lumber standards, however, specify a minimum board width of 6 inches for the FAS grade and 4 inches for select. The standard lengths are 4 through 16 feet. This means if you're buying 50 BF of random stock, the dealer can fill your order with any combination of board sizes within these limits. You can request specific board sizes, but there will be an extra charge. Random widths and lengths can be an advantage, because the variety increases the chances of finding the exact size board you need for your project.

Another nebulous practice is the use of quarters of an inch to specify the thickness of rough-sawn lumber. For example, a 1¼-inch-thick board is called "five-quarter" (⁵⁄₄). Lumber dealers sell their hardwood rough or planed to your specifications at extra cost. If the dealer offers presurfaced boards, it's customary to "surface two sides" (S2S) and let the edges rough. If boards are available "surfaced four sides" (S4S), the width will be ⅜ inch less than the rough dimension. The following chart shows the minimum standard thicknesses for hardwoods:

	Thickness	
Rough		*Surfaced*
(⁴⁄₄) 1 inch		¹³⁄₁₆ inch
(⁵⁄₄) 1¼		1¹⁄₁₆
(⁶⁄₄) 1½		1⁵⁄₁₆
(⁷⁄₄) 1¾		1½
(⁸⁄₄) 2		1¾

Softwood. Softwoods, such as pine or spruce are popular for many projects because of their workability and low cost. Most of the softwoods sold are surfaced four sides (S4S) and are graded as "appearance category" construction lumber. The following chart shows the minimum standard dimensions for softwoods (note the variance from hardwoods):

Thickness

Rough	Surfaced
(⁴⁄₄) 1 inch	¾ inch
(⁵⁄₄) 1¼	1
(⁶⁄₄) 1½	1¼
(⁸⁄₄) 2	1½

Width

Rough	Surfaced
4 inches	3½ inches
6	5½
8	7¼
10	9¼
12	11¼

Have a tape measure handy when buying surfaced lumber because dimensions can vary. If you end up with a board that's ¹⁄₆₄ inch too heavy in your project, it can take a lot of unnecessary time to correct.

Sources of Materials. One of the most readily available suppliers of materials is the home-improvement centers that seem to be springing up everywhere. If your project requires a softwood, you'll probably be able to find what you want. Hardwoods are a different matter. Oak and poplar are sometimes available in limited sizes, but walnut and cherry would be a rare find. Count on the stock at these places being surfaced with pricing by the board.

Traditional lumberyards can be the best places to shop. They are almost always staffed with knowledgeable people who can help you with a variety of woodworking questions. The types of wood available can vary from a few of the basic hardwoods to dozens of varieties including the exotics. Perhaps the lumberyard's greatest value is being able to provide the specific sizes on your stock list and surface the boards to your requirements. If you have a specific concern such as grain direction, ask if you can help pick your boards from the pile.

Sometimes the best lumber deals are in the classified sections of woodworking magazines and local newspapers. The sources behind these ads vary from specialty lumber supply houses to a farmer who has taken a fallen tree to the sawmill. If the seller is a full-time business, his stock is probably kiln dried (KD), which is a rapid way of seasoning wood under controlled conditions. But beware of the local one-time deal—the wood was probably air dried, and that's okay only if it was done properly. Check for flatness, dirt, and stains, all of which should run up the red flag or dramatically reduce the price. Finally, if the boards are in the rough, you need to have a source and price for surfacing. With all of this said, some of my best buys have been through the local classifieds.

DRAWING YOUR PATTERNS

Many projects have irregular-shaped parts that have to be transferred onto the stock. These parts could be laid out directly on the boards, but it's more convenient to make patterns that can be moved around for the best position and then traced. Drawing the parts on your stock is the first step of any project. We're all anxious to see the sawdust fly, but up-front planning can save wasted stock later.

My favorite method for making patterns is to start with a thin sheet (about ¹⁄₆₄ inch thick) of poster board. It can be cut easily with a scissors, but it's stiff enough to trace. I buy the 22-by-28-inch size for a mere 50 cents apiece at arts and crafts or stationery stores.

Each irregularly shaped part in this book has a grid overlay for enlargement. Begin by finding the grid size on your plans. Mark off the grid points along all four edges of the poster board and draw the lines with a straight yardstick as shown in Figure 4. Using Figure 3 as an example, identify the grid lines on the plans and poster board with letters

FIG. 3

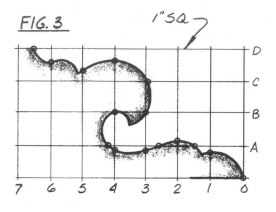

1" SQ.

FIG. 4

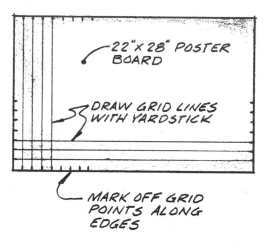

22" x 28" POSTER BOARD

DRAW GRID LINES WITH YARDSTICK

MARK OFF GRID POINTS ALONG EDGES

and numbers to aid in keeping track for the next step. This is particularly helpful when going back and forth from plan to pattern on large parts. Now, starting with the plans, estimate where the part outline intersects with each grid line and duplicate these locations with dots on the poster board grid. Lightly sketch in the part using the dots as a guide, then use a french curve to put a smooth edge on your sketch. (An inexpensive french curve can be found in the drafting section of an office-supply store.)

Enlarging plans on a photocopier can be a simple alternative to the grid system. Many of the parts requiring patterns will fit on 11-by-17-inch paper, and for those that don't, copy in sections and tape together. You may have to go through a number of trial copies before you get the enlargement correct. Check the dimensions in both directions before running the final copy.

HAND TOOLS AND SHARPENING

Many operations can be done just as well with hand tools as with power tools, and in some cases better. The square mortise, the blind dovetail, and the cabriole leg all are easily done with basic hand tools but would require specialized power equipment.

When you buy a hand tool, shop for quality and be prepared to pay a premium for it. Good hand tools are a delight to use and, if properly cared for, will last for generations. Many of the favorites in my tool chest are more than 150 years old. Antique-tool dealers are a source to consider for good hand tools at reasonable prices. Some have hundreds of hand tools that were used by coopers, joiners, carpenters, and cabinetmakers. Share your interests with the dealer and have him show you his better pieces. Any tool you buy should be sound and free of serious rust on the cutting edge.

The key to top performance on cutting-edge hand tools is keeping them sharp. Unfortunately, most new tools like planes, chisels, spokeshaves, and drawknives are sold with their edges ground but not honed to the required sharpness. Consequently, many buyers become frustrated with the performance of their new purchase and abandon it as a bad investment. Dull tools, new or old, require you to exert an excessive amount of force to do the work, resulting in unnecessary fatigue. Also, control of the tool becomes difficult and increases the chance of injury. How sharp is sharp enough? If your cutter or chisel can shave some hair from your arm, you're there. If sliding a razor edge next to your arteries makes you a little uncomfortable, try cutting a thin shaving on the end grain of a pine board without pulling the grain. Whichever test you choose, if your tools don't pass, they are wasting your energy.

The Perfect Edge. A good sharpening setup is the cornerstone of any size shop. At minimum it should consist of a bench grinder with a 6-inch, 80-grit, white aluminum-oxide wheel; an 8-inch-long, coarse-fine combination India benchstone; a 6-inch-long, hard white Arkansas benchstone; and a leather strop, either a flat piece of leather or a leather wheel charged with polishing compound.

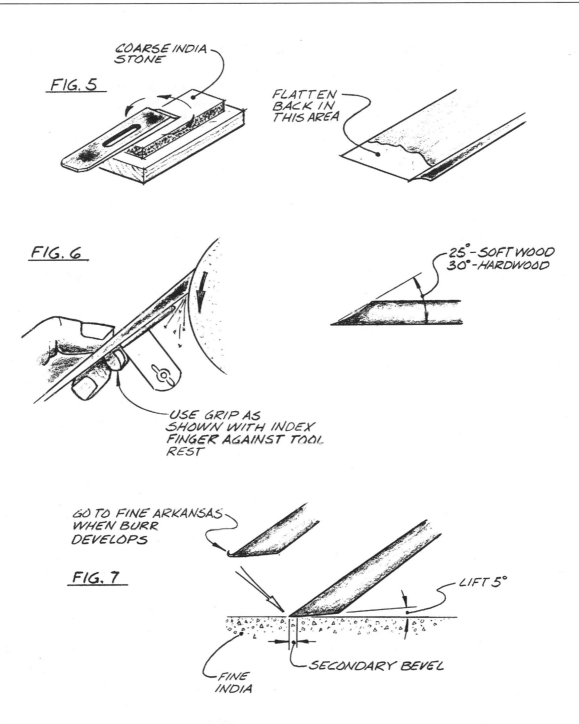

FIG. 5

COARSE INDIA STONE

FLATTEN BACK IN THIS AREA

FIG. 6

USE GRIP AS SHOWN WITH INDEX FINGER AGAINST TOOL REST

25°-SOFT WOOD
30°-HARDWOOD

GO TO FINE ARKANSAS WHEN BURR DEVELOPS

FIG. 7

LIFT 5°

SECONDARY BEVEL

FINE INDIA

There are four steps to sharpening a plane iron or chisel for the first time:

Step 1. The back of a blade needs to be perfectly flat so that it can be honed later without missing any spots along the cutting edge. Start with the coarse side of the India stone, and make circular passes with the blade using three-in-one oil for lubrication. The oil flushes away metal particles and prevents the stone from glazing. Never use the stones dry. Look at the back of the blade and observe where the cutting action is taking place. You want to eliminate all of the high and low spots for about ¼ inch behind the cutting edge.

Step 2. With the back side of the cutting surface flat, the basic cutting angle can be applied on the bench grinder. Use an angle of 25 degrees for softwoods and 30 degrees for hardwoods. I found that the best way to grind these angles is with a freehand technique that uses the tool rest as a guide only. Once I get the angle of the blade to the wheel correct, I grip the blade with my index finger against the tool rest for reference. As long as I maintain my hand position on the blade, I can lift the tool away from the grinder to check the cutting angle and go back again without losing my position. When grinding, the hardness can be drawn from the edge by overheating. This problem can be avoided by keeping the blade moving, using light force, and dipping the edge in water after each pass. This process takes some practice, but once mastered, it can be done in a few minutes.

Step 3. To hone the blade, start on the fine side of the India stone. Give it some oil and place the bevel side of the blade on the surface. Raise the blade about 5 degrees and stroke it back and forth about five times. Raising the blade causes the cutting action to be concentrated at the tip of the bevel to form a very small second bevel. This speeds up the sharpening because very little metal needs to be removed. When a burr develops on the back side of the cutting edge, move to the Arkansas stone and sharpen at the same 5-degree angle until all the scratches are removed from the bevel. Staying with the Arkansas, turn the blade over and stroke it flat against the stone to remove the burr. If some of the burr bends to the other side, alternate honing from bevel to back until the burr is gone. If you have trouble holding the 5-degree angle by hand, you may want to consider buying a honing guide. These devices work well but they require time to set up.

Step 4. Pull the bevel and the back over the strop three or four times to attain the final edge. (The strop is simply an 8- to 12-inch long piece of leather that is charged with a polishing compound like emery, tripoli, or jeweler's rouge.) Give your blade one of the tests, and if it doesn't pass, go back to the Arkansas stone in step 3.

This may seem like a lot of work, but flattening is done only once, and the cutting edge can be honed dozens of times before regrinding is necessary. And

once the razor edge is established, maintaining it is easy.

When a blade begins to dull, all that's required is honing to bring the edge back. Of course, each time the edge is honed, the second bevel gets a little bigger and the honing time gets longer, until it becomes more efficient to regrind.

ROUTERS AND ROUTER TABLES

The router has always been a versatile tool, and coupled with one of the latest router table designs, the capabilities are tremendous. This setup will mold, dovetail, mortise, groove, dado, and do biscuit joinery. Best of all, it's quick to set up and easy to use.

What makes the new systems so handy? The router is attached to a subplate, which drops into a close fitting rabbeted hole in the tabletop. The router is held in place by its own weight so that it can be quickly removed to change cutters or to use the router for another purpose. I have two routers each mounted on identical subplates. This arrangement is great for hopping back and forth on two cutting operations such as complex moldings or rails and stiles.

The plunge router style is best for table mounting because its vertical adjustment allows the motor to be quickly dropped for changing cutters. If you're buying a router, consider one with a 3-horsepower motor and a ¼- and ½-inch collet. Many of the new cutters, such as the raised panel and multiform shapes, have a 3-horsepower minimum requirement. When buying cutters, if you have a choice between ¼- and ½-inch shanks, go with the ½-inch, which has less vibration and gives a smoother cut.

The router table can be made in your shop or purchased from one of the woodworking-supply companies offering kits, parts, and complete units. I made mine from a ¾-by-24-by-20-inch piece of plywood covered with plastic laminate for the top and a ¼-by-8-by-10-inch piece of phenolic for the router subplate. My shop is short on space so I put short runners on the bottom of the table for clamping in a portable Workmate bench. That way, when

FIG. 8

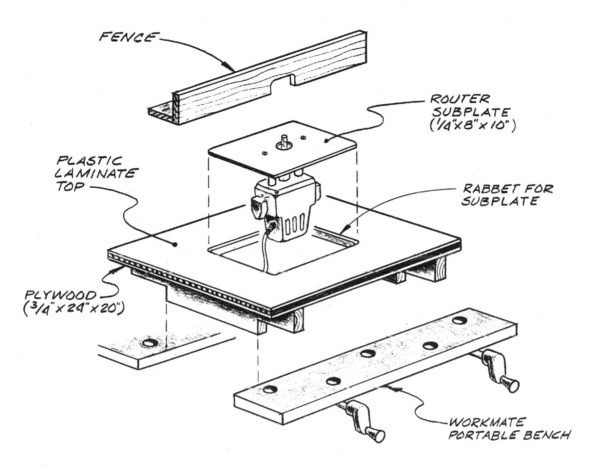

FENCE

ROUTER
SUBPLATE
(1/4"x8"x10")

PLASTIC
LAMINATE
TOP

RABBET FOR
SUBPLATE

PLYWOOD
(3/4"x24"x20")

WORKMATE
PORTABLE BENCH

it's not in use, I can fold up the workbench and hang the table on the wall.

JOINERY WITH BISCUITS

In years past, if a furniture designer wanted to simplify the construction of a dado or mortise joint, dowel pins were usually the answer. Dowels have two major drawbacks, however. First, the holes must be drilled very accurately using jigs. Second, the effective gluing area is small because two sides of the dowel are usually contacting end grain, which makes a poor bonding surface. These two problems are solved with biscuit joinery.

Biscuits are football-shaped splines made from solid beech with the grain running at a diagonal to their length. They are compressed slightly in thickness to provide a loose fit in the mating slots. This allows the joint to slip together freely with some lateral movement for final alignment. As the biscuit absorbs the moisture from the glue, it swells to create a tight fit. Since the sides of the biscuit are flat, the effective area for gluing is much larger than with a dowel. A biscuit can't compare to the through mortise for strength, but it's a good substitute for quick assembly.

There are two methods for cutting the slots. A router with a 5/32-inch slot cutter will do the job. If the parts to be joined are small, a router table would be better for control. A disadvantage with this method is that the slot must be close to the edge of a board because of the limited distance from the cutter to the router base. Another method is to cut

FIG. 9

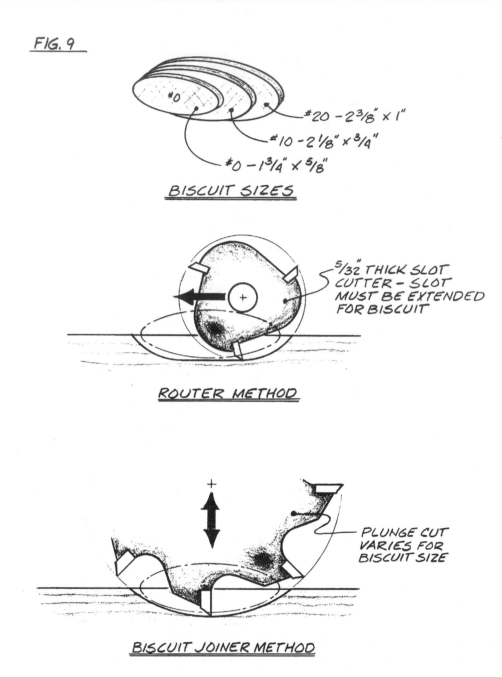

#0

#20 – 2³⁄₈" × 1"
#10 – 2¹⁄₈" × ³⁄₄"
#0 – 1³⁄₄" × ⁵⁄₈"

BISCUIT SIZES

⁵⁄₃₂" THICK SLOT
CUTTER – SLOT
MUST BE EXTENDED
FOR BISCUIT

ROUTER METHOD

PLUNGE CUT
VARIES FOR
BISCUIT SIZE

BISCUIT JOINER METHOD

the slots with a hand-held biscuit joiner. This tool has a 4-inch circular blade that is plunged into the stock. Adjustable guides are provided to cut slots anywhere on the stock, including mitered corners. These tools are easy to use and give excellent results. Currently there are about ten manufacturers offering hand-held biscuit cutters, with a starting price of about $130 (see Sources).

WOOD SCREWS: APPLYING THEM THE RIGHT WAY

Many of us have been in a hurry to complete a project. It comes down to driving a couple of screws, and we decide to take a chance—skip the pilot holes and hope for the best. We're already late, so of course the inevitable happens—the wood splits or the screw head breaks off. This scenario is all too common because drilling pilot holes takes time—three steps in all, for the anchor, shank clearance, and countersink or plug recess.

Many of the screw problems that arise can be attributed to incorrect pilot holes. To get the maximum holding force for a specific screw size, the anchor hole in softwoods should be about 70 percent of the root diameter of the threads, and in hardwoods about 90 percent as in the following chart:

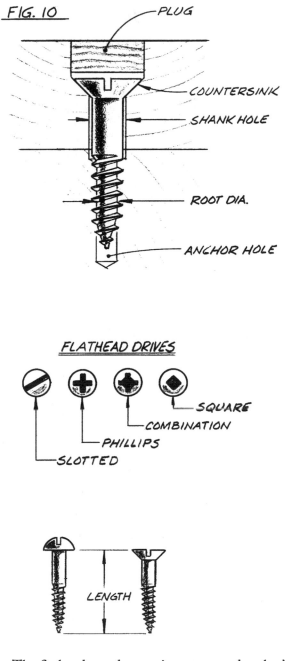

FIG. 10

		Anchor Hole	
Screw size	Shank hole	Softwoods	Hardwoods
#4	$7/64$ inch	$3/64$ inch	$1/16$ inch
#6	$9/64$	$1/16$	$5/64$
#8	$11/64$	$5/64$	$3/32$
#10	$3/16$	$3/32$	$7/64$
#12	$7/32$	$7/64$	$1/8$

The pilot holes and countersink can be drilled individually or in combination. The individual method cuts down on the number of tools lying around, and you can drill any combination. There are several different pilot-drill combination tools that do the hole and countersink in one step. The simplest type is a flat steel bit that is shaped for a specific screw size. This is the least expensive but it lacks adjustability. Another type uses a drill bit with a movable sleeve, that cuts the shank hole and countersink. Each screw size requires a drill bit and sleeve but it's worth it when time counts (see Sources).

In addition to correct size pilot holes, a screw's holding force is determined by wood hardness, grain direction, screw size, and depth. With a softwood, a screw will have to be longer or larger to get the same holding force as in a hardwood. Also, the holding force is about 25 percent less for screws in end grain, so again, you need to compensate by increasing the screw length or size.

If the screws are hard to install, try lubricating the threads with a little soap or wax. This will have little effect on the holding force, and if you're driving the screws with a portable drill, you'll appreciate the extra battery life.

The flathead wood screw is every woodworker's standby. And when it comes to picking the drive for it, my vote goes to the square socket. It tracks straight with the screw gun and the driver bit refuses to cam out of the socket. Its only disadvantage is the special drive bit required, but this has been solved by the combination head that accepts a Phillips or square drive (see Sources).

One oddity with wood screws is how the length

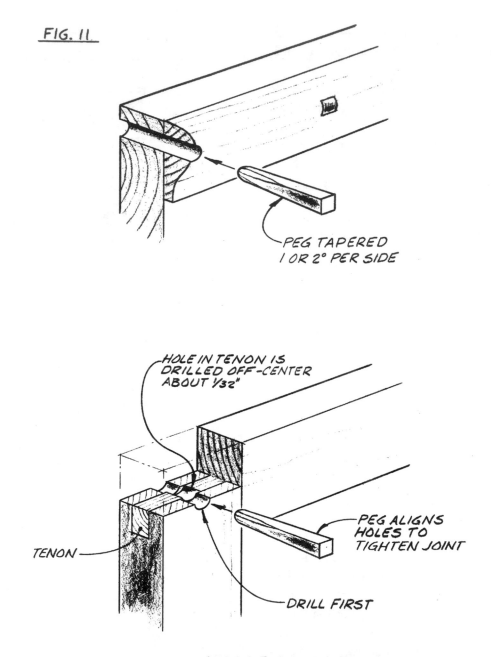

FIG. 11

PEG TAPERED
1 OR 2° PER SIDE

HOLE IN TENON IS
DRILLED OFF-CENTER
ABOUT 1/32"

TENON

PEG ALIGNS
HOLES TO
TIGHTEN JOINT

DRILL FIRST

MORTISE AND TENON JOINT

is specified. Roundhead screws are measured from the underside of the head to the tip, and flatheads by the overall length.

JOINING WITH PEGS
Modern technology has provided us with adhesives that create a bond rivaling the strength of the wood itself. This has simplified furniture construction by making interlocking joints less important. Early American craftsmen, however, had to rely on joinery techniques for the structural integrity of their work.

Joinery pegs played a key role in the construction of early American furniture. Metal fasteners, such as screws and nails, were used sparingly because of their expense; instead, pegs were employed in many creative ways. Many early Pennsylvania German pieces—some of which appear in this book—relied entirely on joinery and pegs for construction.

In some communities joinery pegs were called "tree nails," and for a very good reason. They were used in place of nails to attach moldings and trim boards to furniture carcasses. Unlike modern wooden dowels, pegs were usually square with 1 to 2 degrees of taper on each side and a round nose for starting. As this type of peg is driven into a hole, the slight taper and sharp corners create a very tight fit, and the large end of the peg constantly forces the parts together as it's driven home. I have never encountered precise rules for the shape of the peg or the size of the pilot hole. This isn't surprising, because the hardness of the furniture wood has to be considered. Here are some general guidelines:

1. The pegs can range in size from ⅛ to ½ inch square. Pick a size that is 'in scale' for the parts to be joined.

2. Experiment with the pilot hole size and peg shape using scrap pieces of the same woods as the final piece. Create a tight clamping force, but not so much that splitting occurs in the parts.

3. When working with softwoods such as pine, make the pegs from a harder wood such as birch or maple.

4. With very hard woods such as oak or hard maple, soften the edges of the peg to help it fill the hole better.

5. Make the pegs extralong so that they can be sawn just above flush with the part. You can give your project an authentic look by letting the pegs protrude about ¹⁄₆₄ inch above the part. That way, even if the piece is painted. a shadow of the peg can be seen.

Joinery pegs were also commonly used to draw a mortise and tenon joints tight. First, the peg hole was drilled in the part with the mortise. The joint was assembled and, using the hole just drilled, the tenon hole was located. Now, the tenon member is disassembled and its hole drilled off the mark about ¹⁄₃₂ inch so that the joint will be tightened when the peg is installed. This technique was used to great advantage in making window sashes in colonial buildings. The pegs were allowed to protrude slightly so that they could be tapped out for easy disassembly when making repairs.

STEAM-BENDING WOOD

One of the most intimidating facets of woodworking is the ancient craft of steam-bending wood. It needn't be, however—all you need is a simple steamer, a bending form, the right wood, and a basic understanding of the principals of bending. Several projects in this book require steam-bent parts, and once you've done one, you'll be hooked on the process.

Why bending? When wood is bent, the grain follows the shape of the part, making very strong, lightweight structures possible. Also, this process allows several parts to be combined into one flowing piece to eliminate joints. Canoes, snowshoes, Windsor chairs, and sleighs are just a few traditional wooden products in which this technique is used.

The Right Wood. The first—and most important—step in making bentwood parts is selecting the right material. Although all woods can be bent to some degree, porous-grained woods such as oak, hickory, and ash are preferable because their grain structure reacts most favorably to the steaming operation. The grain in the bending stock must be as straight as possible. Any flaws in the grain, knots, or other surface imperfections can start a fracture during bending. The best stock for bending is green or air-dried wood. Many times perfectly good bending stock can be obtained from firewood dealers. If you can cut or have access to small logs, rive it to rough dimensions and then surface it to size. You can use the stock right away because the steaming process will remove the sap from the wood. Kiln-dried wood is the last choice, but it's possible to bend it with a little extra effort. Give the stock a leisurely soak in water for a couple of days before steaming, and double the time in the steamer. There will also be a higher possibility of breakage during bending

FIG. 12

ONLY STRAIGHT-
GRAINED PART IS
USABLE

SAPWOOD
IS BEST

AVOID WILD
GRAIN

AVOID
PITH

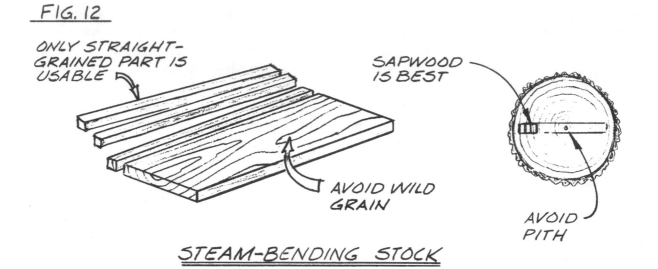

STEAM-BENDING STOCK

than with air-dried stock, so you may want to throw an extra piece in the steamer as a backup.

The Steaming Process. When certain woods are exposed to steam, the wood fibers are sufficiently softened to allow them to move in relation to each other, or become 'plastic'. During bending, the fibers on the outside of the stock are stretched considerably and if not sufficiently softened will pull apart. The fibers on the inside of the bend are being compressed and again if not sufficiently softened will fail by forming compression wrinkles. When bending the stock around the form, using a steady pulling motion allows the wood fibers to slip against each other and minimize these failures.

The amount of time required for steaming is determined by the type of wood, moisture content, thickness, and the efficiency of the steam chamber. If green or air dried stock is used, about one hour per inch of thickness is sufficient. For kiln-dried stock, soak the parts in water for two days and then steam for two hours per inch of thickness. When the stock is sufficiently steamed, remove a piece and test-bend by hand. A ¼-inch-thick strip, which is typical for many of the projects in this book, should bend with very little resistance. Always wear gloves when handling the parts, because at this point they're scalding hot. Once you remove the stock from the steamer, you have fifteen to thirty seconds to bend

and clamp the stock on the form. This means that everything has to be organized—clamps gapped correctly, clamp blocks handy, and bending form mounted. For the first time around, it's a good idea to use an assistant to work the clamps while you bend the stock.

An Inexpensive Steamer. Building an elaborate steamer is an unnecessary burden if you're going to need it for only one or two projects. A simple, inexpensive arrangement can be made in about an hour using a heat source such as an electric hot plate, a cooking pot, and a piece of plastic pipe. My system uses a 1000-watt electric hot plate, which is adequate for steaming small parts. A large propane burner (especially the type plumbers use) will also work. The objective is to have an adequate heat source that will develop a strong head of steam. The more steam there is, the less time the parts have to spend in the steamer.

For a water container, I use a 4-quart cooking pot that is 9 inches in diameter and 5 inches high. This size is adequate for the maximum size of bentwood parts used for the projects in this book, which is about ⅜ inch thick by 60 inches long. If you have a larger heating source, your pot can be bigger; otherwise, stay close to this capacity. The pot can be any type of material, but choose one that can be given up permanently, because a residue develops on the inside that's almost impossible to remove.

The steam chamber is made from schedule 80 PVC plastic pipe, which is suited for high temperatures and can be purchased at a plumbing-supply house. Don't be tempted to use the white schedule 40 pipe found at home-improvement centers. It's rated for low temperatures and will soften and bend when it's subjected to steam. I know—I used it in my first steamer. The base of the pipe has a plywood collar and disk that simply sits on top of the pot. This arrangement is very convenient but it's a little top-heavy, so be careful not to tip it over when loading and unloading parts from the chamber.

I start up my steamer with a full 4-quarts of water and in about fifteen minutes I have a full head of steam. The vertical pipe makes an efficient steam chamber, but it's difficult to unload the parts. To solve this problem, I tie a string onto the end of the stock so that it can be easily retrieved. When running the steamer, always cover the top of the pipe to contain the steam and heat inside the chamber.

How to Make a Spoked Wheel
The most distinctive part of the nineteenth-century children's wagons and carriages are the spoked wheels. At first glance they may appear complex, but they can be made with simple hand tools and

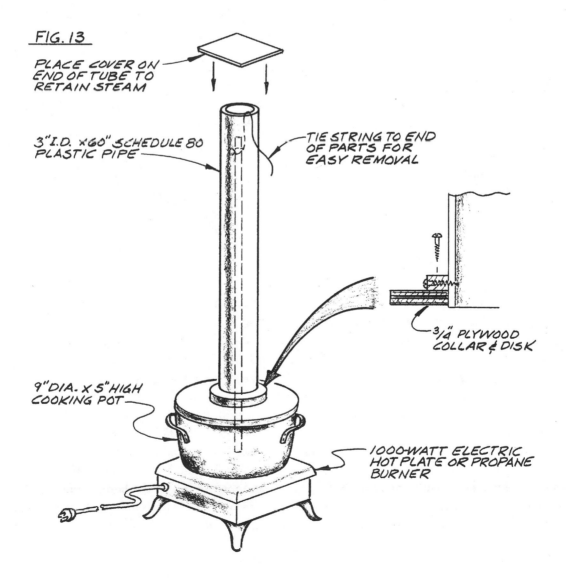

FIG. 13

PLACE COVER ON END OF TUBE TO RETAIN STEAM

3" I.D. x 60" SCHEDULE 80 PLASTIC PIPE

TIE STRING TO END OF PARTS FOR EASY REMOVAL

3/4" PLYWOOD COLLAR & DISK

9" DIA. x 5" HIGH COOKING POT

1000-WATT ELECTRIC HOT PLATE OR PROPANE BURNER

FIG. 14

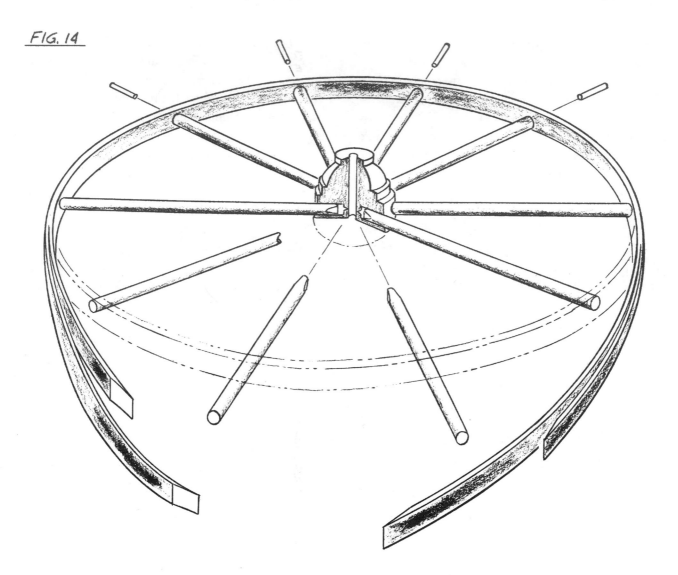

straightforward joinery. The key is in having a good assembly jig that holds all the parts in their correct locations. The following steps describe the sequence of assembly:

Step 1. Making the jig. The jig serves three functions. First, it's a form for steam-bending and gluing up the rim pieces. Second, it's an aid in drilling the spoke holes in the hub. And finally, it holds the rim, spokes, and hub in alignment for gluing up and doweling the spokes.

On a piece of good quality, ¾-inch plywood, lay out the center point, spoke lines, and outside diameter using the dimensions on the project drawings.

Make the lines sharp and clearly visible because they will be used throughout the assembly. Lay out the holes for the clamps on the spoke lines and drill with a 1-inch bit. Finish up cutting out the jig, and add a block for mounting in the vise.

Step 2. Making the rims. All of the wheels for the projects in this book have rims made from two layers of stock. This technique makes the rim stock easier to bend and provides a strong rim splice. The rims are made by first steam-bending the strips, and then gluing up the laminations.

When steam-bending the rim pieces, it's much easier to do one strip at a time for each form. Thus

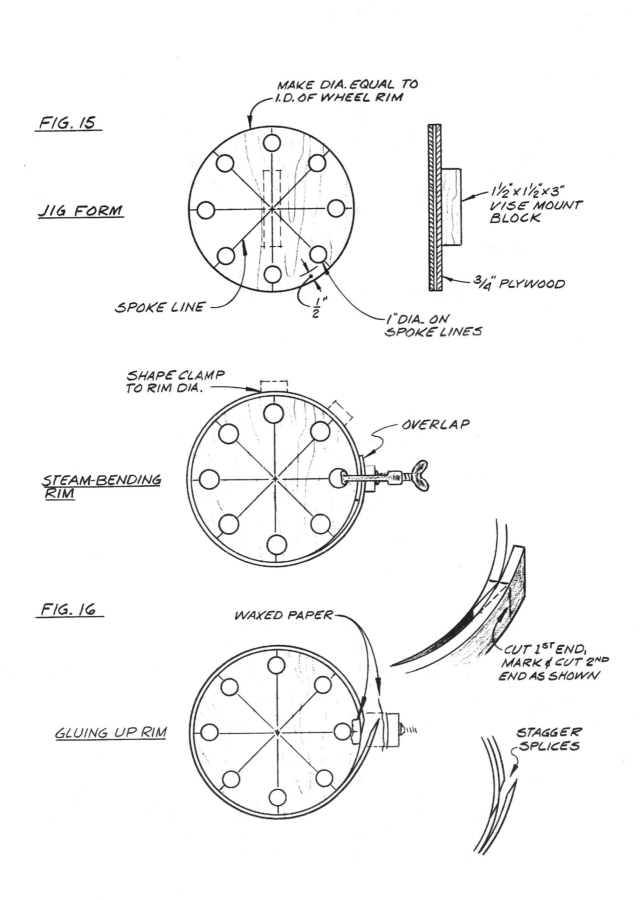

FIG. 15

JIG FORM

MAKE DIA. EQUAL TO
I.D. OF WHEEL RIM

1½" X 1½" X 3"
VISE MOUNT
BLOCK

¾" PLYWOOD

SPOKE LINE

½"

1" DIA. ON
SPOKE LINES

SHAPE CLAMP
TO RIM DIA.

OVERLAP

STEAM-BENDING
RIM

FIG. 16

WAXED PAPER

CUT 1ST END,
MARK & CUT 2ND
END AS SHOWN

GLUING UP RIM

STAGGER
SPLICES

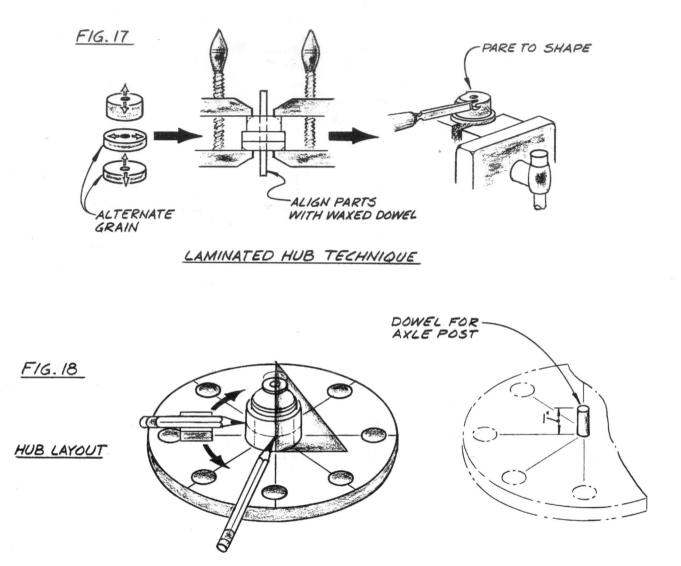

FIG. 17

PARE TO SHAPE

ALTERNATE GRAIN

ALIGN PARTS WITH WAXED DOWEL

LAMINATED HUB TECHNIQUE

DOWEL FOR AXLE POST

FIG. 18

HUB LAYOUT

if there are two wheel sizes, it will take four steaming sessions to do all of the pieces. You can move on to other parts of the project and come back to bending when the forms are free. The steamed pieces can be removed from the forms after about a day of drying. After removing, pull the ends of the strip together and apply a small clamp to prevent excessive spring-back.

The rim laminations are glued up one layer at a time. Cut the bevel on one end of the strip, and then clamp up with the jig. Mark the position of the bevel on the second end and cut it a little on the long side of the line. Now chisel the splice to get

the final fit. Before gluing up the strip, cover the contacting surfaces of the clamp block and jig with waxed paper, and tape in place. After gluing, check the contour of the joint and smooth out with a file if necessary. The second layer of the rim is applied with the same procedure as the first. Finish up by marking the position of each spoke on the side and face of the rim.

Step 3. Making the hubs. There are two ways to make the hubs. If you have a lathe, the hubs should be a routine task. If not, you can get the same results with a little extra effort. Start by dividing the hub into two or three layers so that the mating surfaces coincide with the steps on the hub, as illustrated. Glue and clamp the layers using a dowel for alignment. To prevent the glue from sticking to the dowel, rub candle wax on the dowel prior to assembly. If you alternate the grain direction for each layer, these hubs will be stronger than turned ones. Round the edges of the hubs with a sharp chisel and finish off with a file.

Next, install the axle post. Glue a 1½-inch-long wooden dowel in place, checking for square from several sides. When dry, place the hub on the post and transfer the spoke lines from the jig to the hub. Mark the vertical position of the spokes using the dimension specified in the project drawings.

The spoke holes have to be drilled accurately so that they intersect properly in the center of the hub. The best way to do this drilling operation is right on the jig using a spade with a long shaft bit and a guide block. Keep the bit in the same place and rotate the hub from position to position. Make the guide block out of a good hardwood like oak or hard maple—it has to last for up to forty holes. Measure

the shaft on the bit and make the hole in the guide block ¹⁄₆₄ inch larger. Mark the center of the drill on the guide block and align with one of the spoke lines to assure that the drill will be heading for the center of the hub. To hold the hub securely in place during drilling, position a clamp bar between the spoke lines and mount with two ¼-inch carriage bolts with wing nuts for fast operation. Before you start drilling, mark the hole depth required on the drill shank using a piece of tape next to the guide block.

Step 4. Putting it together. The jig will really pay off on this last step. Before beginning the assembly, make four rim support blocks and attach them to the jig. Use ¾-by-2-inch long oak to take the wear and tear of assembly. The key feature on the blocks is the rim support notch, which can be calculated from the dimensions on the project drawings. Glue and screw the blocks in position between the spoke lines as shown in the illustration. Finish off the support blocks by making the clamp plates that will hold the rim in place.

FIG. 19

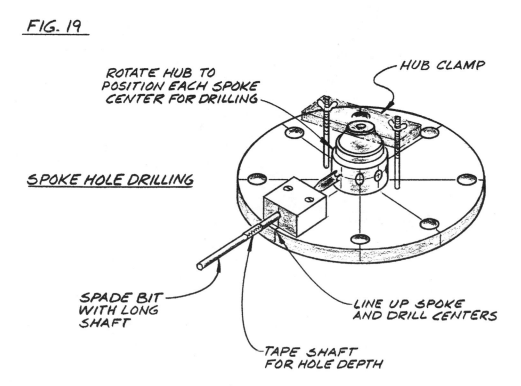

ROTATE HUB TO POSITION EACH SPOKE CENTER FOR DRILLING

HUB CLAMP

SPOKE HOLE DRILLING

SPADE BIT WITH LONG SHAFT

LINE UP SPOKE AND DRILL CENTERS

TAPE SHAFT FOR HOLE DEPTH

FIG. 20

WHEEL ASSEMBLY

SPOKE

"UP" ALIGNMENT
MARK

BEVEL TO CLEAR
ADJACENT SPOKES

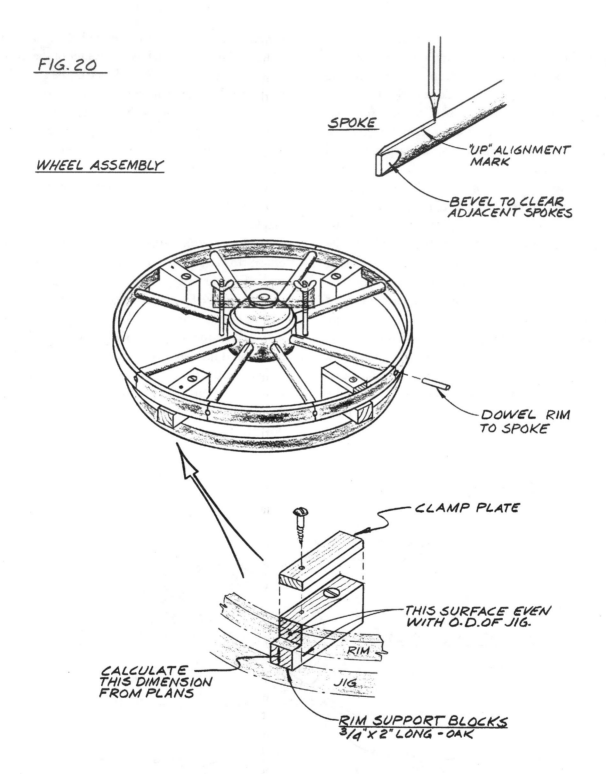

DOWEL RIM
TO SPOKE

CLAMP PLATE

THIS SURFACE EVEN
WITH O.D. OF JIG.

RIM

CALCULATE
THIS DIMENSION
FROM PLANS

JIG

RIM SUPPORT BLOCKS
³/₄" X 2" LONG - OAK

Begin the assembly by lining up the spoke marks on the rim with the spoke lines on the jig, and then clamp the rim in place. Next, cut the spokes to length and make a line on one end to represent "up" for assembly purposes. Using this line for reference, bevel each side of the spoke end to provide clearance at the center of the hub. Insert the spokes into the hub with the "up" lines on top, and test-fit the assembly on the jig . If the spokes seem too long, check the alignment of the "up" line to the hub. If the spokes are still too long, increase the bevel. If the alignment looks okay, remove the spoke assembly for gluing. I like to use a slow-curing glue like G-2 epoxy because of the number of parts that have to be assembled. Glue up the spokes in the hub and place the assembly back onto the jig.

Align the spoke lines on the hub and jig, then secure the hub with the clamp bar. Finish up the assembly by drilling and doweling each spoke to the rim.

DECORATING YOUR PROJECTS

Whether the finish is painted or natural, you can add a touch of class to your projects with some pinstriping and a little filigree. You can do this type of decorating with sign film or by hand painting.

Sign Film. A popular alternative to hand painting for commercial advertising on signs and vehicles is vinyl sign film. This material is sold by the foot and is available in more than two dozen colors. It can be easily cut with scissors or a craft knife and is applied by peeling off a paper backing to expose an adhesive. The film is only 2 to 3 mils thick—about the thickness of a hair—and when it's applied it's difficult to tell the difference from paint. And best of all, it's made for outdoor use, so it's perfect for a wagon or sled project. Two good brands of sign film are Flexcon and 3M Controltac, available from Dick Blick Art Supplies, telephone (800) 447-8192 for orders and (800) 933-2542 for product information.

Hand Painting. Unfortunately, most of us avoid painting stripes and designs because, we say, we're not artists or we don't have a steady hand. Yet painting these details requires not talent—just the right equipment, proper paint consistency, and good technique. Once you've decided to give it a try, the battle is half won.

To get started, you'll need a pair of striping brushes. The first is a #0 or #1 squirrel-hair sword striper. These unusual-looking brushes have short handles and 2-inch-long bristles shaped like a sword when dry. This shape has several advantages. The brush can hold a lot of paint for making long stripes. The bristles taper to a sharp point when wet with paint, and the brush can paint a very straight line because its long bristles are being pulled over the surface at a low angle. Using the tip of the bristles and a high brush angle will create a narrow stripe, and a low handle angle will give a wide stripe. To get a consistent width line, hold the brush as illustrated and support your hand with the tip of your little finger and ring finger on the surface being painted. Maintaining this hand position and angle, drag the brush along the surface. If you need distinct start and stop points, use a piece of cellophane tape at each end.

A second brush that's worth having is the square end highliner. The bristles are straight and have a square tip, so the brush paints a single line width for its diameter. The beginning of a stripe can be painted square because of the square tip on the brush. These brushes are very handy for stripes less than a foot long.

If the area to be striped doesn't allow you to slide your hand freely across its surface, a maulstick may be the answer. You can purchase this tool at an art-supply store or make one from a 3/8-by-24-inch dowel with a 1-inch-diameter cork fishing float glued onto one end. The maulstick provides support for the brush hand when working over top of wet artwork. To use it, hold the stick at the end without the ball and position it over the artwork. The brush hand rests on the stick for detail work or slides along it to do striping. I use the maulstick most of the time because it steadies the hand and gives me better control of the brush.

FIG. 21

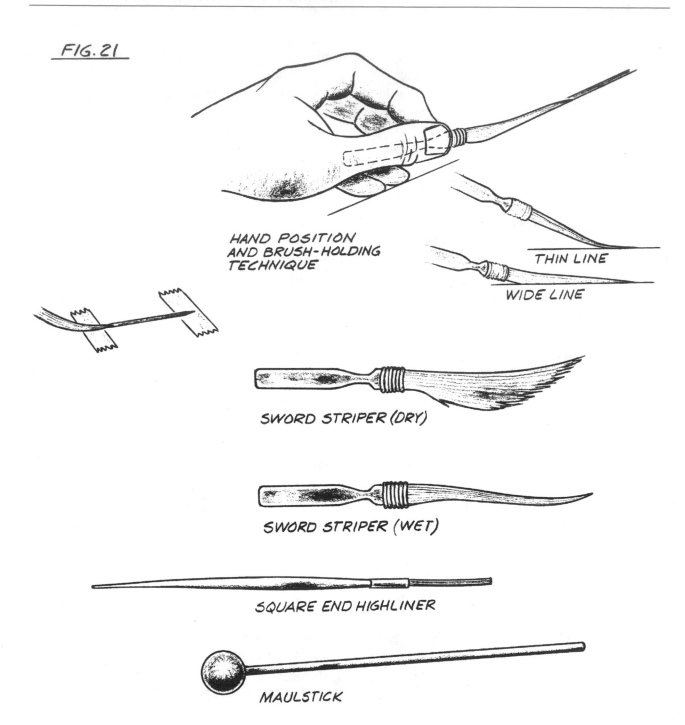

HAND POSITION
AND BRUSH-HOLDING
TECHNIQUE

THIN LINE

WIDE LINE

SWORD STRIPER (DRY)

SWORD STRIPER (WET)

SQUARE END HIGHLINER

MAULSTICK

The final factors in painting good stripes are getting the paint consistency right and practicing. Before attempting to paint the detail on my projects, I first practice on a sheet of thin white poster board. I thin the paint to something less than what I think is needed, and then I try a couple of stripes with each type of brush. If the edge of the stripe is irregular, the paint isn't flowing well enough because it's too thick. If the edge of the stripe is straight but watery, it's too thin. I keep experimenting with the thinner until I get a sharp edge. When the paint is right, I spend about fifteen minutes making stripes and experimenting with the brushes on the poster board before working on my project.

PROJECTS

THE ACROBAT

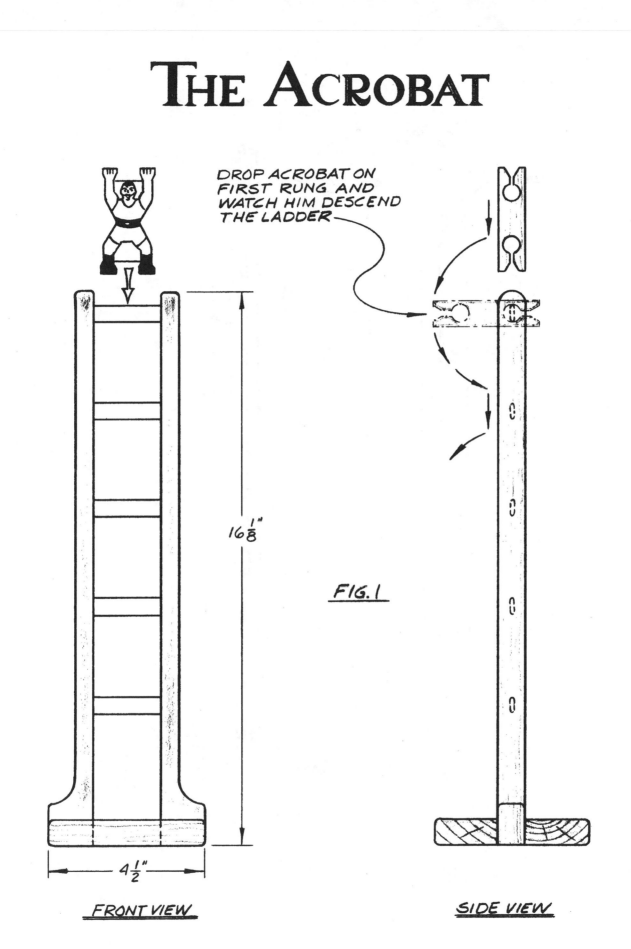

DROP ACROBAT ON
FIRST RUNG AND
WATCH HIM DESCEND
THE LADDER

$16\frac{1}{8}$"

FIG. 1

$4\frac{1}{2}$"

FRONT VIEW

SIDE VIEW

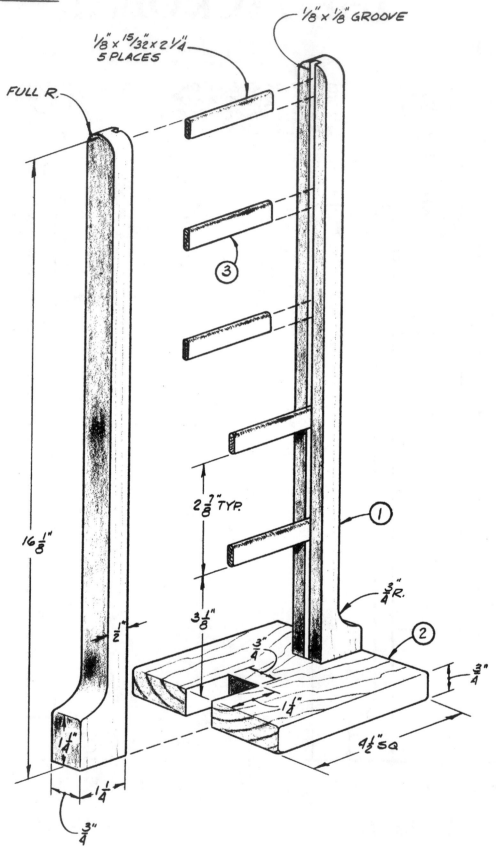

FIG. 2

1/8" x 15/32" x 2 1/4"
5 PLACES

1/8" x 1/8" GROOVE

FULL R.

③

16 1/8"

2 7/8" TYP.

①

3 1/4"

3/4" R.

1/2"

3/4"

3/16"

②

1 1/4"

1 1/4"

4 1/2" SQ

3/4"

1 1/4"

3/4"

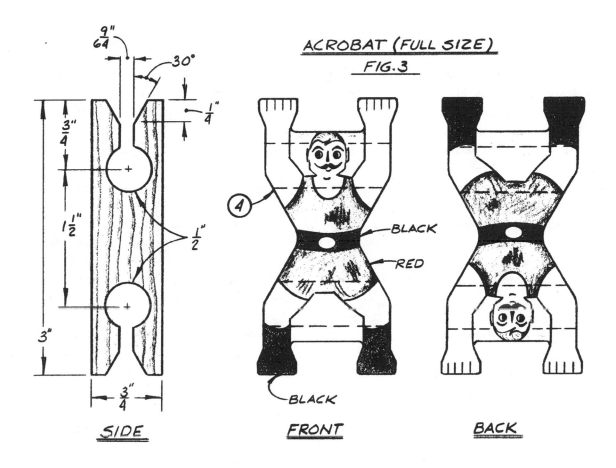

ACROBAT (FULL SIZE)
FIG. 3

SIDE

FRONT

BACK

BILL OF MATERIALS

Stock (inches)	Quantity	Item	Part
¾ × 4½ × 24 hard maple	1	①	ladder sides (two)
		②	ladder base (one)
		③	acrobat (one)
⅛ × ¹⁵/₃₂ × 12 hard maple	1	④	rungs (five)

27

THE ACROBAT

The Acrobat is a classic toy that never fails to amuse young children. Just drop the acrobat on the first rung and watch him climb down the ladder. Simple, yet very entertaining.

How does it work? The acrobat has a keyhole-shaped opening at each end. The straight part of the keyhole is a close fit on the rung, holding the acrobat vertical so that it can slide from one rung to another. When the rung enters the round part of the keyhole, the acrobat is free to swing around the rung until the slot once again aligns with the rung. The acrobat then repeats the process and drops to the next rung.

Note in Figure 3 that the top half of the acrobat is exactly the same shape as the bottom half. This allows an identical man to be painted upside down on the back of the piece. The purpose of this is to make the acrobat look like he is always swinging on the rung with his hands as he descends the ladder.

MAKING THE ACROBAT

Begin with a ¾-by-1⅝-by-3 inch piece of hard maple. Measure and mark the positions of the ½-inch holes and intersecting slots as shown in the side view of Figure 3. Drill the ½-inch holes first, using a Forstner or brad point bit and drill press to ensure accuracy. Retract the bit frequently to clear the chips—bits have problems clearing chips in deep holes, causing them to bind and wander. Next, cut the slots and bevels with a band saw, and then test with a piece of ⅛-inch stock. It should be a slip fit without excessive play.

Figure 3 shows the acrobat full size. The best way to make the pattern is to photocopy the drawing, then cut out the pattern of the man and trace onto the stock. Use a scroll saw to cut out the shape, staying to the outside of the line. Once cut, smooth down the edges and keyhole surfaces using files and sandpaper.

If you don't want to paint the man freehand, you can glue a photocopy of him on each side of the wooden piece, then paint in the details, followed by a coat of varnish for durability. If you plan to paint the man directly onto the piece, put a sealer coat on the wood first. I like to use two coats of shellac thinned 50 percent, rubbing with steel wool after each coat. The color details are enamel, topped off with a protective coat of varnish. If you prefer water-based paints, stick with them for the primer as well as the top coat to ensure compatibility. Whatever finish you choose, make sure that the paint, stain, and glue are all nontoxic.

MAKING THE LADDER

The ladder illustrated has five rungs, but you can add more if you wish to create a more dramatic descent for the acrobat. Increase the size of the base proportionally to maintain stability. To build the ladder as shown in Figure 2, start by ripping two pieces of hard maple to ¾-by-1¼-by-16⅛ inches for the ladder sides. Now rip a ⅛-by-⅛-inch groove down the center of the ¾-inch face of each piece and add the remaining features with a scroll saw or band saw. Make the rungs by ripping a ⅛-inch strip from ¾-inch stock and then ripping again to a width of ¹⁵⁄₃₂-inch. Cut five rungs to a length of 2¼ inches and round the edges over with sandpaper. Cut a piece of hard maple ¾-by-4½ inches square for the base. Add the ¾-by-1¼-inch notches for the ladder sides and round the outside edges with sandpaper.

Now that all of the pieces are cut, begin the assembly by marking the positions of the rungs on the ladder sides. Test-fit the sides, rungs, and base and give the acrobat a try. If acceptable, disassemble and redo with glue and clamps. Complete the project by giving the ladder a final sanding with 220- through 320-grit sandpaper and applying a nontoxic finish of your choice.

SMALL WAGON

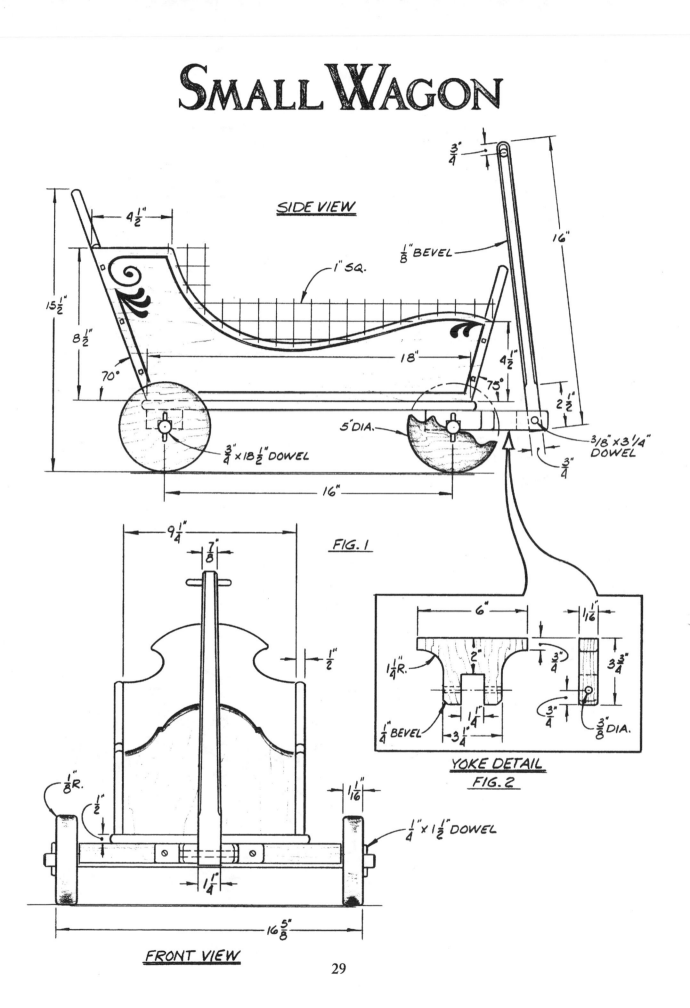

SIDE VIEW

4 1/2"

1" SQ.

3/4"

1/8" BEVEL

16"

15 1/2"

8 1/2"

18"

4 1/2"

70°

75°

5" DIA.

2 1/3"

3/4" × 18 1/2" DOWEL

3/8" × 3 1/4" DOWEL

3/4"

16"

FIG. 1

9 1/4"

7/8"

1/2"

YOKE DETAIL
FIG. 2

6"

1 1/16"

1 1/4"R.

2"

3/4"

3 3/4"

1/4" BEVEL

1 1/4"

3 1/4"

3/4"

3/8" DIA.

1/8"R.

1/2"

1 1/16"

1/4" × 1 1/2" DOWEL

1 1/4"

16 5/8"

FRONT VIEW

29

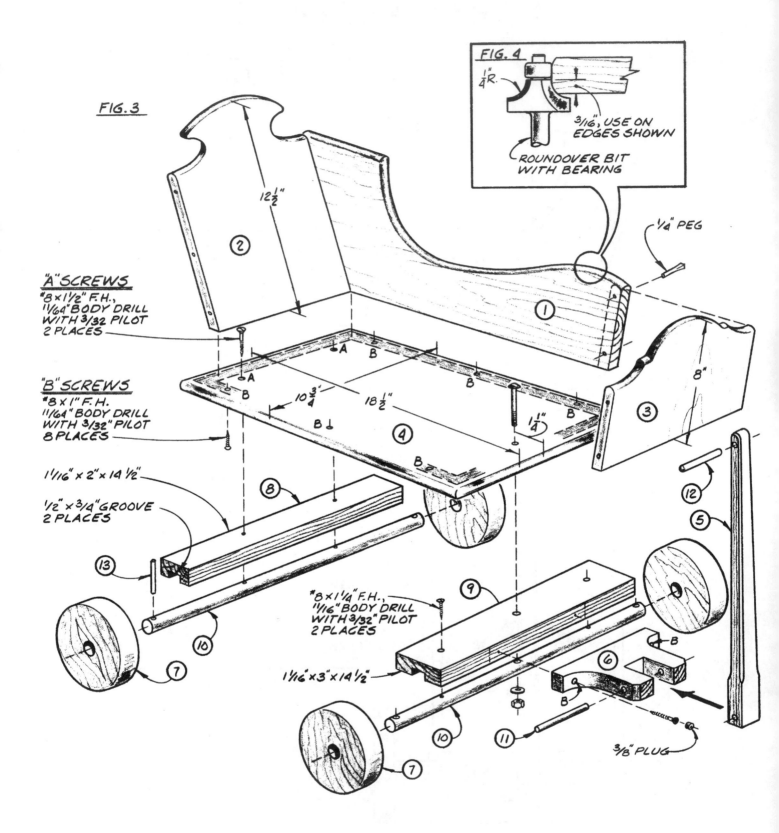

FIG.3

FIG. 4

$\frac{1}{4}$"R.

3/16", USE ON
EDGES SHOWN

ROUNDOVER BIT
WITH BEARING

$\frac{1}{4}$" PEG

12$\frac{1}{2}$"

②

①

"A" SCREWS
#8×1$\frac{1}{2}$" F.H.,
11/64" BODY DRILL
WITH 3/32 PILOT
2 PLACES

"B" SCREWS
#8×1" F.H.
11/64" BODY DRILL
WITH 3/32" PILOT
8 PLACES

A   B
  A
B

10$\frac{3}{4}$"   18$\frac{1}{2}$"

B

④

B

B

B   B

③

8"

$1\frac{1}{4}$"

⑧

1$\frac{1}{16}$" × 2" × 14$\frac{1}{2}$"

$\frac{1}{2}$" × $\frac{3}{4}$" GROOVE
2 PLACES

⑤

⑫

⑬

⑩

⑨

⑥

B

B

⑦

#8×1$\frac{1}{4}$" F.H.,
11/16" BODY DRILL
WITH 3/32" PILOT
2 PLACES

1$\frac{1}{16}$"×3"×14$\frac{1}{2}$"

⑩

⑪

$\frac{3}{8}$" PLUG

⑦

30

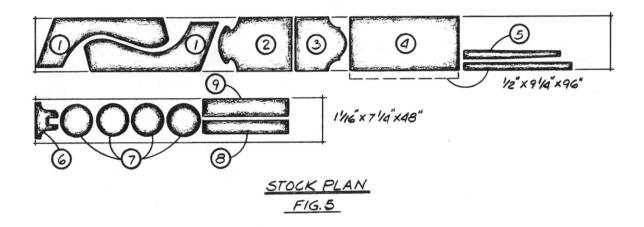

STOCK PLAN
FIG. 5

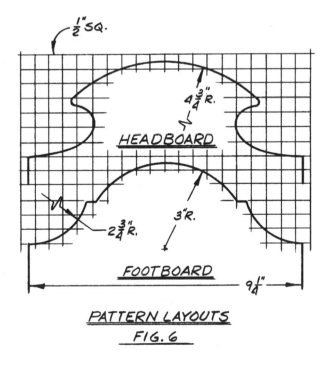

PATTERN LAYOUTS
FIG. 6

31

Bill of Materials

Stock (inches)	Quantity	Item	Part
½ × 9¼ × 96 poplar	1	①	sides (two)
		②	headboard (one)
		③	footboard (one)
		④	floorboard (one)
		⑤	handle (one)
1¹⁄₁₆ × 7¼ × 48 poplar	1	⑥	yoke (one)
		⑦	wheels (four)
		⑧	rear axle bolster (one)
		⑨	front axle bolster (one)
¾ dia. × 36 maple dowel	1	⑩	axles (two)
⅜ dia. × 36 maple dowel	1	⑪	handle pivot (one)
		⑫	handle pull (one)
¼ dia. × 36 maple dowel	1	⑬	retaining pins (four)

Hardware and supplies	Quantity	Description
wood screws	8	#8 × 1" F.H.
	2	#8 × 1¼" F.H.
	2	#8 × 1½" F.H.
carriage bolt	1	¼" × 2½"
locknut	1	¼"
washer	1	¼"

SMALL WAGON

A wagon is one of a child's most prized possessions, and playtime just wouldn't be complete without one of these vehicles to do those heavy hauling jobs from the house to the sandbox. This is a great first wagon for three- or four-year-olds because of its low profile and easy handling. So if you're looking for a present for a preschooler, this one should be at the top of your list.

Early American toys, like this wagon, are highly sought after by antiques collectors today. The original wagon was made entirely of wood, even down to the axles and "tree nail" fasteners. This construction illustrates the economic conditions of the period. Metal hardware was very expensive because of the slow process of making wrought iron (the metal of the day) and the laborious task of having a blacksmith hammer out each piece by hand. Wood, meanwhile, was everywhere and mostly free for the taking. It was easily cured and could be fashioned into many hardware items such as hinges, locks, pulls, and even nails!

Things to Know

Before you begin this project, you'll need to learn or review the techniques discussed in the following sections:
   Drawing Your Patterns
   Joining with Pegs
   Decorating Your Projects

PLANNING THE PROJECT

Unlike the original, the wagon illustrated uses metal screws and slightly different construction to keep the assembly as straightforward as possible. Only the pegs in the sides remain, and even these can be replaced with 1¼-inch brads to speed things up. The original was made from poplar and finished with milk paint. If you prefer a natural finish, con-sider maple, cherry, or walnut. Just stay in the hardwood family.

PATTERNS

The sides ①, headboard ②, and footboard ③ require full size patterns. Lay out the pieces on thin poster board as shown in Figures 1 and 6. When drawn, cut out the patterns and then position them on the stock so that there is generous space between pieces for the saw cuts (see Figure 5). When you're satisfied with the arrangement, trace the patterns and draw the straight pieces.

BED ASSEMBLY

Begin the construction by cutting out the bed assembly pieces ① through ④. If you used the recommended 9¼-inch stock width (the actual width of a 10-inch board), the floorboard will have to be glued up from two pieces to make the 10¾-inch width. Once all of the pieces are cut, smooth out the curved surfaces with a spokeshave and files, followed by 180-grit sandpaper. To create a soft edge on the pieces, rout the edges with a ¼-inch roundover bit as shown in the exploded view drawing. Then use 180-grit sandpaper to smooth out the round surfaces and at the same time maintain the distinct edge on the faces of the parts.

Start the assembly by gluing the two sides to the footboard and headboard. To ensure twistfree construction, place the assembly right side up on the workbench, then clamp to the benchtop and check for square on the inside corners. When dry, drill and peg the joints if you want to retain the original appearance, or use 1¼-inch brads.

Center up and then trace the inside and outside edges of the assembly onto the floorboard to create a "footprint" of the mating surfaces. Use the footprint to locate the six B screws, then drill the 3/32-inch pilot holes. This way, you know the screws will hit the sides perfectly when driven from the bottom of the floorboard. Dry-clamp the parts together, then turn the assembly over and redrill the pilots and add the countersinks. Disassemble, then redo with glue and #8-by-1-inch flathead screws.

WHEEL AND AXLE ASSEMBLIES

Start by cutting out the yoke ⑥ and front and rear bolsters ⑧ and ⑨ as shown in Figure 5. Cut a ½-by-¾-inch wide axle groove in the center of each bolster using a router or table saw and dado blade. When cutting the width, use the axle material as a gauge to get a tight fit because the diameter of dowel stock can vary.

Using the dimensions in the yoke detail drawing, mark the position of the ⅜-inch handle pivot and drill with a drill press to guarantee a straight hole. If you don't have a drill press, carefully lay out and drill the hole from both sides to minimize error. Check the hole alignment with a ⅜-inch dowel, and if there is a bind, use a round file to bridge the distance between the two holes to correct the problem. Next, mark the position of the yoke on the front bolster and clamp in place. Drill and counterbore for the two B screws that join the assembly, then disassemble and redo with glue, #8-by-1-inch flathead screws, and ⅜-inch plugs.

The front axle is made from ¾-inch dowel stock cut to a length of 17⅞-inches. Center up the axle in the front bolster groove and clamp in place. To attach the axle to the bolster permanently, drill, countersink, and then apply two #8-by-1¼-inch flathead screws as shown in the exploded view drawing.

The front axle assembly is joined to the floor of the wagon using a ¼-by-2½-inch carriage bolt as a pivot. Measure in 1¼ inches from the front of the floorboard and drill a ¼ inch hole for the axle pivot. Next, turn the axle assembly upside down and drill a ¼-inch hole through the center of the axle and bolster plate. Join the axle assembly to the wagon using the carriage bolt, washer, and locknut.

Measure and mark the rear axle position at 16 inches from the center line of the front axle. Glue and clamp the rear bolster ⑧ at the rear axle position. The rear axle is also a piece of ¾-inch dowel

stock cut to a length of 17⅞-inches. Once cut, position the axle in the bolster groove and clamp in place. Starting from the axle side, mark the positions of the "A" screws and drill the ³⁄₃₂-inch pilots through the axle, bolster, and floorboard. This way, you know the screws will hit the axle perfectly without critical measurements. Flip the wagon over and finish the holes by drilling the body holes and countersinks. Complete by adding the two #8-by-1½-inch flathead screws.

Now cut out the four wheels using a scroll saw or band saw. Finish the curved surfaces with a file followed by a sandpaper block, then break the edges using a router and an ⅛-inch-radius roundover bit. Complete the wheels by drilling the ¾-inch holes using a Forstner bit and a backup block to prevent tear-out. Test-fit the wheels on the axles. If they won't go on or are tight, sand down the axle until they run smoothly, then rub the end of a small candle on the insides of the holes for lubrication. Next, make the retaining pins ⑬ from ¼-inch dowel stock cut to a length of 1½ inches. Place a double thickness of cardboard (a tablet back is good) behind the wheels to establish some clearance, then locate the pins and drill. Remove the cardboard and test-fit a pin, but don't glue it in place at this time because it's easier to finish the wagon in pieces.

HANDLE

The handle ⑤ is the last part to make on the wagon. Cut the handle to a starting size of ¾-by-1¼-by-16 inches. Mark the positions and drill the holes for the ⅜-inch pivot shaft ⑪ and handle pull ⑫. On the 1¼-inch face, measure in 2½ inches for the pivot end and mark an equal-sided taper down to ⅞ inch. Cut the taper with a band saw and smooth the surfaces with a jointer or hand plane. Round the end of the taper, and then cut ³⁄₁₆-inch bevels with a spokeshave or a router table and chamfer bit. Now cut the handle pull from ⅜-inch dowel stock, round the ends, and glue in place. Finish the handle by making the pivot pin also from ⅜-inch dowel stock. Again, test-fit the handle but don't glue the pin in place until after the wagon is finished.

FINISHING TOUCHES

With the wagon disassembled, go over all of the pieces with 220- and then 320-grit sandpaper.

Apply the finish of your choice. The striping and filigree can be applied to a natural or painted finish using the tape or hand-painted technique. After the finish has dried, install the wheels and handle and glue the pins in place.

SMALL CHILD'S CHAIR

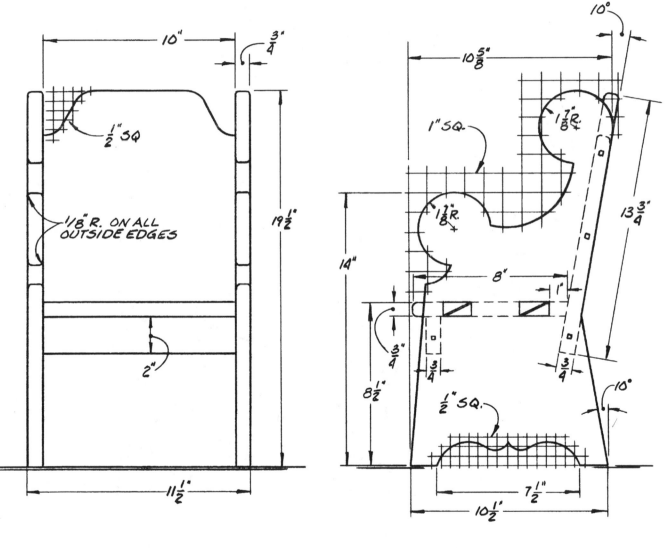

FRONT VIEW FIG. 1 SIDE VIEW

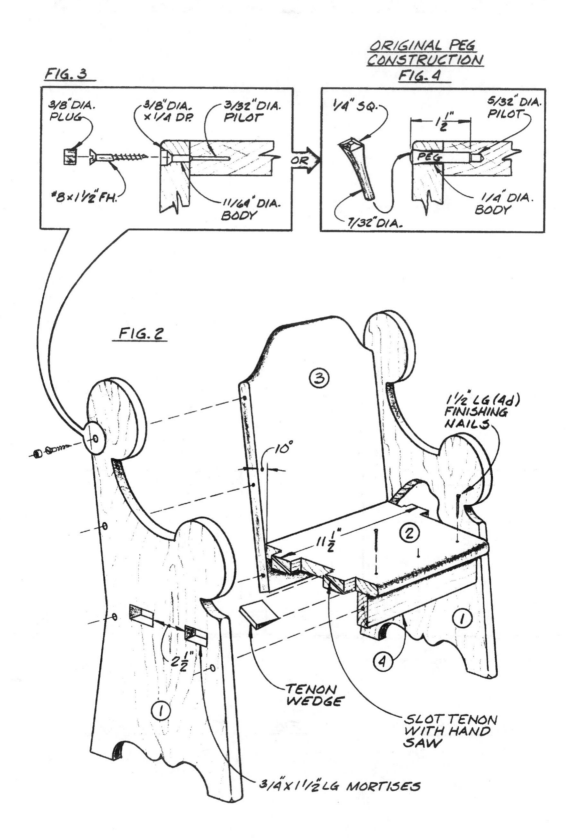

ORIGINAL PEG
CONSTRUCTION
FIG. 4

FIG. 3

3/8" DIA.
PLUG

3/8" DIA.
x 1/4 DP.

3/32" DIA.
PILOT

1/4" SQ.

5/32" DIA.
PILOT

"8 x 1 1/2" FH.

11/64" DIA.
BODY

OR

PEG

1 1/2"

7/32" DIA.

1/4" DIA.
BODY

FIG. 2

③

1 1/2" LG (4d)
FINISHING
NAILS

10°

②

11 1/2"

①

TENON
WEDGE

④

①

2 1/2"

SLOT TENON
WITH HAND
SAW

3/4" x 1 1/2" LG MORTISES

38

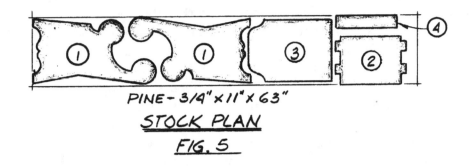

PINE - 3/4" × 11" × 63"
STOCK PLAN
FIG. 5

BILL OF MATERIALS

Stock (inches)	Quantity	Item	Part
¾ × 11 × 63 pine	1	①	sides (two)
		②	seat (one)
		③	back (one)
		④	support (one)
⅜ × 36 dowel maple	1	–	screw plugs (eight)

Hardware and supplies	Quantity	Description
wood screws	8	#8 × 1½" F.H.
finishing nails	3	1½"

Small Child's Chair

Children's chairs have always been a favorite, and you can build this unusual nineteenth-century country piece in little more than a weekend. The size is appropriate for toddlers up to three or four years old, and when they outgrow the chair you'll have an interesting display piece that's filled with memories.

This chair is a typical example of early country furniture: simple in form and sturdy in construction. Country cabinetmakers didn't take pains to hide the joinery and left mortise and dovetail joints exposed and used pegs or "tree nails" to make simple joints and apply moldings. Many of these pieces would be used without a finish or possibly with a coat of colored milk paint. This finish was easily brewed in the kitchen, starting with buttermilk as a binder, adding lime to thicken, and tinting with animal blood or plant material. Original country pieces with this kind of finish are prized possessions of antiques collectors today.

Things to Know

Before you begin this project, you'll need to learn or review the techniques discussed in the following sections:
Drawing Your Patterns
Joining with Pegs

Planning the Project

The first decision to be made is the type of construction. Follow the plans as shown in Figure 1 for the traditional construction, or use screws as shown in Figure 3 to replace the pegs and mortise and tenon joints. The original was made of pine and painted with a mustard yellow milk paint. Walnut, cherry, maple, or poplar are also acceptable, although pine is preferred because it is light, strong, and easy to work.

Patterns

The first step in making the chair is laying out the parts on your stock as shown in Figure 5. Make full-size patterns of the sides ① and back ③ on thin poster board. Cut out the patterns, then position them on the stock so that there is generous space between pieces for the saw cuts. When you're satisfied with the arrangement, trace the patterns and draw the straight pieces.

Cutting the Parts

Start by rough-cutting the sides ① from the stock. Then cut the final shape with a band saw or jigsaw and smooth out the curved surfaces with a file and the straight surfaces with a hand plane. Break all of the sharp edges with a router and a ¼-inch roundover bit except where the back joins the side and the scroll on the bottom. Identify which side is left and which is right, and then put them aside for now. Cut the remaining parts. When cutting the seat ②, leave the tenons uncut because they must be matched to the mortises later in the assembly. After the parts are cut, finish them by routing the top of the back and the front of the seat with a ⅜-inch roundover bit. Complete the parts with a first sanding of 180-grit sandpaper.

Mortising the Sides

The seat and sides are attached with a double mortise and tenon joint to provide the main structural support for the chair. The easiest way to do this joint is to cut the mortise first, then fit the tenon to it. Start by laying out the mortises on both sides of the side pieces. This is important because you'll be working on both sides as you cut the hole. From the outside surface of the side piece, begin the mortise by drilling a starter hole for a jigsaw, then cut to the inside of the line. Check the inside surfaces of the mortise for square with the face of the side, and correct with a sharp chisel if required. When the mortises are done, cut the tenons in the seat slightly wider than necessary so that they can be fitted to the mortises. Compare the tenon positions to the mortises on the outside of the side pieces (that's the fit you're going to see when the joint is together), then mark the corrections and number the joints. Pare the sides of the tenons with a sharp chisel until they just enter the mortises. Now test-fit the tenons from the inside of the side piece and do the final trimming on the mortise until you get full engagement. Finish up the tenons by cutting diagonal wedge slots ¾-inch deep with a back saw.

The next step is assembling the sides with the seat. Cut four tenon wedges about 1½ inch long by ⅛ inch thick, tapering to a sharp edge. If you are using pine for your piece, make the wedges from a light colored hardwood like maple so it can stand the force of being driven into the joints. Now fasten the support ④ to the seat with glue and 1½-inch finishing nails or pegs as shown in Figure 4. When dry, test-fit all the parts for the chair and check for square. If the alignment looks acceptable, lay the back aside for now and redo the seat and sides

with glue and clamps, then drive the wedges into the joints using a hammer and a wooden block. Don't overdo it with the hammer; when the wedge has tightened the joint, you're there. Finish up the joints by cutting the wedge excess to slightly above flush with a handsaw, then pare flush with a sharp chisel.

ATTACHING THE BACK

Glue the joint surfaces, then slip the back into position and clamp in place. If you prefer to use screws for the joints, drill the counterbore and pilot holes for the #8-by-1½-inch flathead screws as shown in Figure 3. Follow up with the screws, and glue the plugs in place. When dry, use a chisel to trim down the plugs and sand flush. For pegged joints, let the glue dry overnight and then apply the pegs as shown in Figure 4. Rough cut the peg excess with a handsaw and pare to slightly above flush so that they can be seen through the finish. Sand the chair with 220-grit sandpaper, and then apply the finish of your choice.

RING TOSS

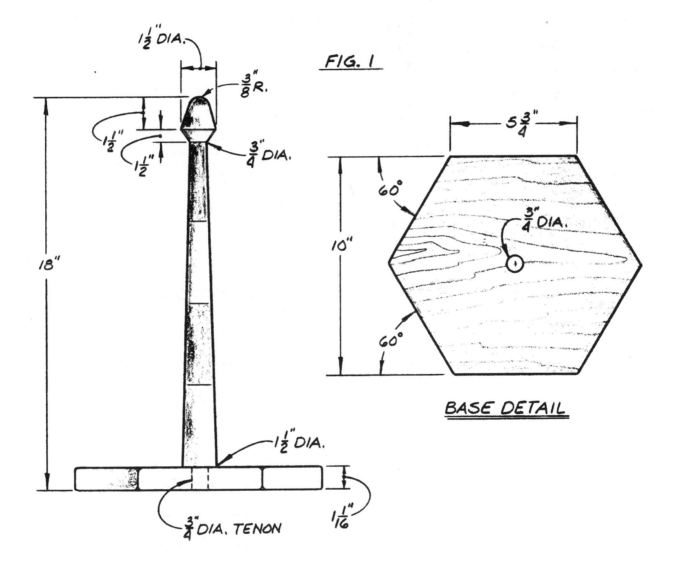

FIG. 1

$1\frac{1}{2}$" DIA.

$\frac{3}{8}$" R.

$1\frac{1}{2}$"

$1\frac{1}{2}$"

$\frac{3}{4}$" DIA.

18"

$1\frac{1}{2}$" DIA.

$\frac{3}{4}$" DIA. TENON

$1\frac{1}{16}$"

$5\frac{3}{4}$"

60°

10"

$\frac{3}{4}$" DIA.

60°

BASE DETAIL

FIG. 2

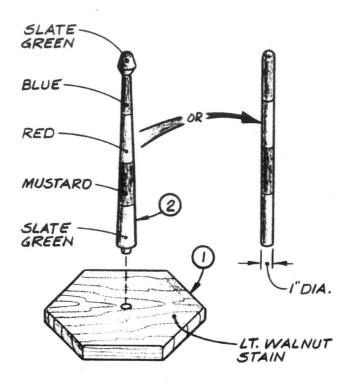

SLATE GREEN

BLUE

RED

MUSTARD

SLATE GREEN

②

①

1" DIA.

LT. WALNUT STAIN

OR

RING SET
(MADE FROM EMBROIDERY HOOPS)

FIG. 3

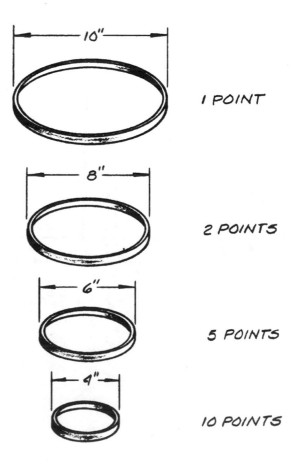

10"

1 POINT

8"

2 POINTS

6"

5 POINTS

4"

10 POINTS

44

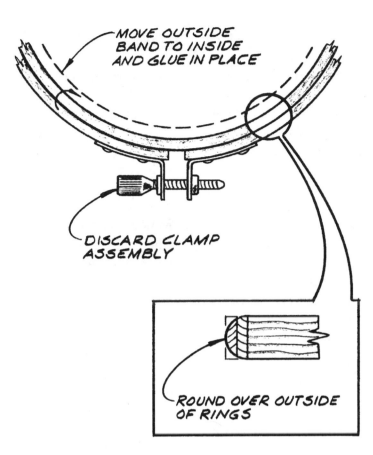

MOVE OUTSIDE
BAND TO INSIDE
AND GLUE IN PLACE

DISCARD CLAMP
ASSEMBLY

ROUND OVER OUTSIDE
OF RINGS

FIG. 4

BILL OF MATERIALS

Stock (inches)	Quantity	Item	Part
1¹⁄₁₆ × 10 × 12 pine	1	①	base (one)
1½ × 1½ × 18 maple	1	②	post (one)

Hardware and supplies	Quantity	Description	
embroidery hoops	2	4" dia.	
	2	6" dia.	
	2	8" dia.	
	2	10" dia.	

Ring Toss

Ring Toss is an age-old summertime game that offers competition for the whole family. It's simple to play and children love the challenge of trying to encircle the post with the different size rings. The game consists of a post on a base and one or more sets of rings ranging from 4 to 10 inches in diameter. The rings are made from embroidery hoops, and each set is painted a different color for scoring purposes.

The rules are flexible. The game can be played by one or more people, each requiring a set of rings. Step off a distance from the post that is appropriate for the skill of the players. Starting with the largest ring, each player in turn tries to toss a ringer on the post. When all of the rings have been thrown, the ringers are tallied for each player using the point values given in Figure 3. The first player to reach twenty-five points wins the game.

For two players, you can use a more competitive variation. When a ringer is made, the points are canceled if the opponent can top the ring with one of the same size. The player with the highest number of points for a round must toss first on the next round. Again, the first player to reach twenty-five points wins the game.

Post Assembly

The piece illustrated was manufactured by an unknown maker around 1930. It had a gaily painted post that was turned from 1½-inch-square hardwood stock. This part is a snap to make with a lathe, but if you don't have one, you can substitute an 18-inch length of 1-inch dowel as shown in Figure 2. Paint the post, following the suggested color scheme or one of your own, before joining to the

base. Start with a coat of sanding sealer followed by an oil-based enamel for the color bands. Paint the light-colored areas first, then the darker bands so that coverage won't be a problem. Now make the base from pine and finish with a medium walnut stain and a top coat of varnish. Glue the post into the base and check for square.

Making the Rings

The game requires a set of four rings for each player as shown in Figure 3. These pieces can be easily made from inexpensive embroidery hoops, available at fabric stores and some craft stores. To achieve sufficient strength, both bands of the hoops are used to make the rings. Begin by carefully removing the clamp assemblies from the outer bands by drilling out the attaching rivets (see Figure 4). Then cut the outer band to fit inside the inner band. When you're satisfied with the fit, glue and clamp in place.

The last step is rounding over the outside surface of the rings as shown in Figure 4. This is important, as it allows the rings to sail through the air properly. If you have a router table, the task is easy. Make a circular guide and use a ¼-inch-radius roundover bit. Alternatively, shape the roundover with a spokeshave or small hand plane. Smooth out the curves with 180-grit sandpaper followed by 220.

All that remains is applying the finish. Make each set of rings a different color for scoring. The originals were painted, but a clear finish is acceptable if you use different color stains to distinguish the sets. Give the finish a few days' drying time for durability, and then head for the yard and let the competition begin!

DOLL CRADLE

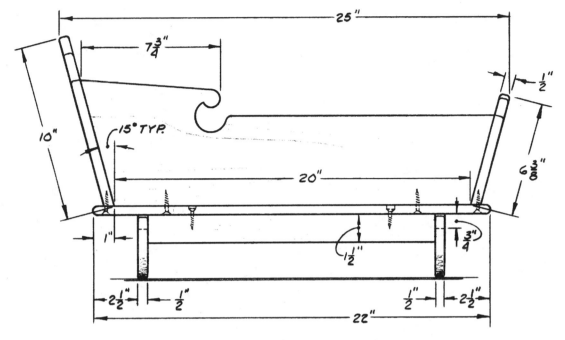

SIDE VIEW

FIG. 1

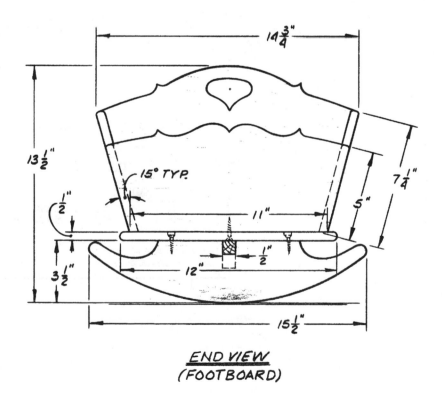

END VIEW
(FOOTBOARD)

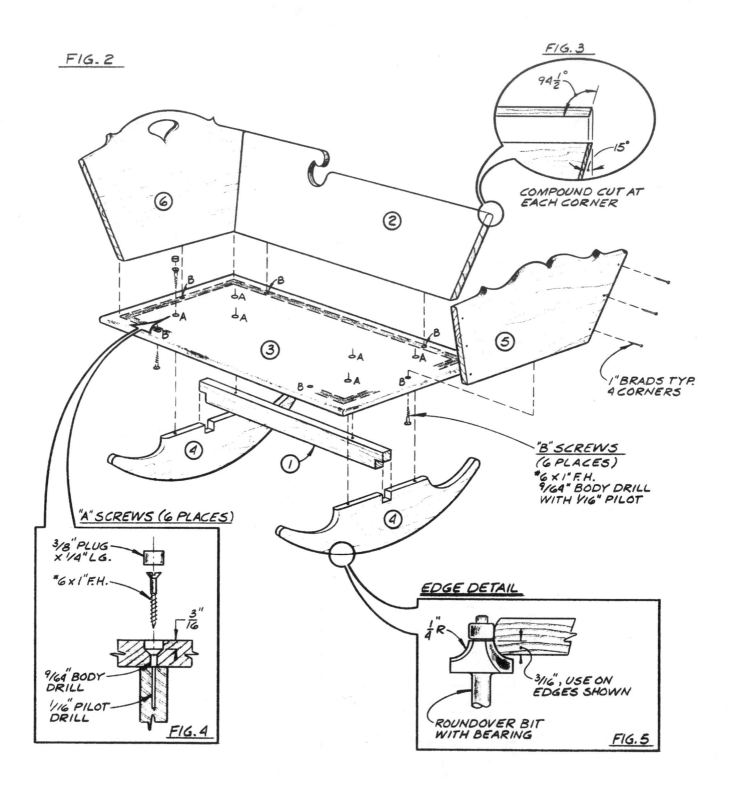

FIG. 2

FIG. 3

$94\frac{1}{2}°$

15°

COMPOUND CUT AT
EACH CORNER

⑥

②

⑤

B

B

A

A

③

A

A

B

B

A

A

B

B

④

①

④

1" BRADS TYP.
4 CORNERS

"B" SCREWS
(6 PLACES)
#6 X 1" F.H.
9/64" BODY DRILL
WITH 1/16" PILOT

"A" SCREWS (6 PLACES)

3/8" PLUG
X 1/4" LG.

#6 X 1" F.H.

$\frac{3}{16}$"

9/64" BODY
DRILL

1/16" PILOT
DRILL

FIG. 4

EDGE DETAIL

$\frac{1}{4}$" R

3/16", USE ON
EDGES SHOWN

ROUNDOVER BIT
WITH BEARING

FIG. 5

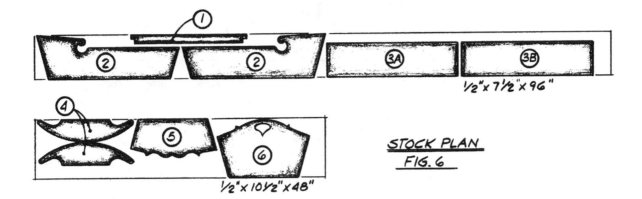

1/2" x 7 1/2" x 96"

STOCK PLAN
FIG. 6

1/2" x 10 1/2" x 48"

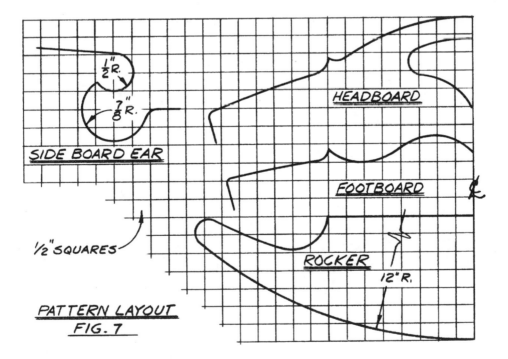

1/2" R.

7/8" R.

SIDE BOARD EAR

HEADBOARD

FOOTBOARD

1/2" SQUARES

ROCKER

12" R.

PATTERN LAYOUT
FIG. 7

Bill of Materials

Stock (inches)	Quantity	Item	Part
½ × 7½ × 96 pine	1	①	floorboard support (one)
		②	side boards (two)
		③A	floorboard (one)
		③B	floorboard (one)
½ × 10½ × 48 pine	1	④	rockers (two)
		⑤	footboard (one)
		⑥	headboard (one)
⅜ × 36" dowel, maple	1		screw plugs (six)

Hardware and Supplies	Quantity	Description
wood screws	12	#6 × 1" F.H.
brads	16	1"

Doll Cradle

Every little girl has a favorite doll that rarely leaves her side. When bedtime arrives, this attractive cradle can provide a special place to tuck in her inseparable friend. This 25-inch-long cradle is perfect for medium-size dolls, and best of all, you can build it in a couple of weekends and put a big smile on a little girl's face.

Things to Know

Before you begin this project, you'll need to learn or review the techniques discussed in the following section:

Drawing Your Patterns

Planning the Project

Old doll cradles were made from many different kinds of wood in both natural and painted finishes. I used pine with a walnut stain because I wanted to keep the weight to a minimum. Whatever wood you choose, don't be tempted to substitute ¾-inch for the ½-inch stock called for, because the material will look out of scale for the size of the piece and add unnecessary weight. If you can't find a source for the ½-inch stock, have a custom cabinet shop plane your material down to size. Most shops, especially the small ones, will do a few boards for a reasonable charge.

Patterns

Figure 5 shows the placement of the parts on the stock. Make patterns for the parts with irregular shapes by drawing the ½-inch square grid and shapes shown in Figure 2, then cutting with a sharp knife. Use these patterns to lay out complete parts on poster board. Cut out the patterns, then position them on the stock so that there is generous space between pieces for the saw cuts. When you're satisfied with the arrangement, trace the patterns and draw the straight pieces.

ROCKER ASSEMBLY

The best way to build this cradle is from the floor up. Start by cutting out the floorboard pieces ③Ⓐ and ③Ⓑ, then glue and clamp together. While this assembly is drying, cut the rocker pieces ④ and the floor support ① to size. Each end of the support has a ½-by-¾-inch tongue that fits snugly into a notch on top of one of the rockers. Cut the tongue first, then cut the notch slightly undersize with a table saw. Test-fit the joint and mark the corrections for final cutting. Now smooth out the rocker curves with a hand plane and spokeshave.

Finish up the rockers and floorboard by adding a half-round on the edges using a router and ¼-inch-radius roundover bit as shown in the edge detail drawing. Use 180-grit sandpaper to smooth the half-round surfaces and at the same time maintain the distinct edge at the faces of the board. This treatment gives the parts a soft look and increases the durability of the edges.

Start the assembly by gluing the two rockers to the floorboard support. To assure twistfree construction, place the assembly on your workbench with the rockers up; then apply clamps and check for square between the rockers, bench, and support. When dry, center the rocker assembly on the floorboard, then trace the assembly's periphery with a sharp pencil to create a "footprint" of the mating surface. Put an identifying pencil mark on one rocker and its location on the floorboard to prevent reversing during reassembly. It's now an easy task to mark the positions of the #6 screws onto the "footprint" and drill the pilot holes into the floorboard. Once drilled, use the "footprint" to match the assembly and dry-clamp in place. Turn the assembly over and redrill the pilots for the #6-by-1-inch flathead screws and the counterbores for the plugs. Disassemble, then redo with glue and screws. Glue the ⅜-inch screw plugs in place, and when dry, trim flush with a chisel.

MAKING THE SIDE BOARDS

The first operation in cutting out the side boards ② and end boards ⑤ and ⑥ is ripping the 15-degree angle on the bottom of the parts. If the parts are laid out as shown in the stock plan, this cut can easily be made by putting the opposite edge of the board against the table saw fence to guide the cut. That way, you can avoid putting your saw blade tight against the fence.

The most critical cuts in this project are the 15-by-94½-degree compound angles that are on the ends of the sideboard as shown in Figure 3. You need to be certain that the 94½-degree angle is in the right direction and that you end up with a left- and a right-hand side board. To ensure success, make the 15-degree end cuts slightly oversize and at 90 degrees. Now identify and mark which is left and which is right (determined by the 15-degree angle on the bottom), and mark the direction of the 94½-degree angle at each corner. Set your table saw blade to 4½ degrees off vertical and your miter gauge to 15 degrees and cut to the lines. Finish cutting the parts by removing the waste from the top edges using a scroll saw or jigsaw.

The last parts to cut are the headboard ⑥ and the footboard ⑤. The sides of these parts also require 15-by-94½-degree compound angles, so use the same procedure for layout and cutting as described for the sideboards. Remove the waste from the top edges and heart-shaped cutout using a scroll saw or jigsaw. Finish up the side boards and end boards by routing the same half-round on the top edges as was done on the rocker assembly. After routing, follow up with a chisel and files to complete the roundovers on the inside corners.

Begin the assembly by driving three 1-inch brads into each joining edge of the end boards as shown in the exploded view drawing. Dry-fit a joint together and drive the brads halfway home. Repeat for the remaining three corners, then disassemble. Redo with glue and then drive the brads home. Check the assembly for warps and for square. If necessary, clamp into shape until dry.

PUTTING IT ALL TOGETHER

The last step is mounting the sideboard assembly onto the rocker assembly. Position, then trace the inside and outside edges of the sideboard assembly onto the floorboard to create a "footprint" of the mating surfaces. Mark the positions of the six #6 screws on the "footprint" and drill the pilot holes into the floorboard. Once drilled, use the "footprint" to match the floorboard and sideboard assembly, then dry-clamp in place. Turn the cradle over, and redrill the pilots and add the countersinks for the #6-by-1-inch flathead wood screws. Disassemble, then redo with glue and screws. Give the whole cradle a final sanding with 240-grit sandpaper.

APPLYING THE FINISH

You can use any kind of finish for your cradle, as long as it's nontoxic. Old doll cradles were sometimes painted, and if it was a country piece, milk paint was often used. I used a medium walnut stain followed by two sealer coats of shellac thinned 50 percent. I lightly rubbed out each coat with #0000 steel wool and then applied two coats of satin lacquer for the final finish.

PIGS IN CLOVER

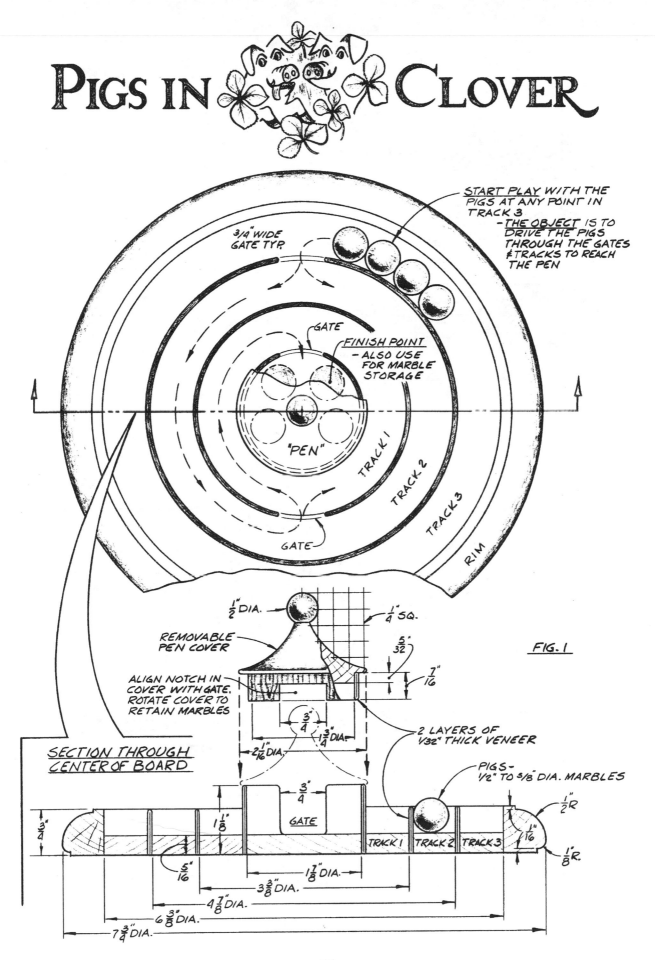

START PLAY WITH THE PIGS AT ANY POINT IN TRACK 3 - THE OBJECT IS TO DRIVE THE PIGS THROUGH THE GATES & TRACKS TO REACH THE PEN

3/4" WIDE GATE TYP.

GATE

FINISH POINT - ALSO USE FOR MARBLE STORAGE

"PEN"

TRACK 1

TRACK 2

TRACK 3

RIM

GATE

FIG. 1

1/2" DIA.

1/4" SQ.

REMOVABLE PEN COVER

5/32"

7/16"

ALIGN NOTCH IN COVER WITH GATE. ROTATE COVER TO RETAIN MARBLES

3/4"

1 3/4" DIA.

2 1/16" DIA.

2 LAYERS OF 1/32" THICK VENEER

PIGS- 1/2" TO 5/8" DIA. MARBLES

SECTION THROUGH CENTER OF BOARD

3/4"

GATE

1 1/8"

3/4"

TRACK 1

TRACK 2

TRACK 3

1/2" R

1/16"

1/8" R.

5/16"

1 7/8" DIA.

3 3/8" DIA.

4 7/8" DIA.

6 3/8" DIA.

7 3/4" DIA.

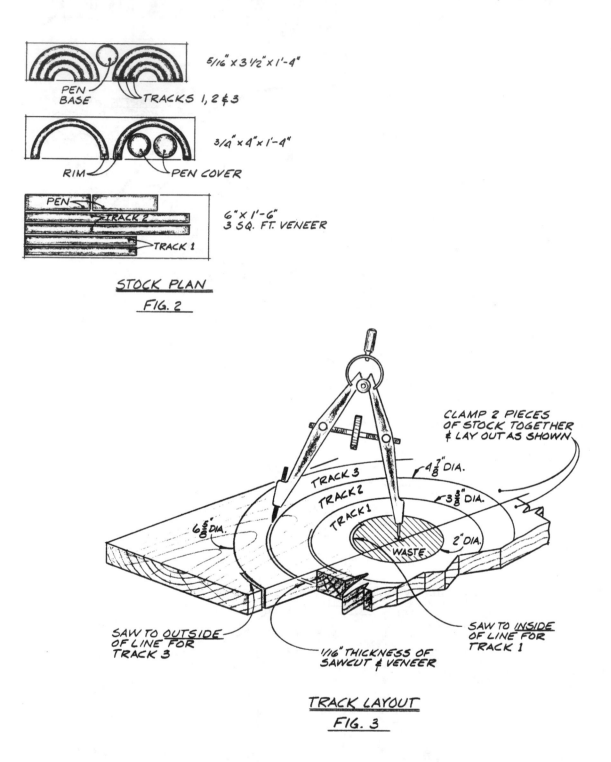

5/16" x 3 1/2" x 1'-4"

PEN BASE

TRACKS 1, 2 & 3

3/4" x 4" x 1'-4"

RIM

PEN COVER

PEN

TRACK 2

TRACK 1

6" x 1'-6"
3 SQ. FT. VENEER

STOCK PLAN
FIG. 2

CLAMP 2 PIECES
OF STOCK TOGETHER
& LAY OUT AS SHOWN

TRACK 3

TRACK 2

TRACK 1

4 7/8" DIA.

3 9/16" DIA.

2" DIA.

WASTE

6 3/16" DIA.

SAW TO OUTSIDE
OF LINE FOR
TRACK 3

1/16" THICKNESS OF
SAWCUT & VENEER

SAW TO INSIDE
OF LINE FOR
TRACK 1

TRACK LAYOUT
FIG. 3

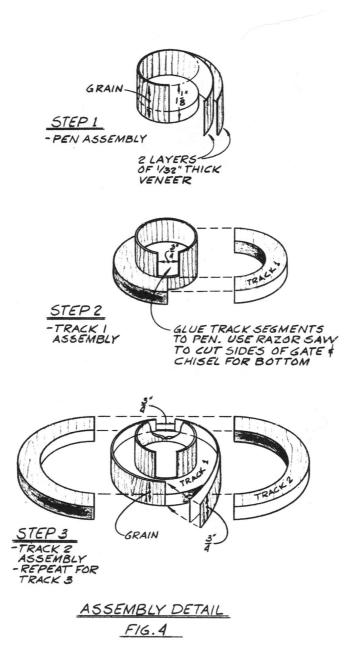

GRAIN

$1\frac{1}{8}"$

STEP 1
- PEN ASSEMBLY

2 LAYERS
OF 1/32" THICK
VENEER

$\frac{3}{4}"$

STEP 2
- TRACK 1
  ASSEMBLY

GLUE TRACK SEGMENTS
TO PEN. USE RAZOR SAW
TO CUT SIDES OF GATE &
CHISEL FOR BOTTOM

TRACK 1

$\frac{3}{4}"$

TRACK 1

TRACK 2

GRAIN

$\frac{3}{4}"$

STEP 3
- TRACK 2
  ASSEMBLY
- REPEAT FOR
  TRACK 3

ASSEMBLY DETAIL
FIG. 4

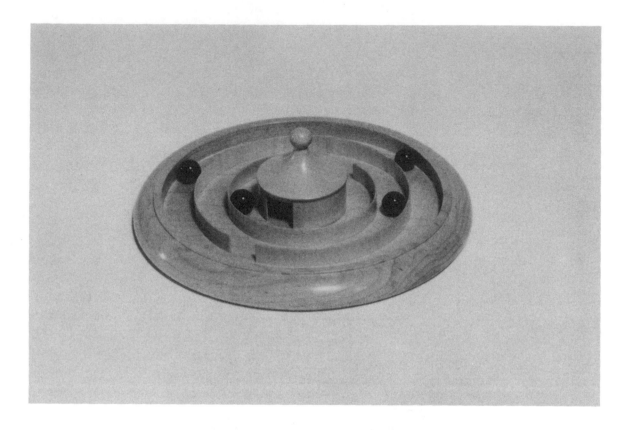

PIGS IN CLOVER

If you build only one project in this book, it has to be Pigs in Clover! This exciting game of skill will test the mettle of everyone who tries to master the technique of "driving home the pigs." Hold the board in your hands and tilt it slightly to maneuver the four marbles (the pigs) from the outside track (a field of clover) through the succeeding gates and tracks and into the center compartment (the pen). It sounds easy, but it's not. The difficulty is in keeping the marbles in a group as they're worked through the gates; if one gets away, the trouble begins.

The game was introduced to the public by toy inventor C. M. Crandall in 1889. What followed made history in the toy industry. Within three weeks of operation, Crandall's factory was working around the clock to produce fifty thousand games per week, and even at that rate he was already a month behind in production. Everyone in America wanted Pigs in Clover; even president Harrison was shown in a New York newspaper cartoon "driving home the pigs" with some of his cabinet members. The game quickly spread to Europe and was welcomed with similar enthusiasm. The game is great for all ages, and it's just a lot of fun!

PLANNING THE PROJECT
The original Pigs in Clover was simply a 6-inch wooden disk with pasteboard partitions to form the tracks. For my version, I wanted to keep the same dimensions and turn it into an attractive woodworking project. All of the parts can be made with a router and a jigsaw except for the pen cover, which requires a lathe. If you don't have one of these tools, a flat cover and brass knob would make an attractive replacement.

When choosing a wood, select a hard, tight-grained variety so that the marbles can roll smoothly without sticking. My favorite is hard maple, but cherry and birch are good substitutes. Also, make sure that a veneer is available in the wood that you choose. A good selection is available from the Woodworkers Store, 21801 Industrial Boulevard, Rogers, MN 55374-9514, telephone (800) 279-4441.

LAYING OUT AND CUTTING THE STOCK

One of the most important aspects of the project is matching the thickness of the veneers with the width of the saw cut for cutting out the tracks (see Figure 3). The closer you get, the less fitting you will have to do at assembly, so verify the thickness of your veneer (should be about $1/32$ inch) and pick a jigsaw blade with a kerf width equal to two layers of veneer. Make a test cut into a piece of scrap, then insert two layers of veneer to check for a snug fit.

From your $5/16$-inch piece of stock, rough-cut two blanks for the track parts and clamp together as shown in Figure 3. Next, draw the diameters of the tracks and the saw cuts between tracks 1, 2, and 3 so that it will be clear where to make the cuts. Finish up by drawing the $1\,7/8$-inch diameter pen base.

When cutting out the parts, always be conscious of which side of the line you should be cutting. Start with the pen base and cut to the outside of the line. Now go to the track segments and remove the waste pieces by cutting to the inside of the line as shown in Figure 3. Continue cutting tracks 1, 2, and 3, using the saw cut lines drawn.

PEN ASSEMBLY

Figure 4 shows the step-by-step procedure for building up the veneer partitions and track segments. If you were able to buy 6-inch wide veneer as shown in Figure 2, cut three $1\,1/8$-inch wide strips with the grain running widthwise and square up the ends. Smooth out the rim of the pen base with a file and sandpaper block. Test-fit one of the strips around the base as shown in step 1. If it feels like it's going to break, temporarily put a strip of masking tape on the outside surface of the strip and try again.

When wrapped, the ends of the strip should be short of touching; this will be filled in later. Apply epoxy glue, then wrap the strip around the base and clean up the excess glue with lacquer thinner. Clamp the strip in place with a generous piece of masking tape, and then clean all excess glue. When dry, cut, fit, and glue the remaining piece using tape to hold alignment.

Apply the second layer of veneer the same way as the first, staggering the starting point for the strip. If you develop gaps between the veneers or feel the need for an extra hand, use small paper clips to hold the strips together or make about a dozen clamps from small, spring-operated, clothespins. To prevent the clamping force from distorting the partition, cut the width of the jaws down to about $1/8$ inch.

Next join the track 1 segments to the pen assembly as shown in step 2. First check to make sure the veneer is even with the bottom of the pen, and sand flush if necessary. Test-fit the segments and remove material where required. Match the grain direction of the segments with the pen base, and then glue and clamp. Verify that the bottom of the pen assembly is flush with the segments. This will guarantee that the top surfaces are also flush and that the marbles can roll from track to track without steps. Lay out the $3/4$-inch wide gate so that its position is with the grain as shown in step 2 (this will allow the bottom of the gate to be sanded flush with the grain). Cut each side of the gate with a razor saw and the bottom with a sharp knife. Finish off the bottom with a sharp chisel and sand smooth.

Follow the same procedure with the segments and partitions for tracks 2 and 3, alternating the gate position for each track and keeping the grain in the same direction for all the segments.

MAKING THE RIM

Draw the two rim pieces on your stock as shown in Figure 2. Because the outside of the rim will receive a routed edge, cut just the outside of the parts at this time so that there's material left to hold. Smooth out the rim with a file to provide a clean, stepless curve for the router to follow. Now rout the top molded edge with a $\frac{1}{2}$-inch roundover bit, then turn over and repeat for the bottom edge using a $\frac{1}{8}$-inch roundover bit. Cut the insides of the rims next, staying to the inside of the line. Once cut, smooth out the inside of the curves with a contoured sandpaper block and test-fit with the track assembly. When gluing in place, match the direction of the grain with the assembly.

COVERING THE PEN

The pen cover serves two purposes: First, it makes play more difficult by hiding the position of the pigs (marbles) that were driven into the pen. Forget them for a moment and they'll pop out while you're going for the others. Second, the cover can retain the marbles in the pen for storage. The notch in the side of the cover is aligned with the gate for play and rotated away from the gate for storage.

If you have a lathe, draw a template of the cover illustrated in the section view and make it from the leftover stock. If you don't have a lathe, simply make the cover from two disks, the bottom one $1\frac{3}{4}$ inches diameter by $\frac{5}{32}$ inch to mount the veneer skirt and the top $2\frac{1}{16}$ inches diameter by $\frac{1}{4}$ inch. Finish off with a brass knob. However you make the cover, you'll need to add a veneer skirt to retain the marbles. Cut two $\frac{7}{16}$-by-6 inch strips of veneer and attach using the method described for the track partitions. Finish up by cutting the $\frac{3}{4}$-inch notch.

FINISHING TOUCHES

Carefully sand a full radius on the edges of the track partitions and gates to prevent chipping. Then sand everything with 220- and then 320-grit sandpaper. Apply the finish of your choice.

For a final touch, add a layer of felt on the bottom. This comes in various size sheets with self-adhesive backing. If you can't find a source in your area, call the Woodworkers Store at (800) 279-4441. The best-quality marbles can be purchased at most arts and crafts stores. They should be smooth, perfectly round, and between $\frac{1}{2}$ inch and $\frac{5}{8}$ inch in diameter. The next time you're at a party that needs a boost, liven it up with your Pigs in Clover game.

Marble Solitaire

FIG. 1

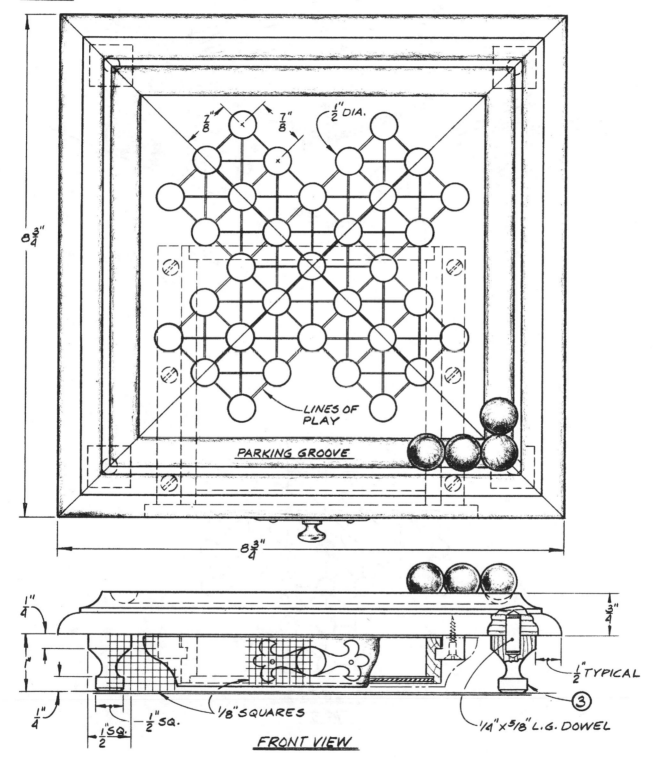

8¾"

½" DIA.

7⅞" 7⅞"

LINES OF PLAY

PARKING GROOVE

8¾"

¼"

¼"

¼"

½"SQ.

½ "SQ.

⅛"SQUARES

¾"

½"TYPICAL

③

¼"X⅝" L.G. DOWEL

FRONT VIEW

61

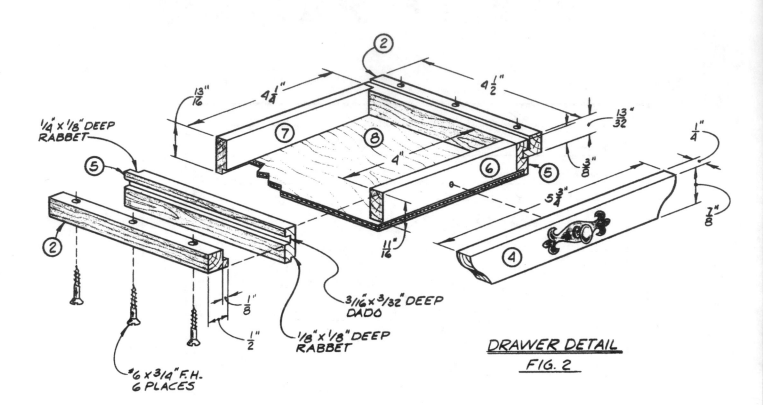

13"/16

1/4" x 1/8" DEEP
RABBET

4 1/4"

②

4 1/2"

13"/32

⑤

⑦

⑧

4"

⑥

⑤

1/4"

②

4"

5 3/4"

7/8"

11"/16

④

1/8

1/2

3/16" x 3/32" DEEP
DADO

1/8" x 1/8" DEEP
RABBET

#6 x 3/4" F.H.
6 PLACES

DRAWER DETAIL
FIG. 2

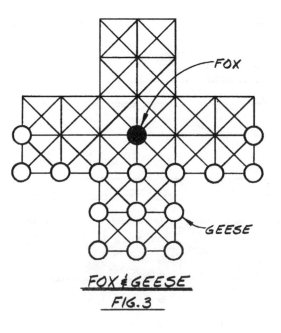

FOX

GEESE

FOX & GEESE
FIG. 3

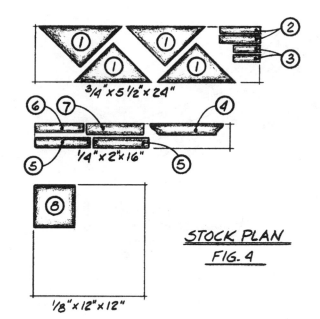

3/4" x 5 1/2" x 24"

1/4" x 2" x 16"

STOCK PLAN

FIG. 4

1/8" x 12" x 12"

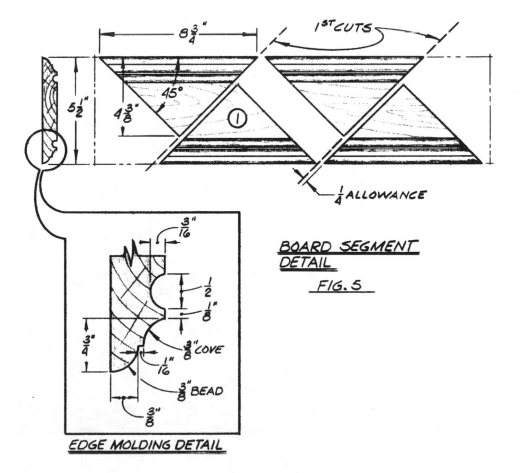

8 3/4"

1ST CUTS

45°

5 1/2"

4 3/8"

1/4 ALLOWANCE

BOARD SEGMENT
DETAIL

FIG. 5

3/16"

1/2"

1/8"

3/4"

3/8" COVE

1/16"

3/8" BEAD

3/8"

EDGE MOLDING DETAIL

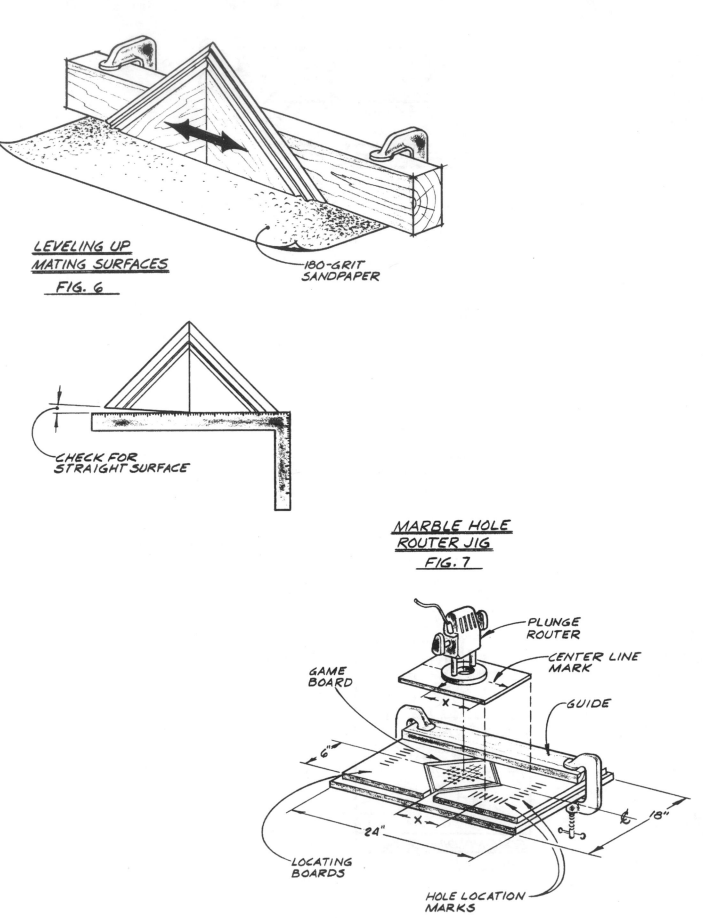

LEVELING UP
MATING SURFACES
FIG. 6

180-GRIT
SANDPAPER

CHECK FOR
STRAIGHT SURFACE

MARBLE HOLE
ROUTER JIG
FIG. 7

PLUNGE
ROUTER

CENTER LINE
MARK

GAME
BOARD

GUIDE

6"

X

X

18"

24"

LOCATING
BOARDS

HOLE LOCATION
MARKS

BILL OF MATERIALS

Stock (inches)	Quantity	Item	Part
¾ × 5½ × 24 walnut or cherry	1	①	board segments (four)
		②	drawer guides (two)
		③	feet (four)
¼ × 2 × 16 walnut or cherry	1	④	drawer face (one)
		⑤	drawer sides (two)
		⑥	drawer front (one)
		⑦	drawer back (one)
⅛ × 12 × 12 birch plywood		⑧	drawer bottom (one)
¼ dia. × 36 maple dowel	1	–	foot dowels (four)

Hardware and Supplies	Quantity	Description
wood screws	6	#6 × ¾" F.H.
brass knob	1	½" diameter
marbles	32	white
marble	1	black
felt	1	9" × 12" green
brass plate	1	1⁄32" × ¾" × 2¼"

MARBLE SOLITAIRE

This project is an ideal use for that short piece of exotic hardwood you've been hoarding under your workbench. All it takes is one board foot of lumber to make Marble Solitaire. This game is easy to learn but difficult to master. The object is simple: A single player tries to clear the board by jumping adjacent marbles. Play is over when you run out of moves or you achieve the perfect game of one marble remaining, and in the center position— which isn't easy!

The solitaire board also can be used for a game for two players called Fox and Geese (see Figure 3). One player assumes the role of the fox (the dark marble in the center), and the other the geese. The fox tries to eliminate the geese from the board by jumping them, while the geese try to trap the fox into an unmovable position.

Marble Solitaire was conceived in Europe during the early eighteenth century. Since then, many designs have appeared, ranging from the ornate to a simple board with holes and wooden pegs. For this project, I chose a classy piece that was in the middle of the range and then modified the design so that it can be done with router cutters in my shop. The board features a parking groove on the rim for holding marbles taken out of play, and a drawer for marble storage.

Rules of Play for Solitare. Play begins with thirty-two marbles in all except the center hole. Marbles are removed from the board by jumping one at a time with an adjacent marble, moving forward, backward, or sideways, but never diagonally. The only moves allowed are by jumping, and play ends when no more moves can be made. A perfect game is when the last marble finishes in the center hole. When you become an ace at the game and are looking for a greater challenge, replace one of the marbles with a different color and try to finish with this marble in the center hole.

Rules of Play for Fox and Geese. The game is played with two people, one being the fox and the other the geese. Play begins with an odd-colored marble in the center position for the fox and thirteen marbles arranged as shown in Figure 3 for the geese. Play alternates with the fox moving first, one position at a time and in any direction including diagonally. He can eliminate geese by jumping one or more at a time, although jumping isn't mandatory. The geese move one position at a time and in any direction *except* diagonally. They may jump other geese, but not the fox. The game ends when the fox reduces the geese to five or the geese have trapped the fox into an unmovable position.

MAKING THE BOARD

Make this handsome piece from a fine cabinet wood such as walnut or cherry. When choosing a board for the playing surface, look for one that has a grain that will create an interesting effect when the four segments are assembled. Begin construction by laying out the board segments ① on the stock as shown in Figures 4 and 5. Rough-cut the material for items ②, ③, and ④ and lay it aside for later. Next, cut the molding detail on each edge of the stock as shown in Figure 5. This is best done on a router table, but a hand-held router will also do the job. First rout the ⅜-inch cove using a core box bit, and take three or more passes to arrive at the dimension to prevent cutter tear-out.

Next, route the ⅜-inch bead using a roundover bit. Finish up the molding by routing the ½-inch marble groove using a core box bit. Again, make the cut in several passes to prevent tear-out.

With the edges molded, the segments can be cut from the stock. Carefully set your saw for a 45-degree angle to make the cuts shown in Figure 5. Any deviation in this angle will show up later as a gap in the assembly, so as a precaution, cut two test pieces from scrap and check with a straight-edge as shown in Figure 6. When you're satisfied with the setup on the saw, cut the segments from the stock.

Now glue up the segments. Do them in pairs, because it's easier to clamp and align the parts together, and you can correct any angular error that may exist before joining the two halves. If you need to straighten the edge, use the setup shown in Figure 6. Then test-fit the two halves, and glue and clamp together.

THE MARBLE HOLES

There are two ways to do the holes. You can drill them if you don't mind the appearance that the drill tip creates on the bottom of the hole, or you can route them to create a smooth depression (a jig and plunge router are required).

For drilling, lay out the pattern on the board and carefully center punch each position; any variation is likely to be seen after drilling. Use a $\frac{1}{2}$-inch diameter Forstner bit to avoid tear-out and drill $\frac{3}{16}$-inch deep.

For routing, Figure 7 illustrates a jig that will accurately position the holes. The base can be made from anything handy, but the locating boards should be $\frac{3}{4}$-inch stock because the top surface must be even with the top of the game board. Mount the router on a $\frac{1}{4}$-by-6-by-12-inch piece of plywood and mark the cut line for two axes. When the game board is fixed in place, establish the center lines on the game board face and transfer onto the locating boards. From the center lines, mark the location points for the router to cut the hole pattern as shown in Figure 7. Make a test piece from $\frac{3}{4}$-inch scrap and rout the hole pattern using a $\frac{1}{2}$-inch diameter core box bit. Make the required adjustments for the positioning lines, then rout the final piece.

CUTTING THE FEET

To make the feet ③, cut two blanks, $\frac{3}{4}$ inch square by $2\frac{1}{4}$ inches, from the leftover board segment stock. Make a pattern of the concave shape on thin cardboard (cereal box material is perfect) and transfer onto the stock. Draw two feet on one blank with the small end of a foot facing each end of the stock. That way, one foot can be clamped in a vise, leaving the other free for shaping. Cut the tight radiuses with a scroll saw, and smooth out the curves with files and sandpaper.

When shaped, cut the pieces to length and install $\frac{5}{8}$-inch-long pieces of $\frac{1}{4}$-inch dowels as shown in the front view drawing. Mark the positions of the feet on the bottom of the board, then carefully drill the dowel holes to a controlled depth to prevent breaking through. Glue the feet in place. When dry, finish-sand everything with 220- and then 320-grit sandpaper.

DRAWER ASSEMBLY

Figure 2 shows the dimensional detail for the drawer parts. Start by cutting the face ④, front ⑥, back ⑦, and sides ⑤ to size from $\frac{1}{4}$-inch stock. Cut the rabbets and dadoes next, using a table saw or router table. Test-fit the parts, then reassemble with glue and clamps, checking for square. The drawer bottom ⑧ is made from $\frac{1}{8}$-inch birch plywood, which can be purchased in small pieces at hobby-supply stores. Measure the opening for the drawer bottom, then cut to size and glue in place. Finish the construction by gluing the face to the drawer and, when dry, finish sand.

Now is a good time to make the escutcheon plate for the pull knob. It takes an extra hour or so to make, but the results are worth it. Using the front view in Figure 1, make a pattern of the plate on thin cardboard by drawing with the grid technique or simply enlarge to size on a photocopier. Using a sharp pencil, transfer the design onto $\frac{1}{32}$-inch thick brass, which can be purchased in small sheets at hobby supply and hardware stores. Use a jeweler's saw or scroll saw with a #0 metal blade to cut the shape, then bevel the edges with needle files. Drill a hole for the pull knob and two for brads as shown in the front view. Finish with a buffing wheel and compound, then spray on a protective coat of lacquer. Mount the $\frac{1}{2}$-inch-diameter brass knob and the plate after the finish has dried. You can order the knob (stock #02622) from Woodcraft, telephone (800) 225-1153.

MOUNTING THE DRAWER

Now mount the drawer with the two drawer guides ② as shown in Figure 2. Cut the pieces from the leftover ¾-inch stock, then drill and countersink for the six #6-by-¾-inch flathead screws. Mark the position for one of the guides on the bottom of the game board and clamp in place. With this guide as a reference, add the drawer and the second guide. Adjust for alignment and smooth sliding, then drill the pilot holes and add the screws.

FINISHING TOUCHES

Go over the parts one more time with 320-grit sandpaper, then apply the finish of your choice. When dry, mount the escutcheon and pull knob and cover the drawer bottom with a piece of felt. You can purchase the marbles from a crafts-supply store or from Meisel Hardware Specialties, telephone (800) 441-9870 (ask for stock #MWH). The green felt can also be ordered from Meisel (#7355).

DIABOLO

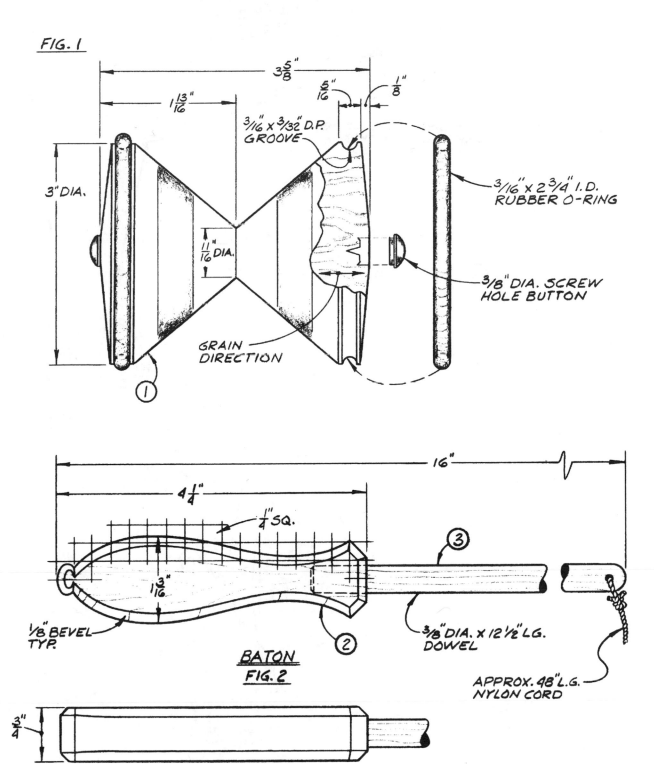

FIG. 1

3 5/8"

1 13/16"

5/16"

1/8"

3/16" x 3/32" D.P. GROOVE

3" DIA.

11/16" DIA.

3/16" x 2 3/4" I.D. RUBBER O-RING

3/8" DIA. SCREW HOLE BUTTON

GRAIN DIRECTION

①

4 1/4"

16"

1/4" SQ.

③

1 3/16"

1/8" BEVEL TYP.

②

BATON
FIG. 2

3/8" DIA. x 12 1/2" LG. DOWEL

APPROX. 48" L.G. NYLON CORD

3/4"

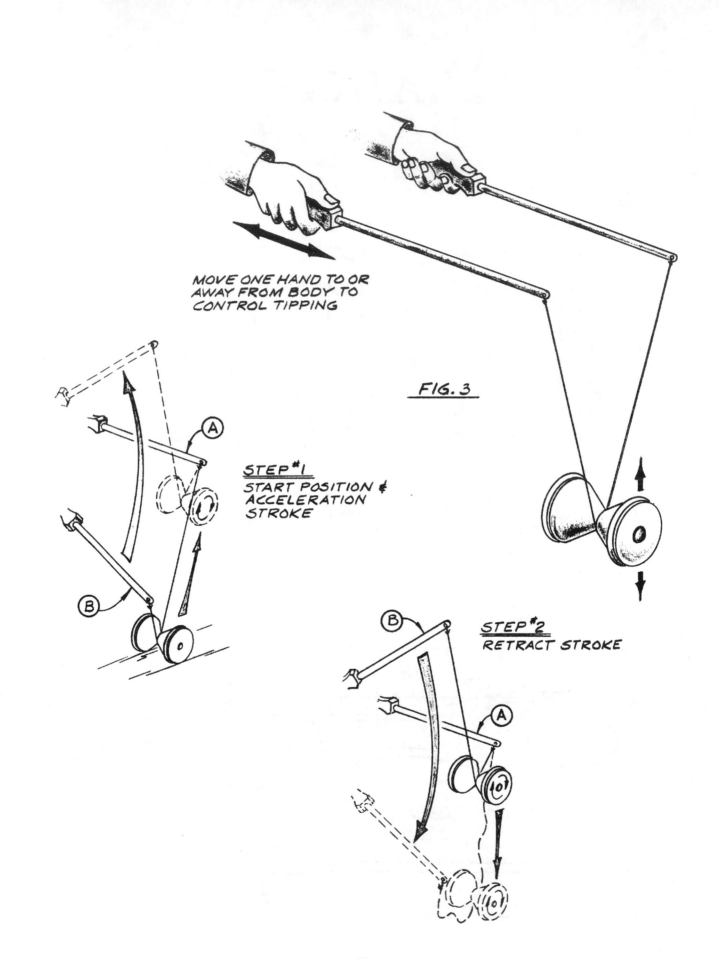

MOVE ONE HAND TO OR
AWAY FROM BODY TO
CONTROL TIPPING

FIG. 3

(A)

(B)

STEP #1
START POSITION &
ACCELERATION
STROKE

(B)

(A)

STEP #2
RETRACT STROKE

70

BILL OF MATERIALS

Stock (inches)	Quantity	Item	Part
3×3×5 hard maple	1	①	top (one)
¾×1¼×9 walnut	1	②	handle (two)
⅜ dia.×36 walnut dowel	1	③	baton (two)

Hardware and Supplies	Quantity	Description
O-rings	2	³⁄₁₆" × 2¾" I.D.
screw hole button	2	⅜" dia.

DIABOLO

The more action a game has, the better young people seem to like it, and this challenging game of dexterity has enough action for anyone. It takes two minutes to explain and years to master. The first step in the game is to get the diabolo spinning, using a cord attached to two batons. Then it can be thrown in the air and caught again, walked across the floor, or tossed to another player. The first step can be accomplished after a few tries, and from there it's practice, practice, practice. Diabolo is exciting to play, inspires competition, and best of all, can be made in a week end.

Diabolo is considered a member of the top family. It originated in China where it was played for hundreds of years under the name of *Kouen-Gen*. In the late eighteenth century, it found its way to Europe, where it caught on at once. It was played by kings and queens and their court as well as youngsters in the street. Across the continent, thou-sands of people formed clubs for social and serious play. More than a century later, Parker Brothers introduced the top in America, and it became an instant success as it had in Europe. Unlike most games, which quickly pass as fads, Diabolo has earned its place within the privileged group of classics that will be enjoyed for generations.

Basic Play. The objective is to get the top into a high rate of continuous rotation by stroking it with a cord. Step 1 in Figure 3 shows the starting position; the top is resting on the floor with baton B held close to the top and baton A held high to keep the cord taut. Start the action by raising baton B at a moderate speed; the top will roll along the string. This is the basic acceleration stroke. When the top gets close to baton A, drop the tip of baton B at a rate equal to the falling top as shown in step 2. Stop baton B at a point that prevents the top from hitting the floor and repeat the acceleration stroke; this time, do it a bit more aggressively to increase the speed of the top. As the acceleration strokes are repeated and the speed increased, the top will become more stable.

In addition to controlling the speed of the top, you have to maintain the balance. If the top starts to tip on the cord, move one of the batons in or out (depending on the direction of rotation) to correct the balance as shown in Figure 3. Have your first practice session outside, or make sure all lamps and vases are safely out of your practice zone.

Advanced Play. Once you've mastered the speed and balance of the toy, try tossing the top in the air at the end of the acceleration stroke and catching it with the cord. Other feats include making the top walk on the floor like a yo-yo or climb your baton stick. The real fun starts when a group of advanced players pass the spinning top among each other and try to match tricks.

MAKING THE TOP

The top is made from 3-by-3-by-5-inch hard maple stock. You can use other woods, but stick to the hardwoods, because this toy will see a lot of abuse.

This is a perfect first project for a wood lathe. The only critical part in turning is having the $^{11}/_{16}$-inch diameter exactly in the middle of the top to ensure proper balance. After turning, apply the finish of your choice while the top is still in the lathe. Then remove the top from the lathe, saw off the scrap ends, and drill and attach $^3/_8$-inch screw hole buttons as shown in Figure 1 for a decorative touch. You can purchase the buttons from McFery's, telephone (800) 443-7937 (ask for stock #BH-1103).

To protect the top from chipping on those hard landings, a $^3/_{16}$-by-2$^3/_4$ inside diameter rubber O-ring is installed on each end by rolling them over the ends of the top and into the $^3/_{16}$-inch retaining grooves. O-rings can be purchased at the larger hardware stores and bearing supply companies.

MAKING THE BATONS

I made my baton handles from $^3/_4$-inch walnut, but any hardwood will do. Lay out the pattern for the handle on thin cardboard (a cereal box is good), then cut and trace onto the stock. Cut the handles to shape using a scroll saw, and drill holes for $^3/_8$-inch dowels. Glue the dowels in place and apply $^1/_8$-inch bevels with a half-round file. Finish sand with 220- and then 320-grit sandpaper. Apply the finish of your choice.

When dry, attach a piece of 50-pound nylon cord between the batons. Start with a 4-foot length, and adjust to what feels most comfortable.

NINE MEN'S MORRIS

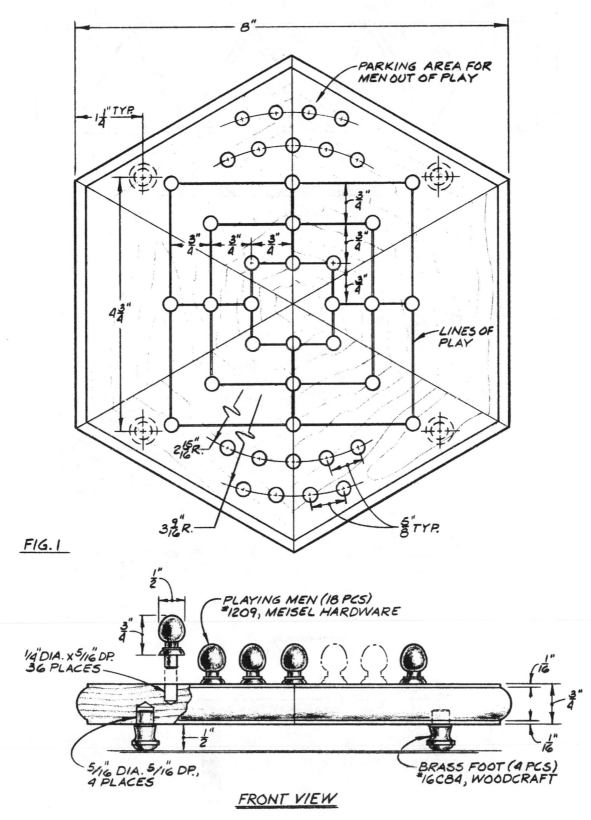

PARKING AREA FOR
MEN OUT OF PLAY

8"

1¼" TYP.

¾"

¾" ¾" ¾"

¾"

¾"

4¾"

LINES OF
PLAY

2 15/16" R.

3 9/16" R.

⅝" TYP.

FIG. 1

½"

¾"

PLAYING MEN (18 PCS)
#1209, MEISEL HARDWARE

¼" DIA. x 5/16" DP.
36 PLACES

1/16"

¾"

1/16"

½"

5/16" DIA. 5/16" DP.,
4 PLACES

BRASS FOOT (4 PCS)
#16C84, WOODCRAFT

FRONT VIEW

75

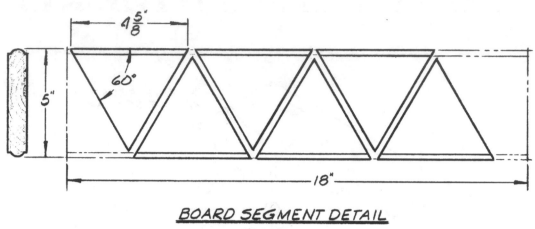

BOARD SEGMENT DETAIL
FIG. 2

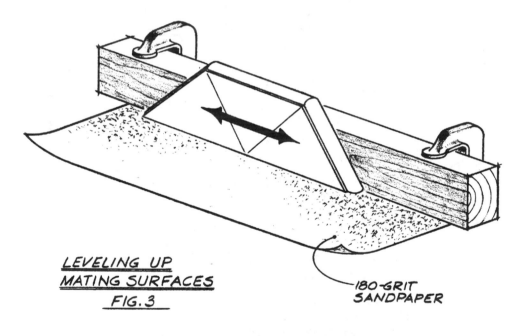

LEVELING UP
MATING SURFACES
FIG. 3

180-GRIT
SANDPAPER

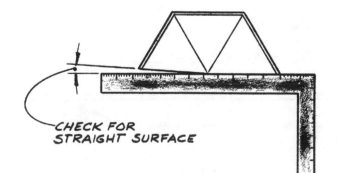

CHECK FOR
STRAIGHT SURFACE

76

NINE MEN'S MORRIS

If your family and friends like games of strategy, build Nine Men's Morris. This ancient English game, played by two people, combines the simplicity of tic-tac-toe with the strategy of chess. Six-year-olds will easily master the rules, and adults will enjoy the battle of wits. This classic game has entertained people for centuries and will likely continue to do so for many more.

The playing field consists of twenty-four playing positions arranged in three concentric boxes. The positions within the boxes are connected with a series of lines of play. On each end of the field, a nine-position parking area is used for the men not in play. The men are small wooden finials that can be purchased from Meisel Hardware Specialties, telephone (800) 441-9870 (ask for stock #1209). If you have a lathe, you can turn the men in the shape of your choice. Use a different color wood for each side.

Rules of Play. Each player has nine men of the same color. Starting with an empty board, players in turn can place a man anywhere on the board to make three in a row along the lines of play. If accomplished, an opponent's man is removed from the board, but not from a row of three unless there is no other alternative. When all of the men have been played, the game continues with the players alternately moving men into free adjacent positions to try for another three in a row. Once formed, the row cannot be repeated on the same line in succession. To win the game, the opponent must be reduced to two men or placed in an unmovable position.

MAKING THE BOARD

For your board, choose a hardwood with a tight grain such as cherry, maple, or birch to provide a smooth playing surface. Begin construction by drawing the board segments on the stock as shown in Figure 1. Before cutting out the segments, rout the edge molding on each side of the stock using a ⅝-inch diameter fingernail (half-radius) bit. You can purchase this bit from Woodworker's Supply, telephone (800) 645-9292 (ask for stock #819-839).

Next, carefully set your saw for the 60-degree cuts required for the board segments. Any deviation in this angle will show up later as a gap in the joints, so as a precaution, cut three test pieces from scrap and check with a straightedge as shown in Figure 3. When the setup looks okay, cut the segments from the stock. Glue up the segments three at a time, because it's easier to clamp and align the parts together, and you can correct any angular error that may exist before joining the two halves. If you need to straighten the edge, use the setup shown in Figure 3. Then test-fit the two halves, and glue and clamp together.

FIELD OF PLAY

Measure and mark the hole positions for the field of play and the parking area. If you bought the finials recommended for the men, check the diameter of the tenons on the bottom and use a drill bit that is at least 1/64 inch bigger for the holes so that the game pieces will not stick in the board. With the hole locations marked, carefully define the location with an awl, and then drill with a bradpoint bit to eliminate tear-out at the mouth of the hole. These bits are available in 1/64-inch increments at most hardware stores.

FINISHING TOUCHES

The last task in the construction is the addition of the brass feet, available from Woodcraft, telephone (800) 535-4482 (ask for stock #16C84). Measure and mark the positions of the feet and drill 5/16 inch deep with a 5/16-inch bit. Don't install the feet until you have applied the finish.

Finish-sand the board starting with 180-grit and progressively working to 320-grit sandpaper. Because of the segment construction, sanding across the grain is inevitable, so thoroughly sand the top with the final grits and check for scratches and then apply the finish of your choice.

When the finish is dry, apply the lines of play. Paint the lines with a highliner brush and an enamel color that contrasts with the wood or use pinstriping tape. Finish the board by pressing in the brass feet.

Finishing the men is a matter of preference. If you paint the men, choose colors that complement the wood in the board. Alternatively, you can stain one group of men and apply a natural finish to the others.

TWIRLER TOPS

FIG. 1

BALLERINA

SOUTHERN BELLE

SHOWN
FULL SIZE

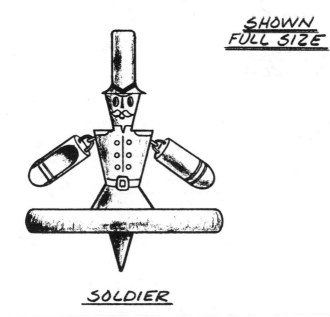

SOLDIER

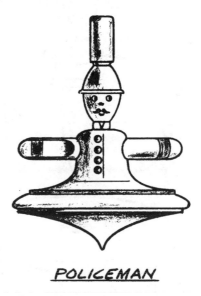

POLICEMAN

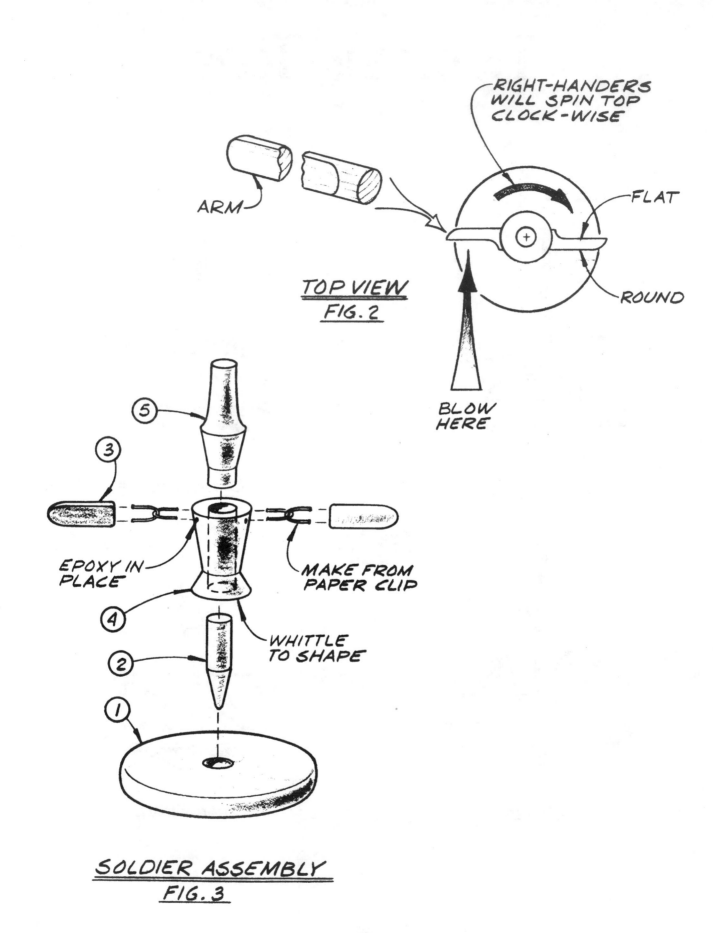

RIGHT-HANDERS
WILL SPIN TOP
CLOCK-WISE

ARM

FLAT

ROUND

TOP VIEW
FIG. 2

BLOW
HERE

5

3

EPOXY IN
PLACE

MAKE FROM
PAPER CLIP

4

WHITTLE
TO SHAPE

2

1

SOLDIER ASSEMBLY
FIG. 3

80

Bill of Materials

Stock (inches)	Quantity	Item	Part
¼ × 2 × 2 hard maple	1	①	disk (one)
¼ dia. × 36 hard maple dowel	1	②	point (one)
		③	arms (two)
⅝ × ⅝ × 13/16 hard maple	1	④	body (one)
7/16 × 7/16 × 1¼ hard maple	1	⑤	head (one)

Hardware and Supplies	Quantity	Description	
paper clip	1	small metal	

TWIRLER TOPS

Here's your chance to let those creative juices flow. Children have always been fascinated with the motion of tops and the challenge of seeing who can make them spin the longest. Twirler tops—the kind spun with the fingers—are a favorite of youngsters because they're easy to put into motion. They have been made in an endless assortment of shapes and sizes, but the most interesting variation is the wind driven type. They are made to look like a variety of characters with projecting arms for wind propulsion. Once the top is in motion, blowing on the arms will keep it going until the player runs out of breath. Just a few possibilities are illustrated here. Make these or come up with your own ideas.

MAKING THE TOP

All of the tops shown are full size. If you have a lathe, making the different shapes shouldn't present a problem. If you don't have a lathe, use the construction technique shown in the exploded view drawing. Simply use a 2-inch diameter disk, a ¼-inch dowel for the bottom part, and whittle the body to shape for the character of your choice. When making the parts, carefully identify the center on each part and try to keep the shape balanced about these points; the better the symmetry, the longer the spin time.

MAKING THE ARMS

The arms add to the appearance of the character, but you may also want to try a top without them. An armless top will spin for about thirty seconds until air resistance—the main reason a top slows—brings it to a stop. If a top has arms, the spin time can be extended by blowing at the proper place on the top. Figure 2 shows how and why this works.

The top is put in motion using the thumb and middle finger. Right-handed players will spin the top clockwise and left-handers counterclockwise, and it is important to shape the arms for the direction of rotation. The back of the arm is round, or slightly pointed, to reduce air resistance and the front is flat to provide a surface to blow on. For left-handed spinners, reverse the features from those shown in the figures.

The easiest way to mount the arms is by gluing them into drilled holes in the body. Another variation is to have them movable on wire hinges; when spun, the arms will raise, creating an interesting motion. Make the hinges by bending pieces of a paper clip into staples and then inserting the ends into drilled holes with epoxy. *Important:* This type of top should not be left with small children, because the arms can be easily pulled from the body.

Rocking Horse

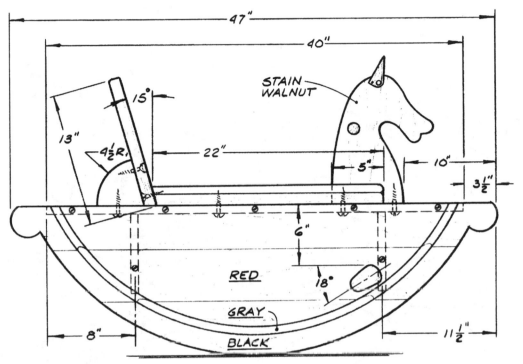

47"

40"

STAIN
WALNUT

15°

13"

4½ R.

22"

5"

10"

3½"

6"

RED

18°

GRAY

BLACK

8"

11½"

SIDE VIEW

FIG. 1

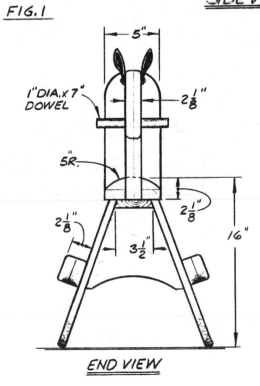

5"

1" DIA. × 7"
DOWEL

2⅛"

5 R.

2⅛"

2⅛"

3½"

16"

END VIEW

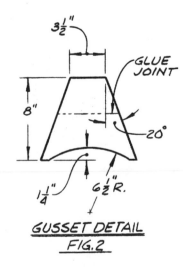

3½"

GLUE
JOINT

8"

20°

1¼"

6½ R.

GUSSET DETAIL
FIG. 2

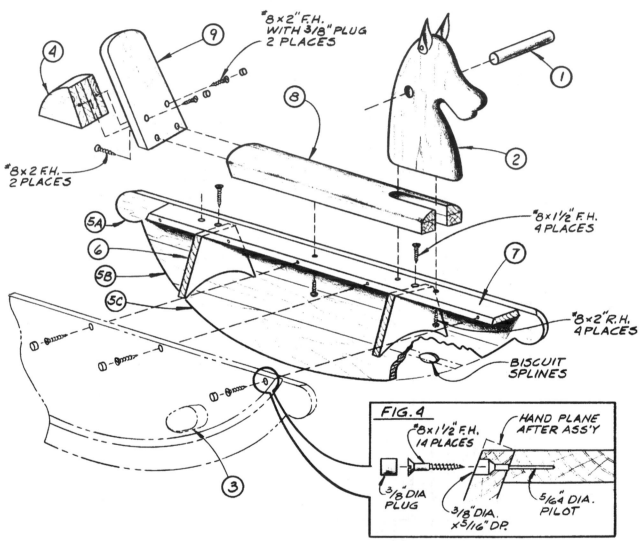

FIG.3

#8×2" F.H.
WITH 3/8" PLUG
2 PLACES

④

⑨

#8×2 F.H.
2 PLACES

⑧

①

②

5A

⑥

5B

5C

#8×1½" F.H.
4 PLACES

⑦

#8×2" R.H.
4 PLACES

BISCUIT
SPLINES

③

FIG.4

#8×1½" F.H.
14 PLACES

HAND PLANE
AFTER ASS'Y

3/8" DIA
PLUG

3/8"DIA.
×5/16" DP.

5/64" DIA.
PILOT

84

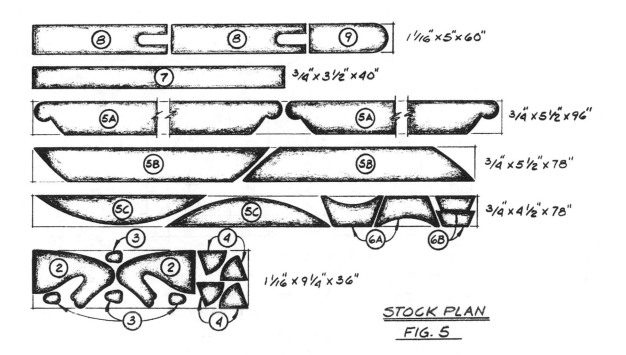

1¹/₁₆" × 5" × 60"

³/₄" × 3¹/₂" × 40"

³/₄" × 5¹/₂" × 96"

³/₄" × 5¹/₂" × 78"

³/₄" × 4¹/₂" × 78"

1¹/₁₆" × 9¹/₄" × 36"

STOCK PLAN
FIG. 5

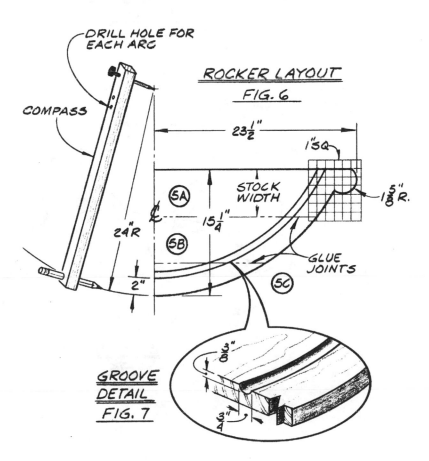

DRILL HOLE FOR
EACH ARC

COMPASS

ROCKER LAYOUT
FIG. 6

23¹/₂"

1"SQ

STOCK
WIDTH

1³/₈"
R.

24"R

15¹/₄"

2"

GLUE
JOINTS

GROOVE
DETAIL
FIG. 7

³/₈"

³/₄"

85

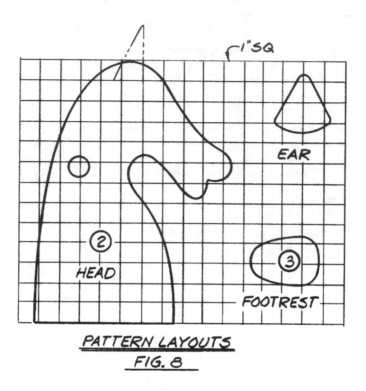

1" SQ

EAR

② HEAD

③ FOOTREST

PATTERN LAYOUTS
FIG. 8

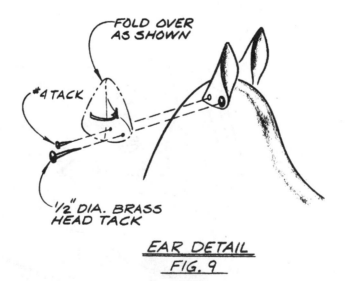

FOLD OVER
AS SHOWN

#4 TACK

1/2" DIA. BRASS
HEAD TACK

EAR DETAIL
FIG. 9

86

BILL OF MATERIALS

Stock (inches)	Quantity	Item	Part
1 dia. × 3b hardwood dowel	1	①	handle (one)
1¹⁄₁₆ × 9¼ × 36 pine	1	②	head pieces (two)
		③	foot rests (four)
		④	back braces (four)
¾ × 5½ × 96 poplar	1	⑤A	rocker sections (two)
¾ × 5½ × 78 poplar	1	⑤B	rocker sections (two)
¾ × 4½ × 78 poplar	1	⑤C	rocker sections (two)
		⑥A	gussets (two)
		⑥B	gussets (two)
¾ × 3½ × 40 poplar	1	⑦	filler plate (one)
1¹⁄₁₆ × 5 × 60 pine	1	⑧	seat pieces (two)
⅜ dia. × 36 maple dowel	1	⑨	seat back (one)
	1	–	screen plugs (sixteen)

Hardware and Supplies	Quantity	Description
wood screws	18	#8 × 1½" F.H.
	4	#8 × 2" F.H.
	4	#8 × 2" F.H.
finishing nails	25	1½"
biscuits	12	#20
upholstery tacks	2	½" dia.
steel tacks	2	#14
leather (4 to 5 oz.)	1	4" × 6"

ROCKING HORSE

If I had to vote for the single most popular toy, it would have to be the rocking horse. Children love the feeling of motion from the day they're born. And this wooden steed will give the three- to five-year-old all the action he or she wants. Best of all, this project takes just a couple of weekends at the workbench.

In early America, toys were usually miniatures of objects of adult life, and children used them to imitate their parents' world. Since the horse was the major mode of transportation until the turn of the century, its not surprising to see it used as the theme for all sorts of toys. Antique rocking horses ranged from simple to complex. An affluent colonial family might commission an artisan to carve a miniature replica of a horse; a family of simpler means would make their own using available materials.

The original of this piece was probably made in the early twentieth century. The straightforward style and tasteful combination of painted and natural wood make this rocking horse very attractive.

Things to Know

Before you begin this project, you'll need to learn or review the techniques discussed in the following sections:
    Drawing Your Patterns
    Joinery with Biscuits

PLANNING THE PROJECT
Think twice and cut once is good advice for this phase of the project. There are many irregular shapes that can waste material if not carefully arranged on the stock. The stock plan in Figure 5 shows how to position these parts for the correct grain direction and good utilization of the material. Note that the rockers ⑤Ⓐ, ⑤Ⓑ and ⑤Ⓒ and gussets ⑥Ⓐ and ⑥Ⓑ are made from several pieces edge-glued together. Narrow boards are easier to find without defects, and the

chance of warpage is reduced when boards with different grain directions are joined together.

Consider how you plan to finish the piece before selecting the wood. The original used poplar for the rocker parts and was painted red with gray and black trim (see side view). The seat and head were pine with a medium walnut stain. If you decide not to use this scheme, make sure you use a hardwood for the parts in the rocker assembly ③, ⑤, ⑥ and ⑦. Rocking horses receive considerable stress when in use, so make yours as strong as possible by gluing all joints and adding screws as shown.

PATTERNS
Draw the patterns of the irregularly shaped pieces, starting with the rocker parts ⑤Ⓐ, ⑤Ⓑ and ⑤Ⓒ shown in Figure 6. Use thin poster board for your pattern material, and draw only half of the rocker since the ends are identical. If you don't have a beam compass for the large arc, make one from scrap ¾ in square by 30 inches long. Fit a pencil into one end and a sharpened nail in the other end to create the pivot for the 24-inch arc. Mark the pivot positions for the groove arcs and drill undersized holes for a tight fit with the nail pivot (see Figure 6).

Because the dimensions of lumber yard stock can vary, measure the exact width of your boards for parts ⑤Ⓐ, ⑤Ⓑ and ⑤Ⓒ and mark them on the pattern (see Figure 6). Cut out the pattern and trace each part onto the stock allowing, ½-inch between parts for rough-cutting. Be careful to align the glue joint marks with the edge of the board. This procedure will assure a smooth curve later when the parts are joined.

Complete the pattern work for the irregularly shaped pieces, then trace the patterns and draw the straight pieces on the stock.

ROCKER PANELS
Start construction by cutting out the rocker parts ⑤Ⓐ, ⑤Ⓑ and ⑤Ⓒ using a band saw or jigsaw. Don't

cut the 20-degree angle on the top edge of the ⑤Ⓐ parts; this operation is easier to do later in the assembly. If you decide to use the biscuit splines for extra strength, cut the pockets now and then test-fit the assembly together. You may find it easier to glue up in two steps. Start with ⑤Ⓐ and ⑤Ⓑ, and add ⑤Ⓒ after the first joint is dry. Clamping on the curved surfaces of ⑤Ⓒ can be difficult. You can do so by reattaching the pieces of waste removed from the curve with double-sided tape to create nonslip, parallel surfaces for the clamps.

When dry, use 120-grit sandpaper to do a first sanding on both sides of the panels. Smooth out the curves using a hand plane, spokeshave, and files for the inside corners. Finish up the panels by adding the decorative groove using a router and a ¾-inch diameter core box bit (see Figure 7). If your router is not equipped with an arc-cutting attachment, make a ¼-inch thick plywood template to guide the router through the arc.

ASSEMBLING THE BASE

The most important task in building the base is matching the 3½-inch dimension on the filler plate ⑦ and gusset ⑥. If this is done accurately, the base will go together easily with gapfree joints.

Start by cutting the 3½-by-40-inch filler plate ⑦ to size. Rip the 20 degree angle on both sides as shown in the end view drawing. Measure 8 inches from each end and mark the locations of the two gussets ⑥. Next, rough-cut the gusset parts ⑥Ⓐ and ⑥Ⓑ from the stock, allowing an extra ½ inch on the width for final cutting. Glue and clamp the ⑥Ⓐ and ⑥Ⓑ parts together, then, when dry, cut the gussets to their final width so that the 3½-inch dimension accurately matches the bottom of the filler plate.

Begin the assembly by dry-clamping the two gussets to the inside of the location lines on the filler plate. Verify that the edges of the gussets are even and square in two planes with the filler plate, then drill and countersink for two #8 screws at each location as shown in the exploded view drawing. Disassemble, then redo with glue and #8-by-1½-

inch flathead screws. Finish up with a final check for squareness.

Position the filler plate and gusset assembly on the inside surface of the rocker panel. Using a sharp pencil, trace the periphery of the assembly on the panel to create a "footprint" of the mating surfaces. Mark the positions of the screws in the "footprint" and drill 5/64-inch pilot holes for the #8 screws. This ensures that the screws are going to hit their mark. Next, dry-assemble the parts by having a helper hold one end of the assembly while you tack everything in alignment with 1½-inch finishing nails driven partway home. When you're satisfied with the results, complete the drilling for the #8 screws and add the counterbores for the plugs as shown in Figure 4. Carefully pull out the nails to disassemble, then redo with glue and #8-by-1½-inch flathead screws.

Repeat the above process for the second rocker panel. After the glue has dried, hand plane the two upper panel corners flush as shown in Figure 4 inset. Now cut the ⅜-inch plugs and glue into the screw counterbores on both panels. When dry, use a sharp chisel to trim the plugs flush, and follow up with a first sanding with 120-grit sandpaper.

The foot rests ③ are the last parts to be added to the base. Rough-cut the parts from the stock to about ⅜ inch oversize for final cutting. Glue the two layers together. When dry, band saw to their final shape and finish sand. Position on the rocker panel as shown in the side view, and then attach with glue and #8-by-2-inch flathead screws from the inside.

HEAD AND SEAT

The head ② is laminated from two pieces of 1 1/16-inch stock. Cut the parts from the stock using a band saw or jigsaw and then glue and clamp together. Smooth out the curves with a spokeshave and use files for the tight spots. Finish off all of the edges, except the base, with a router and a ⅜-inch roundover bit. Drill the 1-inch hole for the handle ① using a Forstner or spade bit. Back up the part with a piece of scrap to prevent bit tear-out. Cut the handle to size and glue in place.

Rip a 5-inch wide piece of stock for the seat and back parts ⑧ and ⑨ as shown in Figure 5. Cut the two seat pieces 22 inches long and glue and clamp together. Use a hand plane and sandpaper to put the 5-inch radius on the top surface. If you don't feel confident doing this operation by eye, make a 5-inch-radius template from poster board. Complete the seat by cutting the 15-degree angle on the back and the 5-inch-long slot to accept the head.

Cut the seat back ⑨ and the gusset ④ pieces to shape. Glue and clamp the four gusset pieces together. When dry, use a sanding block to smooth out the curved surface. Next, join the seat back to the seat with glue and two #8-by-2-inch flathead screws. Attach the gusset to the seat assembly with two #8-by-2-inch flathead screws that are counter-bored and plugged. Glue the head in place to complete the assembly.

FINISHING TOUCHES

For the original finish, prime and paint the base first, using the color scheme indicated on the side view drawing. Stain and varnish the seat assembly, and then attach to the base using four #8-by-2-inch roundhead screws as shown in the side view drawing.

If you prefer an all natural finish, first attach the seat assembly to the base. Finish-sand with 220-grit sandpaper, and then apply the finish of your choice.

The final task is making the ears. Use a pliable 4- to 5-ounce leather in a color that matches your finish. Apply as shown in Figure 9. Leather can be purchased from Tandy Leather Company, telephone (800) 821-0801.

THREE-WHEELED DOLL PRAM

FIG. 1

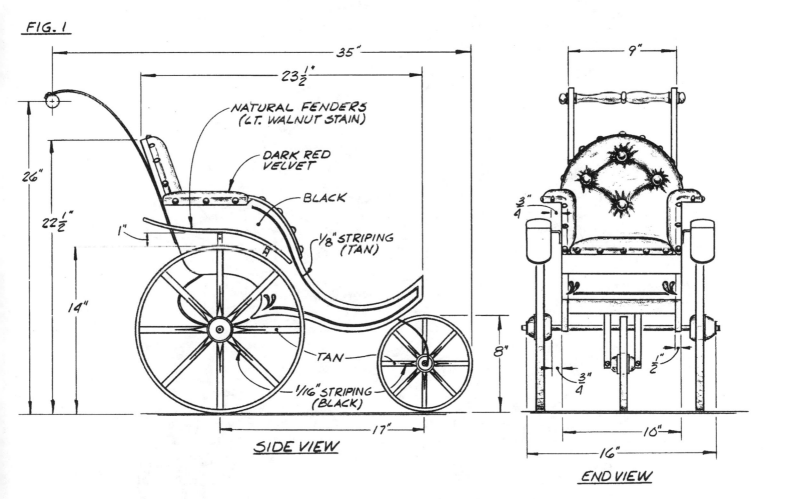

NATURAL FENDERS
(LT. WALNUT STAIN)

DARK RED
VELVET

BLACK

1/8" STRIPING
(TAN)

TAN

1/16" STRIPING
(BLACK)

SIDE VIEW

END VIEW

FIG. 2

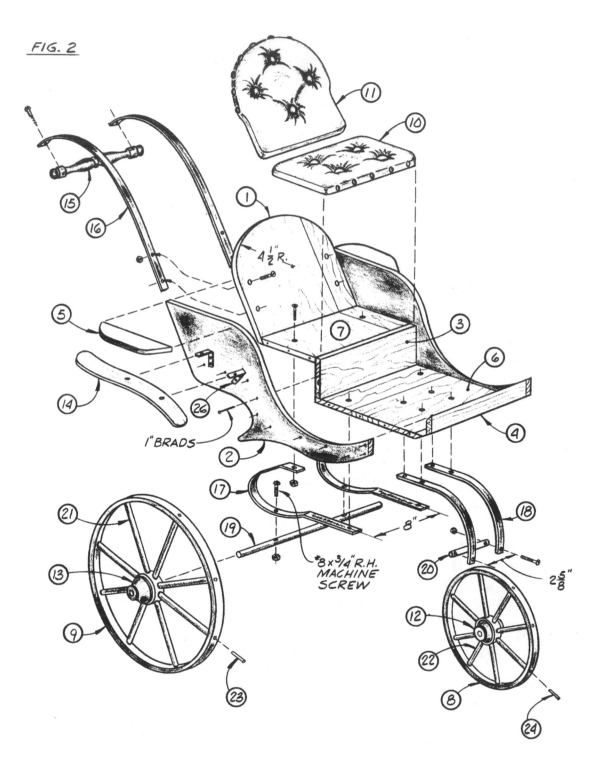

4 ½" R.

1" BRADS

#8 × ¾" R.H.
MACHINE
SCREW

8"

2 ⅝"

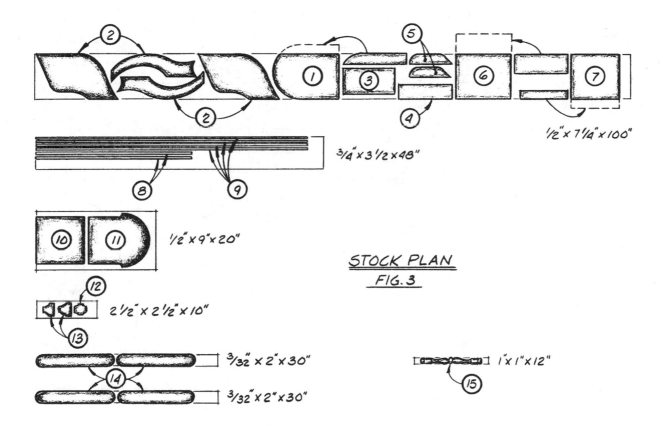

① ②

⑤

④

③ ⑥ ⑦

½" x 7¼" x 100"

¾" x 3½ x 48"

⑧ ⑨

⑩ ⑪   ½" x 9" x 20"

STOCK PLAN
FIG. 3

⑫   2½" x 2½" x 10"

⑬

③⁄₃₂" x 2" x 30"

⑭

③⁄₃₂" x 2" x 30"

⑮   1" x 1" x 12"

93

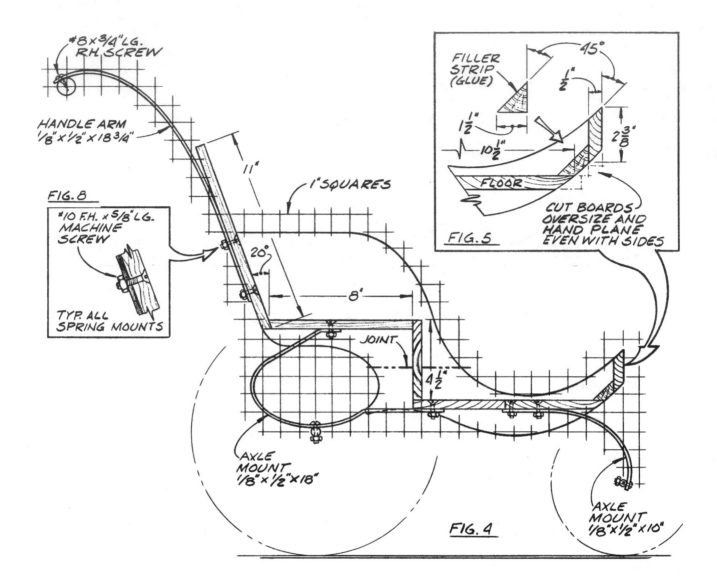

#8 × 3/4" LG. R.H. SCREW

HANDLE ARM 1/8" × 1/2" × 18 3/4"

FIG. 8

#10 F.H. × 5/8" LG. MACHINE SCREW

TYP. ALL SPRING MOUNTS

11"

1" SQUARES

20°

8"

JOINT

4 1/2"

FILLER STRIP (GLUE)

45°

1/2"

1 1/2"

10 1/2"

2 3/8"

FLOOR

CUT BOARDS OVERSIZE AND HAND PLANE EVEN WITH SIDES

FIG. 5

AXLE MOUNT 1/8" × 1/2" × 18"

AXLE MOUNT 1/8" × 1/2" × 10"

FIG. 4

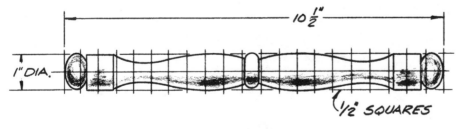

10 1/2"

1" DIA.

1/2 SQUARES

HANDLE FIG. 6

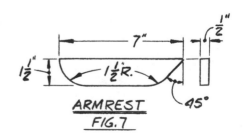

7"

1/2"

1 1/2"

1 1/2" R.

45°

ARMREST FIG. 7

94

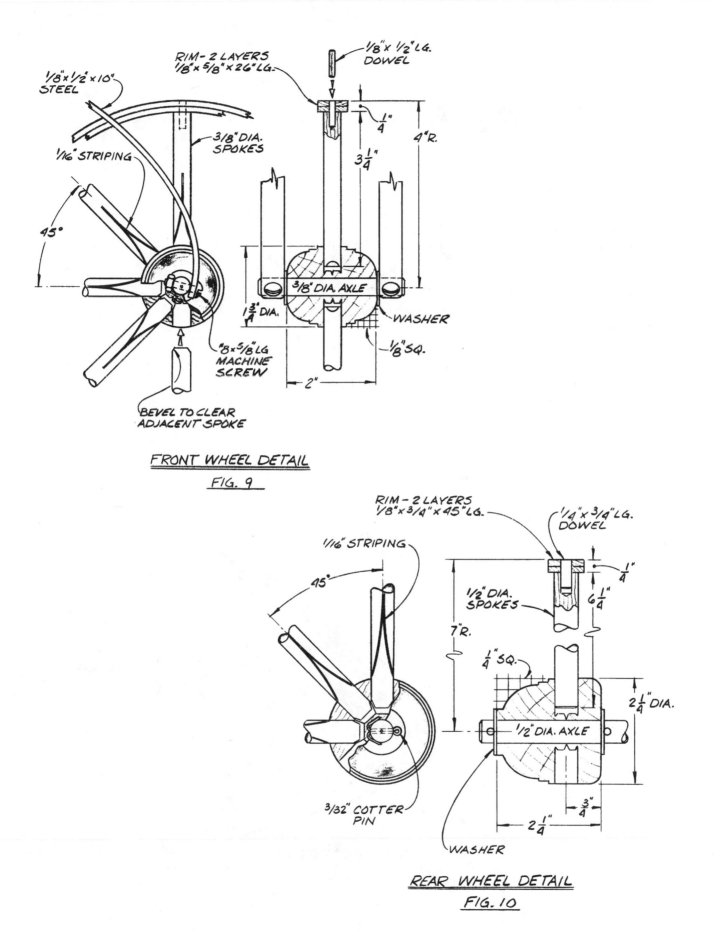

1/8" x 1/2" x 10"
STEEL

RIM - 2 LAYERS
1/8" x 5/8" x 26" LG.

1/8" x 1/2" LG.
DOWEL

1/16" STRIPING

3/8" DIA.
SPOKES

45°

1"
4

4" R.

3 1/4"

3/8" DIA. AXLE

1 3/4" DIA.

WASHER

#8 x 5/8" LG
MACHINE
SCREW

1/8" SQ.

2"

BEVEL TO CLEAR
ADJACENT SPOKE

FRONT WHEEL DETAIL
FIG. 9

RIM - 2 LAYERS
1/8" x 3/4" x 45" LG.

1/4" x 3/4" LG.
DOWEL

1/16" STRIPING

45°

1/2" DIA.
SPOKES

1"
4

6 1/4"

7" R.

1/4" SQ.

1/2" DIA. AXLE

2 1/4" DIA.

3/32" COTTER
PIN

3/4"

2 1/4"

WASHER

REAR WHEEL DETAIL
FIG. 10

95

FENDER DETAIL
FIG. 11

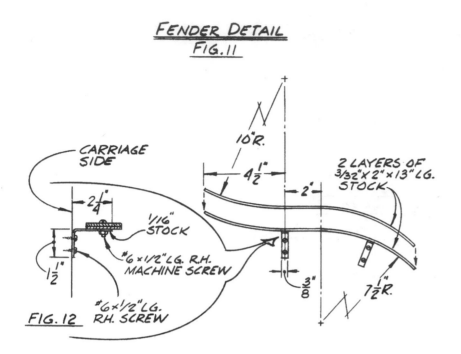

CARRIAGE SIDE

10"R.

4½"

2 LAYERS OF
3/32" × 2" × 13" LG.
STOCK

2¼"

1/16" STOCK

2"

#6 × 1/2" LG. R.H.
MACHINE SCREW

1½"

3/8"

7½"R.

FIG. 12

#6 × 1/2" LG.
R.H. SCREW

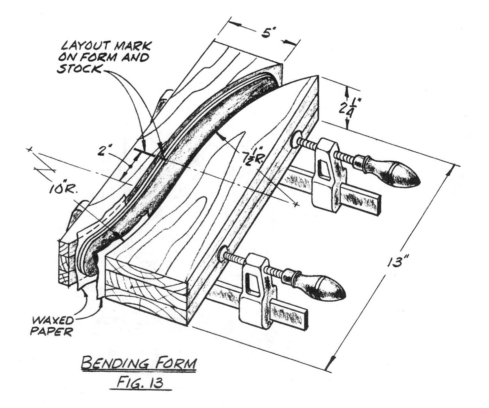

LAYOUT MARK
ON FORM AND
STOCK

5'

2¼"

2"

7½"R.

10"R.

13"

WAXED
PAPER

BENDING FORM
FIG. 13

FIG. 15

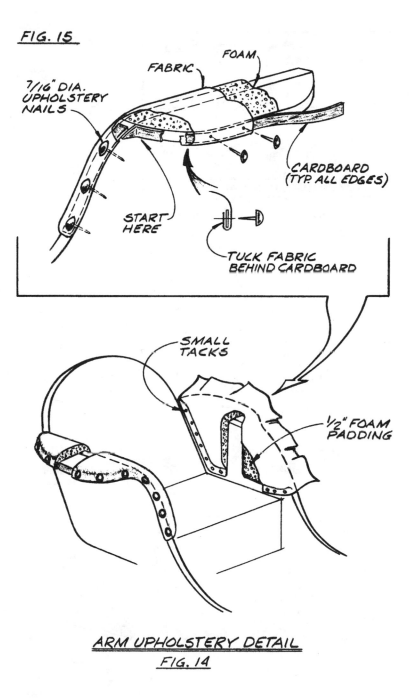

7/16" DIA.
UPHOLSTERY
NAILS

FABRIC

FOAM

CARDBOARD
(TYP. ALL EDGES)

START
HERE

TUCK FABRIC
BEHIND CARDBOARD

SMALL
TACKS

1/2" FOAM
PADDING

ARM UPHOLSTERY DETAIL
FIG. 14

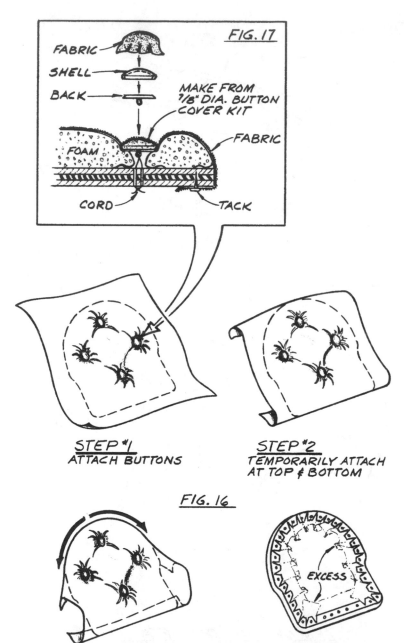

FIG. 17

FABRIC

SHELL

BACK

MAKE FROM 7/8" DIA. BUTTON COVER KIT

FOAM

FABRIC

CORD

TACK

STEP #1
ATTACH BUTTONS

STEP #2
TEMPORARILY ATTACH
AT TOP & BOTTOM

FIG. 16

STEP #3
TEMPORARILY ATTACH
SIDES

STEP #4
1. WORK OUT REMAINING
   WRINKLES & TACK
   IN PLACE.
2. TRIM EXCESS

EXCESS

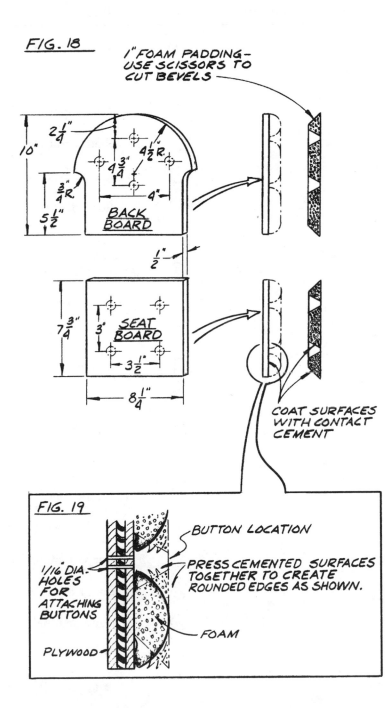

FIG. 18

1" FOAM PADDING –
USE SCISSORS TO
CUT BEVELS

$2\frac{1}{4}"$

$10"$

$4\frac{3}{4}"$

$4\frac{1}{2}"$ R.

$\frac{3}{4}"$ R.

$5\frac{1}{2}"$

$4"$

BACK BOARD

$\frac{1}{2}"$

$7\frac{3}{4}"$

$3"$

SEAT BOARD

$3\frac{1}{2}"$

$8\frac{1}{4}"$

COAT SURFACES
WITH CONTACT
CEMENT

FIG. 19

BUTTON LOCATION

$1/16"$ DIA. HOLES FOR ATTACHING BUTTONS

PRESS CEMENTED SURFACES
TOGETHER TO CREATE
ROUNDED EDGES AS SHOWN.

FOAM

PLYWOOD

BILL OF MATERIALS

Stock (inches)	Quantity	Item	Part
½ × 7¼ × 100 poplar	1	①	seat back (one)
		②	sides (two)
		③	seat support (one)
		④	footboard (one)
		⑤	arm rests (two)
		⑥	floorboard (one)
		⑦	seat (one)
¾ × 3½ × 48 straight-grained oak	1	⑧	front rim strips (two)
		⑨	rear rim strips (four)
½ × 9 × 20 plywood	1	⑩	seat board (one)
		⑪	back board (one)
2½ × 2½ × 10 poplar	1	⑫	front wheel hub (one)
		⑬	rear wheel hubs (two)
3/32 × 2 × 30 oak	2	⑭	fender strips (four)
1 × 1 × 12 oak	1	⑮	handle (one)
⅛ × ½ × 62 steel	2	⑯	handle arms (two)
		⑰	rear axle mounts (two)
		⑱	front axle mounts (two)
½ dia. × 17 steel	1	⑲	rear axle (one)
⅜ dia. × 3¼ steel	1	⑳	front axle (one)
½ dia. × 36 maple or birch dowel	3	㉑	rear spokes (sixteen)
⅜ dia. × 36 maple or birch dowel	1	㉒	front spoke (eight)
¼ dia. × 36 maple or birch dowel	1	㉓	spoke dowels (sixteen)

Stock (inches)	Quantity	Item	Part
⅛ dia. × 36 maple or birch dowel	1	㉔	spoke dowels (eight)
¾ × 5 × 39 pine	1	㉕	bending form (three)
1⁄16 × ⅜ × 16 steel	1	㉖	fender brackets (four)

Hardware and supplies	Quantity	Description
wood screws	8	#6 × ½" R.H.
	2	#8 × ¾" R.H.
machine screws	12	#10 × ⅝" F.H.
	4	#6 × ½" R.H.
	2	#8 × ⅝" R.H.
	2	#8 × ¾" R.H.
nuts	4	#6
	4	#8
	12	#10
washers	4	½"
	2	⅜"
brads	50	1"
upholstery nails	35	7⁄16" dia.
upholstery fabric	1	yard
foam padding	1	sq. ft, ½"
	2	sq. ft., 1"
button cover kit	8	⅞" dia.
cotter pin	2	3⁄32" × ¾"

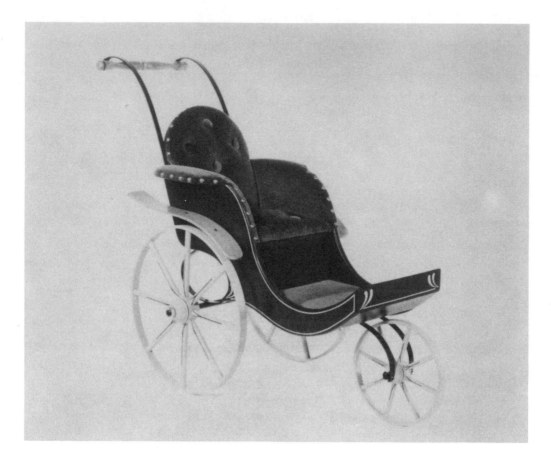

THREE-WHEELED DOLL PRAM

This doll carriage is delightfully elegant with its flowing lines, velvet upholstery, and spoked wheels. And even a three-year-old can enjoy this pram because it's lightweight and petite—the handle is only 26 inches high. This is definitely more than a weekend project, but the construction is straightforward and even the spoked wheels can be easily made with the method described earlier in the book.

Three-wheeled prams—short for perambulators—are of British origin. During the 1840s, four-wheeled baby carriages were considered a menace to pedestrians so they were classed as road vehicles and banned from London sidewalks. The three-wheeled pram was born. Eventually this popular carriage style was used for doll prams both in Europe and America.

Things to Know

Before you begin this project, you'll need to learn or review the techniques discussed in the following sections:
  Drawing Your Patterns
  Steam-Bending Wood
  How to Make a Spoked Wheel
  Decorating Your Projects

PLANNING THE PROJECT

The original pram was painted black with tan wheels, stained wooden fenders, and red velvet upholstery, but you can obtain striking results with other color schemes and woods. A natural walnut or cherry body with a contrasting paint on the wheels would make an attractive variation. The body should be made from a hardwood for durability. If you would like to simplify the project, you can omit the upholstery.

PATTERNS

This project has many irregular-shaped pieces, so do the pattern work before cutting any wood. The body, handle, handle arms, axle mounts (Figures 4 and 6) require full-size patterns. Draw these parts on thin poster board, then cut out and position the wooden body patterns on the stock as shown in Figure 3. Allow sufficient space between pieces for the saw cuts, then trace the patterns and draw the straight pieces.

WHEEL ASSEMBLY

The spoked wheels can easily be made by following the procedures in the sections How to Make a Spoked Wheel and Steam-Bending Wood in the first part of this book. You'll need two jigs, one for each size wheel.

The construction method for the front and rear wheels (Figures 9 and 10) is essentially the same. The hubs are shown as turnings, but if you don't have a lathe, you can achieve the same results by cutting out a cylinder and rounding the edges with a chisel and file. The spokes are simply straight dowels, and the rims are made from two layers of straight-grained ⅛-inch oak with staggered joints. Using a laminate construction on the rim eliminates the influence of grain direction in the individual layers, resulting in a near-perfect round wheel.

If you would like to eliminate the step of making your own rims, substitute with 8- and 14-inch diameter embroidery hoop assemblies. Remove the clamp hardware from the outer hoop, then glue the two hoops together. They aren't as strong as the oak rims, but you can build the wheels in half the time.

Once you've made the steamer and the jigs, the next step is to make the parts for the wheels (Figures 9 and 10). Start by turning the two rear hubs ⑬ and the front hub ⑫. If you don't have a

lathe, you can make the hubs from a lamination of disks cut out with a scroll saw (see page 18). Do not drill the spoke holes at this time; the layout and drilling will be done later on the assembly jig. Complete the hubs by drilling the axle holes with a drill press to ensure squareness.

The spokes are made from ⅜-inch and ½-inch dowel stock. When buying dowels, always check the accuracy of the diameter. I use a small block of wood with a hole drilled to the dowel size. I look for stock that has a slip fit with the gauge, and absolutely avoid the excessively loose or tight ones. Cut sixteen 6¼-inch-long spokes from the ½-inch stock for the rear wheels and eight 3¼-inch-long spokes from the ⅜-inch stock for the front. Also cut eight ⅝-inch-long dowels from the ⅛-inch stock and 16¾-inch-long dowels from the ¼-inch stock for attaching the rims to the spokes.

Next, make the rim strips ⑧ and ⑨. Use a straight-grained wood that has good steam-bending characteristics, such as oak, ash, or hickory. Rip the strips from the stock, and as a precaution, cut an extra piece of each size in case one breaks during bending. Steam-bend the rim pieces (see page 16).

Now assemble the wheel parts (see page 19). The jigs are used in every step of the assembly and consequently become a bottleneck in the process. Making more jigs would help, but I've found it convenient to move on to other parts of the pram and come back to the wheels when the jig becomes available.

BUILDING THE BODY

The assembly details for the body are clearly shown in Figure 4 and the exploded view drawing (see Figure 2). First cut the pieces for the two side panels ② and glue up. Next, cut the inside body pieces ①, ③, ④, ⑥ and ⑦ and mark with their item numbers to prevent confusion. Back ①, seat ⑦, and floorboard ⑥ are each made from more than one piece. Glue these up, then when dry, join the seat, seat support ③, and floorboard with glue and 1-inch brads, and check for square.

Sand down all of the surfaces on the side pieces,

then rout a $^3/_{16}$-inch-radius roundover on the edges except where the arm rest, back, and footboard attach. Draw the positions of the seat and floorboards on the inside surface of each side piece. Once the floor line is established, place the floorboard assembly on the line and trace its periphery to create a "footprint" of the mating surfaces. Now mark brad positions spaced 2 inches apart on the "footprint," then drill $^1/_{16}$-inch pilots through. This way, you're guaranteed that the brads will hit their mark when driven from the other side. Glue, align, and clamp the floorboard assembly to one side piece, then flip over and drive the 1-inch brads. When attaching the second side, use the same procedure and include the back and headboard ④. Finish up the body by adding the arm rests ⑤ and the filler strip shown in Figure 5 inset. When dry, use a hand plane to smooth down the bottom surface of the headboard, filler strip, and floorboard.

METAL PARTS

With the body done, move on to "ironing the carriage," as the old craftsmen would have said. Use the patterns you made earlier for the handle arms ⑯, rear axle mounts ⑰, and front axle mounts ⑱. All of these parts are made from $^1/_8$-inch-by-$^1/_2$-inch mild steel and can be purchased from better-stocked hardware stores or steel supply houses.

When bending parts with flowing curves such as these the goal is to form the stock by gently using your hands to avoid kinks; don't use a hammer. Starting with the handle arms ⑯, clamp the handle end of one piece of stock (about $^3/_8$ inch) in a metal vise so that the bending can be done parallel to the floor. Grip the free end of the stock with one hand and apply a pulling force while using the palm of your other hand to push on the point where you want the bend to occur. Beginning at the vise end, massage the curve into the stock with this hand technique. Do about half of the curve, then remove it from the vise and check it against the pattern. Use a grease pencil to mark where the part strays from the curve, and return the piece to the vise. When

you're satisfied with the shape, cut the piece to length. Use the same technique for the front axle mounts.

The rear axle mounts ⑰ have a sharp bend that requires a hammer. Starting from either end, mark the position of the first sharp bend. Clamp to the bend with the vise and carefully strike at the bend point with a heavy (2-pound) hammer. Use the hand technique for the curved portion and then the hammer again for the second sharp bend. Finish up the parts by adding the holes for the screw hardware, and lay the parts aside for now.

The axles ⑲ and ⑳ are made from mild steel measuring $^1/_2$ by 17 inches for the rear and $^3/_8$ by 3$^1/_4$ inches for the front. Once cut to length, locate the positions of the mounting and cotter pin holes for both shafts, then center-punch. Drill $^3/_{16}$-inch holes for the #8 mounting screws and $^7/_{64}$-inch holes for the cotter pins, then follow up with a countersink tool to deburr both sides of the holes. Lay the finished parts aside for final assembly.

The fender brackets ㉖ (Figures 11 and 12) are the last of the metal parts to be made. Starting with $^1/_{16}$-inch mild sheet steel, lay out four pieces $^3/_8$ by 3$^3/_4$ inches long. Mark the positions of the two mounting screws and drill with a $^5/_{32}$-inch bit. Leave the drilling of the fender mounting screw hole for final assembly. Cut out the brackets with a hacksaw or a scroll saw with a metal-cutting blade. Complete the brackets by smoothing down the edges with a file and making the 90-degree bend.

FENDERS

The method for making the fenders ⑭ is shown in Figures 11 and 13. They are made from two laminations of $^3/_{32}$-inch oak stock that are simply glued and clamped in a form rather than steam-bent. Make the $^3/_{32}$-inch stock by starting with $^3/_4$-inch-by-2-inch oak and resawing an $^1/_8$-inch thick piece off each side with a band saw. This way, you have a smooth surface on each piece. Then, using double-sided tape, stick the smooth side onto a piece of $^3/_4$-inch stock to give it support, and work the thickness down to ³/₃₂ inch with a hand plane or joiner. Cut four pieces to length but don't round the ends until after forming.

Next make the bending form ㉕ by gluing up three pieces of ³/₄-by-5-by-13-inch stock (see Figure 13). Lay out the curve to the dimensions shown, then cut with a band saw. Mark the center line on the form and on the edge of the fender pieces to aid in positioning when clamping up. To prevent excess glue from bonding the pieces to the form, line each clamping face with waxed paper held in place with double-sided tape. Wet the outside surfaces of the fender pieces to aid bending, glue the mating surfaces, and clamp in the form. Leave the fender in the form for one or two days, then remove, round each end, and finish-sand.

HANDLE

Figure 6 shows the detail for the handle ⑮. If you have a lathe, this part should be easy. If not, you can make a simplified version by starting with a 1-inch oak dowel and creating your own shape.

PUTTING IT ALL TOGETHER

Start the final assembly by mounting up the front axle assembly as shown in Figure 4. First, join the front axle and wheel to the axle mounts using #8-by-³/₄-inch roundhead machine screws with nuts. Position the assembly on the bottom of the body so that the axle is even with the headboard, then mark the mounting hole locations. Drill ⁷/₃₂-inch holes and countersink for #10 screws. Attach with four #10-by-⁵/₈-inch flathead machine screws with nuts.

Next, build up the rear axle assembly by joining the rear axle with the rear mounts using #8-by-³/₄-inch roundhead machine screws and nuts. Position the assembly for 17 inches between axles, then mark the hole locations. Drill ⁷/₃₂-inch holes and countersink for #10 screws. Attach with four #10-by-⁵/₈-inch flathead machine screws with nuts.

Now mount up the rear wheels with the hardware shown in Figure 10. Then, using C-clamps, temporarily attach the mounting brackets to the

fenders in the positions shown in Figures 11 and 12. Use the dimensions on the side and end view drawings to position the fenders on the body. When the location looks okay, mark the mounting hole locations and position the brackets on the bottom of the fender. Locate then drill the mounting holes for the #6 screws in the fenders and brackets. Temporarily mount the fenders on the body to check for alignment.

Finish up the assembly by attaching the handle. Join the handle arms to the handle first, using #8-by-³/₄-inch roundhead screws. Clamp this assembly onto the back so that it meets the dimensions shown in Figure 1. When you're satisfied with the alignment, mark the mounting hole locations, then drill ⁷/₃₂-inch holes and countersink for #10 screws. Attach with four #10-by-⁵/₈-inch flathead machine screws with nuts.

FINISHING TOUCHES

The type of finish you choose is a matter of the wood used and personal preference. For my pram, I used an enamel finish on the body and wheels and a natural finish on the handle and fenders. To do the same, disassemble the pram, and give the wooden parts that are to be painted a coat of sandable primer. Thoroughly scrub the metal parts, then spray them with autobody primer. Spray the body and metalwork with two coats of satin black enamel and the wheels with two coats of tan. If you don't have a paint sprayer, the pram is small enough that you can use aerosol spray cans. The decorative striping can be applied with striping tape or hand-painted.

SEAT UPHOLSTERY

Although the upholstery is optional, the appearance it creates makes the extra time worthwhile. For a dramatic look, I used red velvet for my pram, but any flexible fabric will do. The fabric, foam padding, button cover kits, and upholstery nails are available at fabric stores.

Start with the seat and back assemblies (Figure 18). Cut the seat board ⑩ and back board ⑪ from

½-inch plywood stock as shown in Figure 3. Measure and mark the positions of the buttons, then drill two ¹⁄₁₆-inch holes at each location. Trace the outline of the seat and back boards onto 1-inch foam padding, then use a nail to transfer the button locations. Cut out the foam pieces with scissors, beveling at the button hole locations and outside edges. Apply contact cement to the mating surface of each board and the beveled side of the foam pads. When dry to the touch, place the foam pads on each board and press the beveled edges down to create rounded edges around the pieces and buttonholes.

Figure 16 illustrates the steps used to cover the padded parts. First, make eight covered buttons using a ⅞-inch button cover kit as shown in Figure 17. Then, starting with the back board, cut a piece of fabric of sufficient size and attach using the buttons as shown in step 1. Use a temporary knot when attaching the buttons so that they can be adjusted later if needed. Now pull the fabric around the top and bottom and attach with a couple of tacks or staples from the back (step 2). Balance out the wrinkles as you progressively attach the fabric to the back (step 3). Start at the top and hop from side to side, attaching at only three or four places per side. Pull out the fabric between the first tack points to eliminate wrinkles (step 4). Don't pull the fabric too tight; it's okay to have some wrinkles, especially where they won't be seen. When you're pleased with the results, trim off the excess fabric so that the back will lay flat against the body. Finish up by adding the decorative upholstery nails as shown in Figure 1. Repeat this procedure for the seat.

To cover the arms (Figures 14 and 15), make a paper pattern of the area to be covered by the foam padding. Trace the pattern for each arm onto ½-inch foam and cut out with a scissors, again beveling the outside edges of the foam. Attach with contact cement. Next, make a paper pattern for the fabric, allowing several extra inches at the arm rest. Begin attaching the fabric along the seat and back, being careful to avoid wrinkles along the way. Then trim the fabric around the arm rest, allowing an excess of about ⅝-inch for tucking under. To create a straight edge when tacking, use ⅜-inch wide strip of stiff cardboard (such as the back of a tablet), as shown in Figure 15. Wrap the fabric under both cardboard strips, pull in place, and secure temporarily with heavy-duty straight pins. Then start at the front of the arm rest to work out the wrinkles, repinning as you go. When you're satisfied with the results, progressively replace the pins with the decorative upholstery nails. Cover the second arm, attach the seat and back with a screw from the opposite side, and your masterpiece is ready for its new owner!

ROLLING HORSE

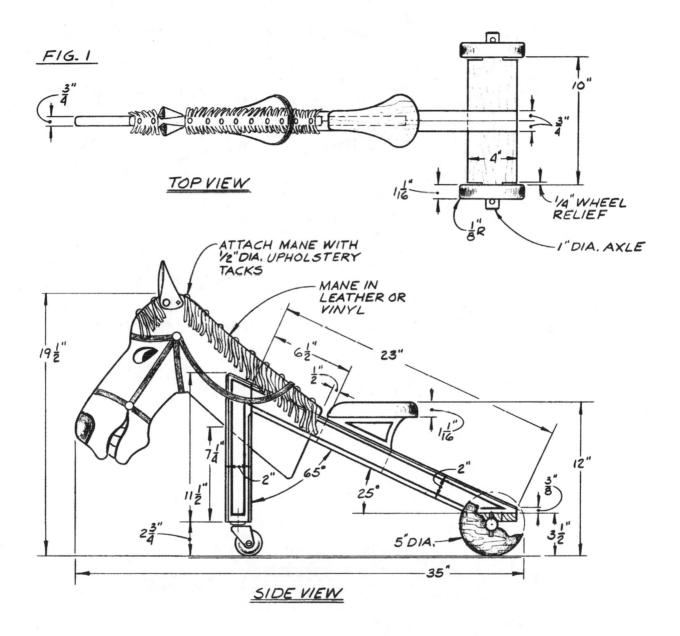

FIG. 1

TOP VIEW

10"

¾"

4"

3"
4

1
16

⅛"R

¼" WHEEL RELIEF

1"DIA. AXLE

ATTACH MANE WITH ½"DIA. UPHOLSTERY TACKS

MANE IN LEATHER OR VINYL

19½"

6½"

23"

½"

1 1/16"

12"

7¼"

2"

65°

11½"

25°

2"

3"
8

2¾"

5"DIA.

3½"

35"

SIDE VIEW

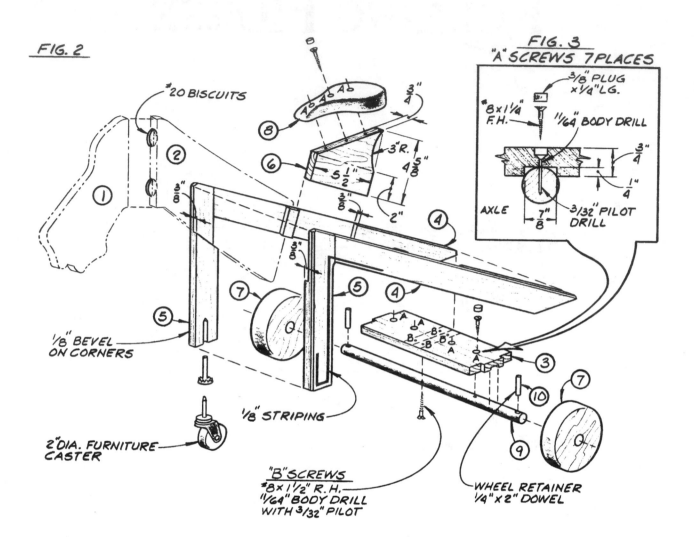

FIG. 2

#20 BISCUITS

②

①

⑧

⑥

⑦

⑤

1/8" BEVEL
ON CORNERS

1/8" STRIPING

2"DIA. FURNITURE
CASTER

"B"SCREWS
#8 x 1 1/2" R.H.
11/64" BODY DRILL
WITH 3/32" PILOT

⑤

④

④

3"R.
5 1/2"
3/8"
2"
3/4"
5/8"
4 3/8"

③

⑩

⑨

⑦

WHEEL RETAINER
1/4" x 2" DOWEL

FIG. 3
"A" SCREWS 7 PLACES

3/8" PLUG
x 1/4" LG.

#8 x 1 1/4"
F.H.

11/64" BODY DRILL

AXLE

3/32" PILOT
DRILL

7/8"

3/4"

1/4"

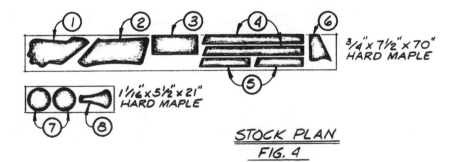

① ② ③ ④ ⑥

3/4" x 7 1/2" x 70"
HARD MAPLE

⑤

1 1/16" x 5 1/2" x 21"
HARD MAPLE

⑦ ⑧

STOCK PLAN
FIG. 4

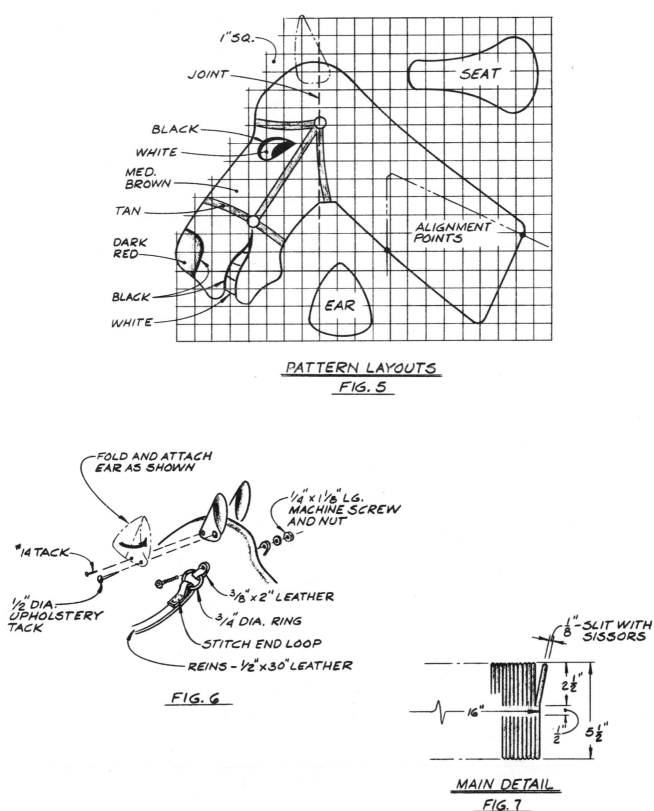

1" SQ.

JOINT

BLACK

WHITE

MED.
BROWN

TAN

DARK
RED

BLACK

WHITE

SEAT

ALIGNMENT
POINTS

EAR

PATTERN LAYOUTS
FIG. 5

FOLD AND ATTACH
EAR AS SHOWN

¼" x 1⅛" LG.
MACHINE SCREW
AND NUT

#14 TACK

½" DIA.
UPHOLSTERY
TACK

3/8" x 2" LEATHER

¾" DIA. RING

STITCH END LOOP

REINS - ½" x 30" LEATHER

FIG. 6

⅛"-SLIT WITH
SISSORS

16"

2½"

½"

5½"

MAIN DETAIL
FIG. 7

Bill of Materials

Stock (inches)	Quantity	Item	Part
¾ × 7½ × 70 hard maple	1	①	head (one)
		②	head (one)
		③	axle board (one)
		④	frame members (two)
		⑤	wheel supports (two)
		⑥	seat support (one)
1¹⁄₁₆ × 5½ × 21 hard maple	1	⑦	wheels (two)
		⑧	seat (one)
1 dia. × 36 maple dowel	1	⑨	axle (one)
¼ dia. × 36 maple dowel	1	⑩	wheel retainers (two)
⅜ dia. × 36 maple dowel	1	–	screw plugs (seven)

Hardware and Supplies	Quantity	Description
wood screws	4	#8 × 1½" R.H.
	7	#8 × 1¼" F.H.
machine screw	1	¼ × 1¼" R.H.
nut	1	¼"
steel rings	2	¾" dia.
upholstery tacks	16	½"dia.
biscuits	2	#20
furniture caster	1	2" dia. stem type
leather rein	1	6- to 8-oz., ½" x30"
mane (leather or vinyl)	1	2- to 3-oz., 5½" × 16"
leather ears	1	4- to 5-oz., 4" × 8"
leather straps	1	4- to 5-oz., ⅜" × 4"
steel tacks	2	#14

Rolling Horse

Looking for an action toy for an energetic preschooler? Here's one that will have that young buckaroo itching to hit the saddle. Indoors or out, this rolling horse is easy to ride and control—just pull on the reins and it'll turn on the spot. And its leather details and irresistible look make this a must-do project.

Things to Know

Before you begin this project, you'll need to learn or review the techniques discussed in the following sections:

Drawing Your Patterns
Joinery with Biscuits
Decorating Your Projects

Planning the Project

The original piece was painted a medium brown with tan leather ears and mane. Color details for the face, bridle, and striping really make this horse come alive. If you prefer to do this project with a natural finish, it can be done with striking results. Choose maple stock that has a consistent cream color and use a clear finish without staining. Make the bridle, mane, and ears dark brown, and the horse takes on a completely different character.

Although choosing the finish is a matter of taste, the wood must be selected for strength. Hard maple is clearly the winner for toys like this one because it resists denting, is extremely tough, and has a compact grain that takes on a glass-smooth finish (you'll appreciate that when its time to paint on the details).

Patterns

Start the project by laying out the patterns on thin poster board as shown in Figure 5. When drawing the head, carefully duplicate all of the details for the face, bridle, and alignment points, because these features will be cut out and traced onto the horse at the end of the project. Mark the joint line on both sides of the head pattern but don't cut; use it for reference when tracing on the stock. Once drawn, cut out the patterns and then position them on the stock as in Figure 4, leaving generous space between pieces for the saw cuts. When the arrangement looks okay, trace the patterns and draw the straight pieces.

Head

Start construction by cutting the head ① and neck ② to size. Begin with the straight cuts for the mating joint, using a table saw or radial arm saw. Then cut the curved surfaces with a jigsaw. Join the head pieces together using two #20 biscuits as shown in Figure 2. Gluing up this assembly can be difficult because of the irregular surfaces. First dry-clamp the pieces together using your workbench top. Clamp the neck to the benchtop with a piece of scrap that's parallel to the joint surface. Now add the head and run a clamp from the forehead to the scrap piece to create a square clamping force. If you're satisfied with the setup, put a sheet of waxed paper on your benchtop and redo with glue. When dry, smooth out the curves with files and a sandpaper block. Complete the head by routing all the edges with a ¼-inch roundover bit and giving everything a first sanding with 180-grit sandpaper.

Frame Assembly

The frame is made from four pieces of ¾-inch stock that are laminated to each side of the head and seat bracket. Start by ripping the frame members ④ and the wheel supports ⑤ to width, then cut then to length with the angles shown in the side view drawing. Now lay out the ⅜-inch recesses for the head and seat by placing the frame halves on the bench as they would be assembled. Use the alignment points on the head pattern for positioning with the frame halves and then trace to mark the cutout. Measure ½-inch from the head and mark the position of the seat cutout. Cut the ends of the recess with a radial arm saw and then cut away the material in between with a spiral fluted, straight bit on a router table. If you're not so equipped, you can use a table saw with a dado blade. Finish up the parts by routing a ⅛-inch bevel on the edges as shown in the exploded view drawing.

Now lay out the position of the frame on the head using the alignment points on the pattern. Test-fit one side of the frame with the head, and if everything looks okay, glue and clamp in place. While drying, cut the seat support ⑥ from the stock so that the grain direction runs toward the seat. Test-fit the seat support and the frame pieces for the second side to the first, and if no adjustments are required, glue and clamp in place. Next, drill the hole in the bottom of the wheel support for the 2-inch furniture caster; if you have a floor-mounted drill press, drilling a straight hole will be easy. Refer to the caster instructions for the hole size. If you use a hand drill, clamp the wheel support to the top of your workbench and use a spacer block between the bit and the bench to guarantee alignment. Try the caster for fit and then lay it aside until final assembly.

Rear Wheel Assembly

Cut the axle board ③ and the axle ⑨ to size. Next, rout the ¼-inch deep groove on the bottom of the axle board as shown in Figure 3. When routing the width, use the axle as a gauge to get a tight fit because the diameter of dowel stock can vary. Position the axle in the groove and clamp in place, then drill the counterbores and pilot holes for the four #8-by-1¼-inch flathead screws as shown in Figure 3. Apply the screws and glue the ⅜-inch plugs in place. When dry, use a chisel to trim down the plugs and sand flush.

Mark the centers of the wheels ⑦ and cut from the stock. A band saw with a ⅛-inch blade is perfect for this operation because it can do a square cut on tight curves. If you use a jigsaw, use a new blade, cut slowly, avoid side pressure on the blade and you should get acceptable results. Once cut, smooth out the rim surfaces with files and a sandpaper block, and then rout the edges with a ³⁄₁₆-inch-radius roundover bit. Drill the axle holes with a 1-inch Forstner bit and a drill press. Test-fit the wheels on

the axle; if they don't go, sand down the axle until you have a very free fit (moisture can make wooden wheels bind if there's insufficient clearance). Position the wheels on the axle so that they are about ¹⁄₁₆ inch away from the axle board, and then mark the locations of the ¼-inch wheel-retaining dowels. Remove the wheels, drill the ¼-inch holes, and test-fit the parts. Don't glue the wheel retainers in place until the horse is finished; the finish is easier to apply with individual pieces.

Complete the Assembly

With the wheel assembly complete, it can now be joined to the frame. Measure and mark the position of the frame on the top surface of the axle board. Make a 25-degree clamp block and apply to the clamp area on the frame with double-sided tape. Now clamp up the frame and wheel assembly and check for alignment. When you're satisfied with the alignment, drill the holes for four #8 screws as shown in the exploded view drawing. Disassemble, then redo with glue and #8-by-1½-inch roundhead screws.

The final woodworking task is making the seat. Use a band saw or jigsaw to cut the seat to size, and smooth out the curves with files and sandpaper. Break the top edges with a router and ⅜-inch roundover bit, and then do a first sanding with 180-grit sandpaper. To attach the seat, start by accurately locating the screw positions on the bottom of the seat and on the seat support. Now drill the body and counterbore holes for #8 screws in the seat, and as a separate operation, drill the pilot holes in the seat support. Attach the seat with glue and #8-by-1¼-inch flathead screws, and finish off with ⅜-inch plugs. Give all the pieces a final sanding with 220-grit sandpaper.

Finishing Touches

Now for the fun—it's time to give this guy some character. First finish the piece as desired: painted head and frame, painted head and natural frame, or all natural. Once the finish has dried, you're ready to do the face.

Carefully cut out the nose, eye, and mouth from the head pattern with a sharp pointed razor knife. Then use a sharp pencil to trace the pattern openings onto both sides of the head. Now cut the bridle free from the pattern and trace the bridle onto the head.

The striping and details for the face can be hand-painted or applied with vinyl sign film. If you decide to use sign film, the surface must be smooth with simple bends. You can outline the nose with the film, but red part must be painted because of its contours. Use black film for the shapes of the eyes and mouth, then paint on the white areas or use a layer of white sign film. Complete the detail by painting the lines that define the teeth.

Now add the leather parts, starting with the rein assembly as shown in Figure 6. Use a piece of 6- to 8-ounce leather, ½ inch wide by 30 inches long, and sew a ¾-inch ring onto each end using heavy waxed thread and a sewing awl. These materials are available at leather-craft stores or from Tandy Leather Company, telephone (800) 821-0801. Mount the completed rein assembly to the head with straps of 4- to 5-ounce leather, ⅜-by-2-inches wide, and a ¼-by-¼-inch roundhead machine screw and nut.

Lay out the two ears on 4- to 5-ounce leather stock. Fold each ear as shown in Figure 6 and attach with a #14 steel tack and a ½-inch-diameter upholstery tack. Make the mane from a soft, pliable 2- to 3-ounce leather or upholstery vinyl so that it will hang with a natural look. Cut the mane as shown in Figure 7 and attach with ½-inch-diameter upholstery tacks.

Finish up by installing the rear wheels. But first, thoroughly rub the end of a candle on the inside surfaces of the holes for lubrication. Pop in the caster wheel, and this guy is ready to hit the trail.

Child's Rocker
Pennsylvania German

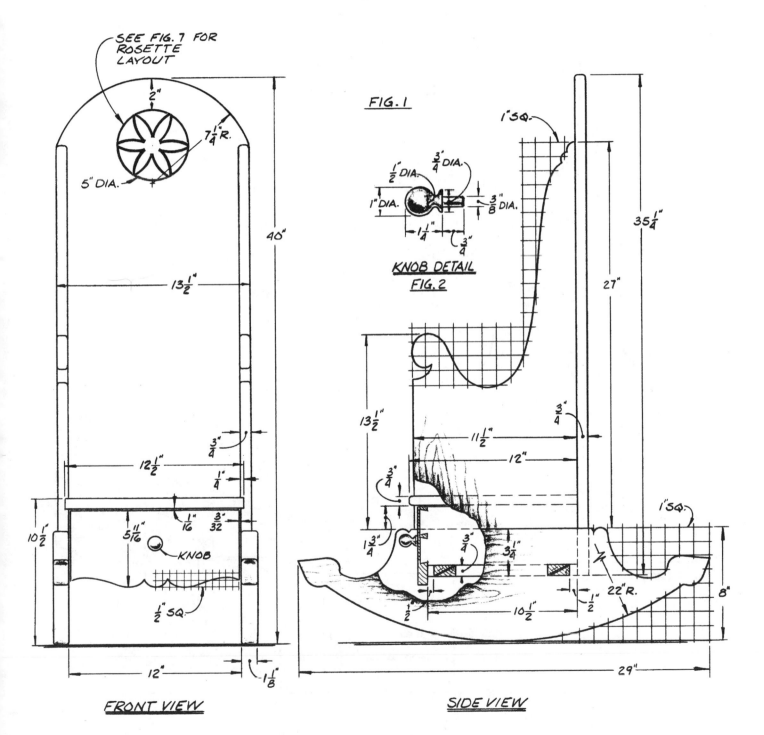

SEE FIG. 7 FOR
ROSETTE
LAYOUT

2"

5" DIA.

7 1/4" R.

40"

13 1/2"

12 1/2"

3/4"

1/4"

10 1/2"

5 11/16"

1/16"

3/32"

KNOB

1/2" SQ.

12"

1 1/8"

FRONT VIEW

FIG. 1

1" SQ.

1" DIA.

3/4" DIA.

1/2" DIA.

1" DIA.

3/8" DIA.

1 1/4"

3/4"

KNOB DETAIL
FIG. 2

35 1/4"

27"

13 1/2"

11 1/2"

12"

3/4"

3/4"

1 3/4"

3/4"

3 1/4"

1/2"

1" SQ.

1/2"

10 1/2"

22" R.

8"

29"

SIDE VIEW

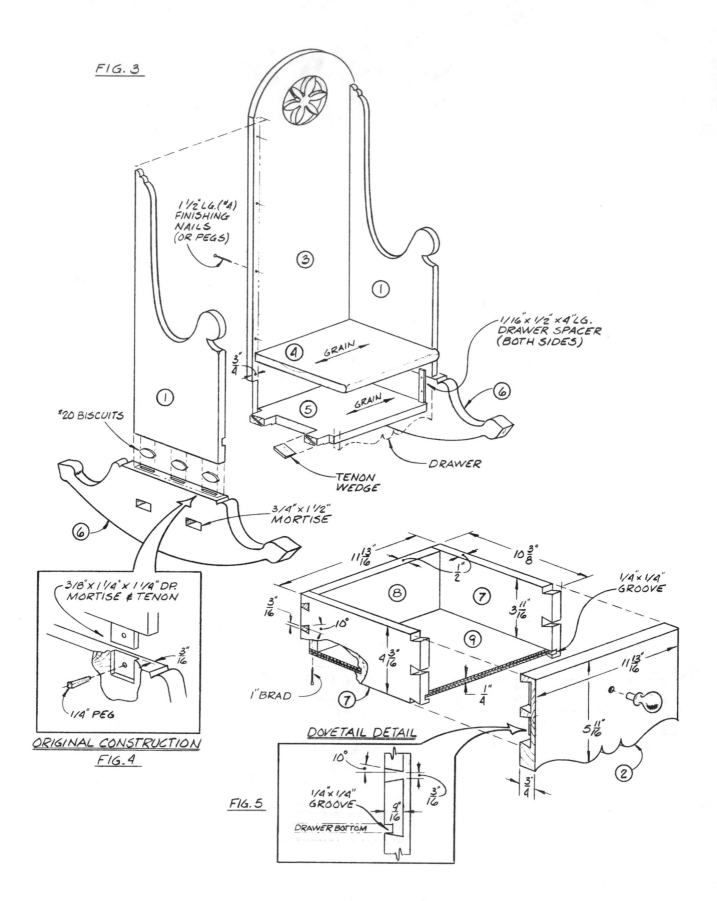

FIG. 3

1½" LG. (#4)
FINISHING
NAILS
(OR PEGS)

③

①

1/16" x 1/2" x 4" LG.
DRAWER SPACER
(BOTH SIDES)

④   GRAIN

⑤   GRAIN

3"/4

⑥

①

⑥   DRAWER

TENON
WEDGE

#20 BISCUITS

3/4" x 1½"
MORTISE

3/8" x 1¼" x 1¼" DP.
MORTISE & TENON

3"/16

1/4" PEG

ORIGINAL CONSTRUCTION
FIG. 4

11 13/16   10 3/8

⑧   ⑦   1"/2

1/4" x 1/4"
GROOVE

3"/16

10°   ⑨

3 11/16

4 3/8

1" BRAD   ⑦

1"/4

11 13/16

DOVETAIL DETAIL   5 11/16

10°   3"/16

1/4" x 1/4"
GROOVE

9"/16

3"/4

②

DRAWER BOTTOM

FIG. 5

116

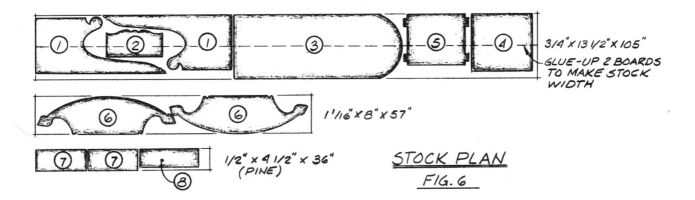

3/4"x 13 1/2"x 105"
GLUE-UP 2 BOARDS
TO MAKE STOCK
WIDTH

1'/16" x 8" x 57"

1/2" x 4 1/2" x 36"
(PINE)

STOCK PLAN
FIG. 6

ROSETTE LAYOUT
FIG. 7

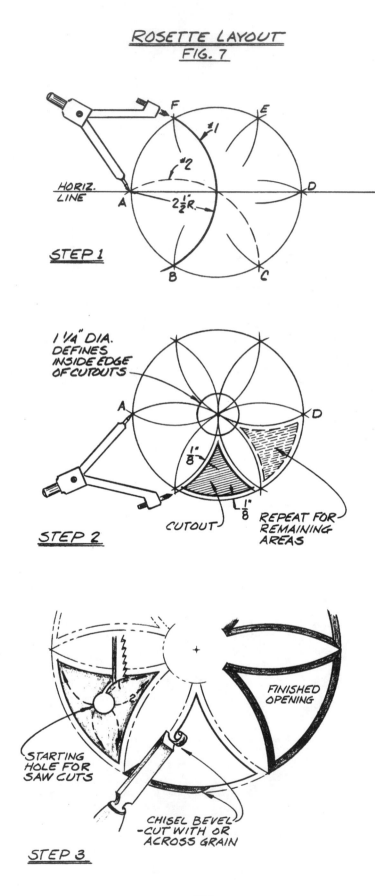

STEP 1

HORIZ. LINE

$2\frac{1}{2}R.$

#1
#2

A   B   C   D   E   F

STEP 2

1 1/4" DIA. DEFINES INSIDE EDGE OF CUTOUTS

A   D

1"/8

1"/8

CUTOUT

REPEAT FOR REMAINING AREAS

STEP 3

FINISHED OPENING

STARTING HOLE FOR SAW CUTS

CHISEL BEVEL -CUT WITH OR ACROSS GRAIN

BILL OF MATERIALS

Stock (inches)	Quantity	Item	Part
$\frac{3}{4} \times 13\frac{1}{2} \times 105$ walnut	1	①	sides (two)
		②	drawer front (one)
		③	back (one)
		④	seat (one)
		⑤	drawer support (one)
$1\frac{1}{16} \times 8 \times 57$ walnut	1	⑥	rockers (two)
$\frac{1}{2} \times 4\frac{1}{2} \times 36$ pine	1	⑦	drawer sides (two)
		⑧	drawer back (one)
$\frac{1}{4} \times 11\frac{5}{16} \times 10\frac{1}{16}$ plywood	1	⑨	drawer bottom (one)

Hardware and Supplies	Quantity	Description
biscuits	6	#20
finishing nails	10	1½" (#4)
brads	2	1"

CHILD'S ROCKER

Rockers are a favorite of all ages, and this one is perfect for preschoolers. The drawer under the seat is great for books, crayons, and other kid stuff. Best of all, the charming style will complement any bedroom decor, and when the children are older, it can serve as a nice accent piece, awaiting the next generation.

I had the good fortune of intercepting this rocker as it entered an antiques shop. I quickly persuaded the dealer, a good friend, to let me borrow it for an evening to make some drawings. I returned the rocker the next morning and within a few hours it was sold. It was in terrible condition, but from the rosette on the top of the backboard down to the teardropped ears on the rockers, it was a fine example of early-nineteenth-century Pennsylvania German design. And as expected, all of the joints were pegged, mortised, or dovetailed to give it quality of craftsmanship as well as character.

Things to Know

Before you begin this project, you'll need to learn or review the techniques discussed in the following sections:
> Drawing Your Patterns
> Joining with Pegs
> Joinery with Biscuits
> Decorating Your Projects

PLANNING THE PROJECT
The drawings illustrate the rocker with some simplifications in the joinery to keep the assembly as straightforward as possible without sacrificing appearance. But if you enjoy traditional woodworking and prefer the original construction, separate views are provided with these details (see Figure 4).

The original rocker was made from walnut, but almost any wood can be used. If you prefer a natural finish, you can substitute cherry or even pine

with an antique glaze or white pickling stain. If you want an authentic-looking painted finish, start with pine or poplar, apply a dark stain with an oil-based enamel on top, then pick the logical wear spots and rub with #0000 steel wool until the stain begins to show through. Top off with a walnut glaze coat.

Unless you have access to extrawide stock, two boards will have to be glued up to make the width required for items ① through ⑤ as shown on the stock plan (Figure 6). If you are planning a natural finish, pick your boards for a matching grain so that the glue line will be less visible. Also, look for a lumberyard that does custom planing so that you can have your boards planed oversize, then glue up and have them planed to the final thickness. This will be a big timesaver.

PATTERNS
Start the project by drawing the irregularly shaped pieces on thin poster board. Cut out the patterns, then position them on the stock so that there is generous space between pieces for the saw cuts (see Figure 6). When the arrangement looks okay, trace the patterns and draw the straight pieces.

BUILDING THE FRAME
Start by rough-cutting the sides ① from the stock and rip to width. Then remove the waste from the curved surfaces using a band saw or jigsaw, and smooth out with files and sandpaper. Mark the position of the ¼-by-¾-inch seat groove on the inside of each side piece (make sure you have a right and a left) and make the cut with a table saw and dado blade. Next, cut the rockers ⑥ on a band saw so that you can get a square cut on the thick stock, and then smooth out the curves. Finish up with a router and a ¼-inch roundover bit to break the edges on the curved surfaces of the rocker and sides. *Do not* round over any of the joined surfaces. Now that the sides and rockers are complete, mark the positions of the biscuits for joining these pieces

together. The joint is offset to make the inside surfaces of the rockers and side pieces flush, so again, make sure you have a right and left. When cut, put the side pieces aside for later in the assembly.

MORTISING THE ROCKER

The mortise and tenon is the strongest of all joints, so it's not surprising to see it used extensively by colonial craftsmen. This joint is used with the drawer support panel to tie the two sides together and provides the main structural support to the chair (see Figure 3). Cut the mortise first, then fit the tenon to it. Start by laying out the mortises on the inside and outside of the rocker pieces. This is important because you'll be working on both sides as you cut the hole. From the outside of the rocker, begin the mortise by drilling a starter hole for a jigsaw, and then cut to the inside of the line. Check the inside surfaces for square with the rocker face and correct with a sharp chisel if required. When the mortises are done, cut the drawer support ⑤, making the tenons slightly wider than necessary so that they can be fitted to the mortises. Compare the tenon positions with the mortises on the outside of the rocker (that's the fit you're going to see when the joint is together), then mark any corrections and number the joints. Pare the sides of the tenons with a sharp chisel until they just enter the mortises. Now test-fit the tenons from the inside of the rocker and do the final trimming on the mortise until you get full engagement. Finish up the tenons by cutting a diagonal wedge slot, 1-inch deep, with a backsaw.

The next step is assembling the rockers with the drawer support. Cut four tenon wedges about 1½ inches long by ⅛ inch thick tapering to a sharp edge. If you are using walnut or cherry for your piece, make the wedges from the same wood, but if your piece is in pine, use a hardwood such as maple so that it can stand the force of being driven into the joint. Glue and clamp the parts together and check for square. Then drive the wedges into the joint using a hammer and wooden block. Don't

overdo it with the hammer; when the wedge has tightened the joint, you're there. When dry, cut the wedge excess to slightly above flush with a handsaw, then pare flush with a sharp chisel.

With the rocker base assembled, the next step is attaching the seat and sides. Cut the seat to size and round over the front edge with a router. Dry-clamp the sides that you made earlier with the seat and base. Check all of the joints for square, and when everything looks good, disassemble and redo with glue.

BACK PANEL

Before you cut the back, verify the 13½-inch width by measuring across the side panels, then rip to size. Mark the positions of the two ¾-inch relief notches on the bottom of the back, verify by measuring the assembly, and then cut to size. Finish up by cutting the 7¼-inch radius on top of the back. Smooth out the curve and rout the edges of the radius with a ¼-inch roundover bit.

Cutting the Rosette. The design on this rocker is unique because the features are cut through the back rather than the more common practice of relief carving on the surface. Figure 7 shows the basic steps for drawing and cutting the rosette. When drawing the design, you can make poster board patterns for tracing or, as the nineteenth-century chairmaker would have done, make the design directly on the wood and end up with faint compass point marks and an occasional construction line in your work—trademarks of a handmade antique. Whichever method you use, start the layout by setting your compass to 2½ inches and drawing a circle as shown in step 1. Draw a horizontal line through the center of the circle to create point A. With the same setting on your compass, place the pivot at A and draw arc BF. Continue drawing the same size arc from point B then C and so on until the rosette is complete.

Step 2 shows how the cutout area and ⅛-inch bevels are described. First, draw the outside edge of the cutouts by making a circle with a compass setting ⅛ inch smaller than the first circle (2⅜ inches). Now draw the first side of the cutout by putting the compass pivot at A and make an arc ⅛ inch larger than the first arc (2⅝ inches). Draw the third side of the cutout with the same arc from point D. Do the remaining cutouts the same way, and then draw a 1¼-inch-diameter circle in the center to complete the layout. If you intend to use patterns, make separate pieces for the circle, rosette, and cutout.

Start the cutouts by drilling starting holes for a jigsaw as shown in step 3. Saw the cutouts, then cut the bevels with a sharp chisel. Cut with, or across, the grain to prevent tear-outs and maintain a 45-degree bevel as you work toward the rosette outline. Use an almost vertical plunge cut to make the inside corner at the tip of each rosette petal. The bevels intersecting at the base of the petals require the same plunge cuts, with the addition of a third plunge cut for the small bevel at the base of the rosette petals. Smooth out the bevels and inside surfaces with a file, and finish-sand. I like to use fingernail emery boards for getting into tight spots. Cut a sharp angle on the end of the emery board and you have a perfect tool for sanding the bevel intersections.

Attaching the Back. Test-fit the back with the frame assembly, and then redo with glue, clamps, and 1½-inch finishing nails. If you decide on pegs in lieu of nails, glue and clamp first, then add the pegs when the assembly is dry. For authenticity, make the pegs with a square or hexagonal cross section and use the same wood as the frame.

DRAWER ASSEMBLY

The drawer is illustrated with its original construction except for the plywood bottom. The dovetails shown in Figure 5 must be hand cut, but if you have a dovetailing jig, you may want to rearrange things for your equipment. If you would like to use a simpler joint than the dovetail, consider a rabbet for the back and a tongue and groove for the front.

Begin construction by cutting all of the drawer parts to size. To make the hand-cut dovetails, start by measuring down 3 ¹¹/₁₆ inches from the top of the drawer to locate the ¼-by-¼-inch grooves on the front and side panels. Cut the grooves, then lay out the dovetails on the inside surfaces of the drawer sides. Use a scroll saw to cut the joint features (tails) into the sides, then clean up the surfaces with a chisel. To assure a perfect-fitting joint, use the tails just cut as a template to mark the positions of the pins. Place the drawer front in a vise with its end facing up and even with the top of the bench. Align the matching end of the side piece with the front piece and trace the tails with a sharp pencil or marking knife. Continue the pin outlines onto the back of the front piece and mark the ½-inch depth of the joint.

Now that the mating features (pins) are defined, the joint can be cut. Using a fine-toothed backsaw, cut along the waste side of the pins. Next, begin removing the waste from between the pins by using a chisel and mallet. When the pockets are close to the required size, lay the mallet aside and hand-chisel to the final fit. Complete the remaining three corners and test-fit the complete drawer. If everything fits well, disassemble and redo with glue and clamps, excluding the drawer bottom. When dry, slip the bottom into the drawer and attach with a couple of 1-inch brads.

Make the knob as shown in Figure 2 for the finishing touch on the drawer. Use a lathe, or make one in a drill press from a 1-by-1-by-1¼-inch block. Glue a ⅜-inch dowel in one end. When dry, carve the knob to its approximate shape with a chisel, and finish up in the drill press with files and sandpaper. Attach the knob, then test-fit the drawer in the rocker. Balance the space around the drawer, and then add spacers as shown on the exploded view drawing to maintain the gap.

APPLYING THE FINISH

Finish-sand everything with 220-grit sandpaper. If you used walnut for your piece, give everything but the pine in the drawer a coat of walnut stain to even out the color, then apply the finish of your choice.

18th Century Cradle
Pennsylvania German

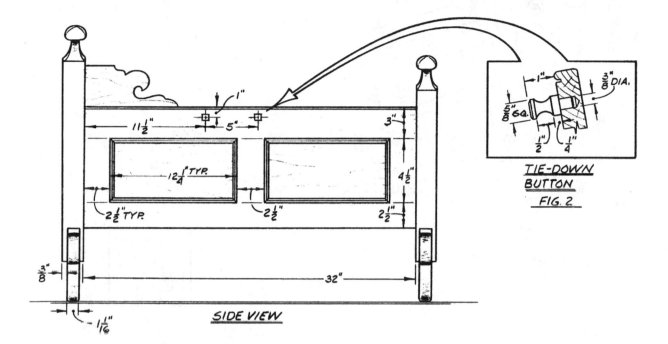

TIE-DOWN
BUTTON
FIG. 2

SIDE VIEW

FIG. 1

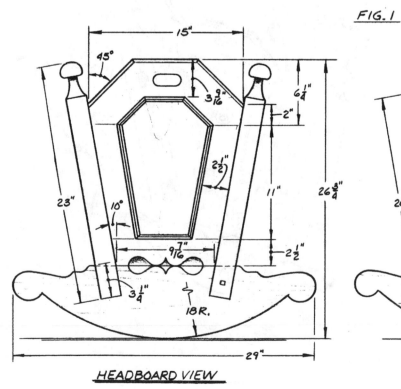

HEADBOARD VIEW

FOOTBOARD VIEW

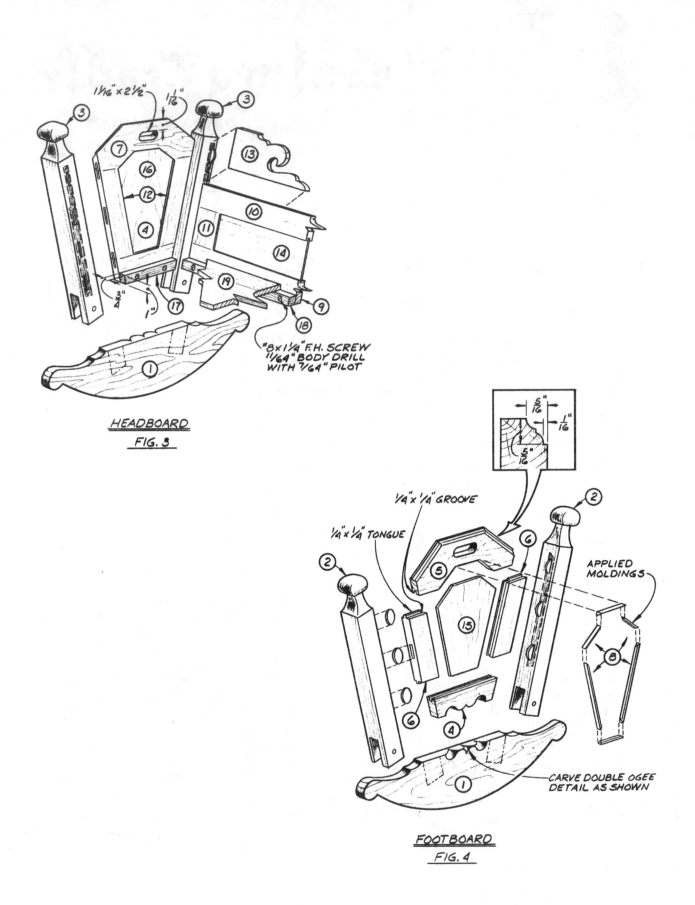

1¹⁄₁₆" x 2¹⁄₂" 1¹⁄₁₆"

③ ③

⑦ ⑬

⑯

⑫

④ ⑩

⑪

⑭

⑲

¾" 1"

⑰ ⑨

⑱

#8 x 1¼" F.H. SCREW
¹¹⁄₆₄" BODY DRILL
WITH ⁷⁄₆₄" PILOT

①

HEADBOARD
FIG. 3

⁵⁄₁₆" ¹⁄₁₆"

⁵⁄₁₆"

¼" x ¼" GROOVE

¼" x ¼" TONGUE

②

② ⑥

⑤ APPLIED
MOLDINGS

⑥

⑮ ⑧

⑥

④

① CARVE DOUBLE OGEE
DETAIL AS SHOWN

FOOTBOARD
FIG. 4

124

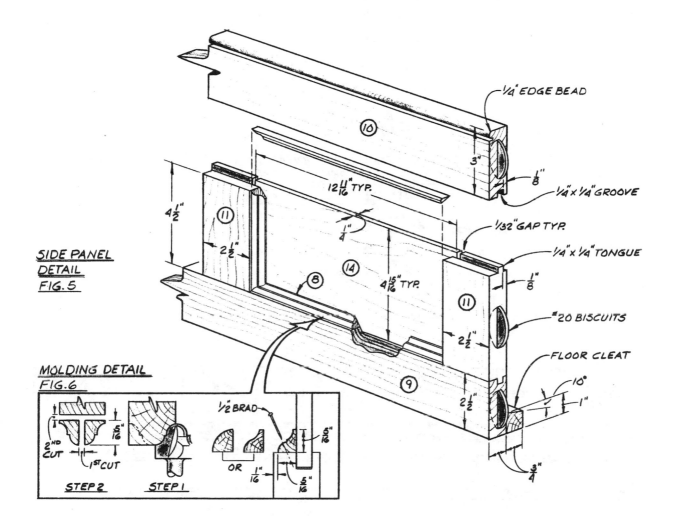

¼" EDGE BEAD

10

3"

⅛"

¼" x ¼" GROOVE

12 ⁴⁄₁₆" TYP.

1/32" GAP TYP.

¼" x ¼" TONGUE

⅛"

#20 BISCUITS

FLOOR CLEAT

10°

1"

¾"

4½"

11

2½"

SIDE PANEL
DETAIL
FIG. 5

¼"

14

8

4 ¹⁵⁄₁₆" TYP.

11

2½"

9

2½"

MOLDING DETAIL
FIG. 6

½ BRAD

1"

⁵⁄₁₆"

2ᴺᴰ
CUT

⁵⁄₁₆"

1ˢᵀ CUT

OR

1/16"

⁵⁄₁₆"

STEP 2

STEP 1

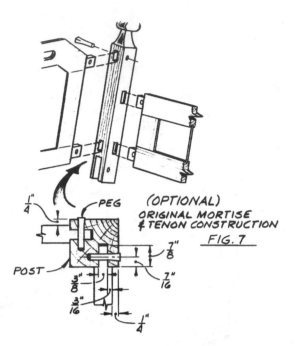

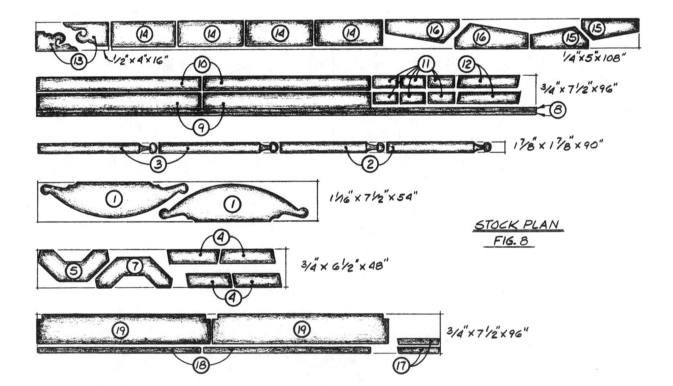

$\frac{1}{4}''$ PEG   (OPTIONAL)

ORIGINAL MORTISE
& TENON CONSTRUCTION
FIG. 7

POST $\frac{7}{8}''$ $\frac{7}{16}''$ $\frac{1}{4}''$

$\frac{1}{2}'' \times 4'' \times 16''$

$\frac{1}{4}'' \times 5'' \times 108''$

$\frac{3}{4}'' \times 7\frac{1}{2}'' \times 96''$

$1\frac{7}{8}'' \times 1\frac{7}{8}'' \times 90''$

$1\frac{1}{16}'' \times 7\frac{1}{2}'' \times 54''$

STOCK PLAN
FIG. 8

$\frac{3}{4}'' \times 6\frac{1}{2}'' \times 48''$

$\frac{3}{4}'' \times 7\frac{1}{2}'' \times 96''$

126

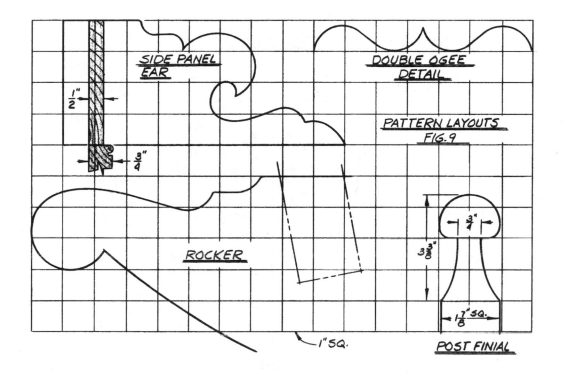

SIDE PANEL EAR

DOUBLE OGEE DETAIL

$\frac{1}{2}$"

$\frac{3}{4}$"

PATTERN LAYOUTS
FIG. 9

ROCKER

$\frac{3}{4}$"

$3\frac{3}{8}$"

$1\frac{7}{8}$" SQ.

1" SQ.

POST FINIAL

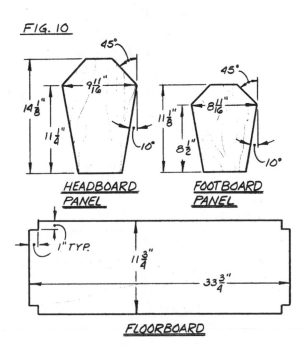

FIG. 10

45°

$9\frac{11}{16}$"

$14\frac{1}{8}$"

$11\frac{1}{4}$"

10°

HEADBOARD
PANEL

45°

$8\frac{11}{16}$"

$11\frac{1}{8}$"

$8\frac{1}{2}$"

10°

FOOTBOARD
PANEL

1" TYP.

$11\frac{3}{4}$"

$33\frac{3}{4}$"

FLOORBOARD

127

STAR LAYOUT
FIG. 11

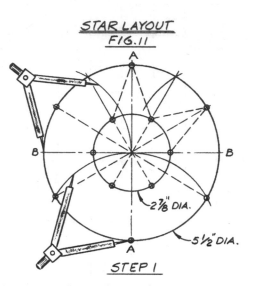

A

B • • B

2 7/8" DIA.

5 1/2" DIA.

A

STEP 1

LT. BROWN

STEP 2

BILL OF MATERIALS

Stock (inches)	Quantity	Item	Part
$1\frac{1}{16} \times 7\frac{1}{2} \times 54$ walnut	1	①	rockers (two)
$1\frac{7}{8} \times 1\frac{7}{8} \times 90$ walnut	1	②	footboard posts (two)
		③	headboard posts (two)
$\frac{3}{4} \times 6\frac{1}{2} \times 48$ walnut	1	④	bottom rails (two)
		⑤	top rail (foot) (one)
		⑥	stiles (foot) (two)
		⑦	top rail (head) (one)
$\frac{3}{4} \times 7\frac{1}{2} \times 96$ walnut	1	⑧	panel moldings (20')
		⑨	bottom rails (side) (two)
		⑩	top rails (side) (two)
		⑪	stiles (side) (six)
		⑫	stiles (head) (two)
$\frac{1}{2} \times 4 \times 16$ walnut	1	⑬	ears (two)
$\frac{1}{4} \times 5 \times 108$ walnut	1	⑭	side panels (four)
	1	⑮	foot panel (one)
		⑯	head panel (one)
$\frac{3}{4} \times 7\frac{1}{2} \times 96$ poplar	1	⑰	end cleats (two)
		⑱	side cleats (two)
		⑲	floorboard (one)

Hardware and Supplies	Quantity	Description
wood screws	10	#8 × 1¼" F.H.
biscuits	28	#20

129

EIGHTEENTH-CENTURY CRADLE

Here's a distinctive piece for that new arrival. This eighteenth-century Pennsylvania German cradle will become a permanent part of the family and serve future generations as well.

Cradles were an essential part of early American family life. The mother's daily chores took her from the kitchen to the fields, and infants needed a safe place that was always close at hand. Some cradles had hoods for protection from the sun and holes were usually cut in the side or end panels for carrying from place to place. Tie-down buttons were placed along the top of the sideboards so that a rope could be used to keep baby and blankets in place. A set of rockers enabled the mother to rock the cradle with her foot while relaxing with some needlepoint.

This cradle is an outstanding example of the colonial period design. The most notable, and unusual, feature is the rail and panel construction. This technique was first used by wagonmakers to reduce weight without sacrificing strength, and it soon became an element of style in architectural and furniture design.

Things to Know

Before you begin this project, you'll need to learn or review the techniques discussed in the following sections:
Drawing Your Patterns
Joining with Biscuits
Joining with Pegs
Decorating Your Projects

PLANNING THE PROJECT
To keep the construction as straightforward as possible, biscuits are used in place of mortise and tenon joints to fasten the end and side panels to the cor-

ner posts. The only visual difference from the original is the absence of the tenon pegs, but these can
be added to create an authentic look. If you prefer
mortise and tenon joinery, use the original construction details shown in Figure 7. The part layouts in the stock plan do not include the tenons;
add 1¾ inch to the length of each tenoned part and
adjust the board lengths accordingly.

Walnut was a popular wood for cradles of this
period and, considering the detail, very appropriate.
Pine could also be used because of the hefty design.

PATTERNS

When there are a lot of similar pieces, as there are
here, it's good to lay out and number all of the parts
on the stock before starting the project. Start by
drawing the patterns shown in Figure 9 on thin
poster board. You can save some time by doing a
half pattern of the rocker. First draw the center line
of each rocker on your stock, then trace the half
pattern, flip, and trace the other half. Complete
the remaining pattern work and draw the straight
pieces.

BUILDING THE SIDE PANELS

Figure 5 shows the construction details for the side
panels. Start with the moldings ⑧, which can be
easily made by routing the shape on a wide piece
of stock and then ripping free. Figure 6 illustrates
several possible shapes; the most interesting is the
⅛-inch-radius cove and bead because of the additional detail. First use a short length of scrap to
make a test piece of the routed edge as shown in
step 1 of Figure 6. When you arrive at the correct
router setting, rout the edges on your stock. Next,
set up your table saw to make the first cut shown in
step 2, and then rip your test piece to verify that
you're making identical moldings (this is important,
because discrepancies will show when the moldings
are joined at the corners). When you're satisfied
with the setup, make the first cut on your stock,
then set up and make the second cut to complete
the moldings. You now have 16 of the 20 feet of
molding required to do the cradle, so make another

5 or 6 feet using the same procedure (it's good to
have a little extra to replace mistakes).

Next, cut the two bottom rails ⑨ and two top
rails ⑩ from the stock. Then cut six stiles ⑪ to a
size of 2½ by 5 inches (4½ inches plus two ¼-
inch tongues) and the four side panels ⑭. Cut the
tongues on the stiles, then position the grooves in
the rails to get the alignment. Use a table-mounted
router and rabbet cutter to cut the waste on one side
of the tongues, then set the cutter for the second
side and remove the waste. To cut the grooves, use a
¼-inch slot cutter in a table mounted router and
cut a test piece to check for fit with the stiles.
When you're satisfied with the fit, mark the position of the grooves on your parts; then groove one
side of the rails and end stiles, and both sides of
the center stiles. Complete the parts by routing a
¼-inch edge bead on the outside edge of the two
top rails.

PANEL ASSEMBLY

Dry-clamp the panel parts together and verify that
the joints are flush, tight, and square. If the mating
surfaces aren't flush within two thicknesses of a
piece of paper, try clamping them flush. If that
doesn't correct the fit, adjust the thickness of the
tongue. The time invested in fitting is much shorter
than trying to sand flush after assembly. When
everything looks okay, disassemble and redo with
glue and clamps.

Next, begin the attachment of the moldings
by cutting the first 45-degree angle on one of the
pieces. Position the cut end of the molding next to
the place it will occupy and mark the second end.
Make the second 45-degree cut on the long side so
that the molding can be fitted to position. A radial
arm saw is good for doing the fitting because you
can make paper-thin cuts on the end of the molding until the length is perfect. Alternatively, you can
shave the end back with a sharp chisel. (With practice, this can be as quick as sawing.) Once fitted,
fasted the molding in place with glue and brads, or
with glue and clamps if you don't want the brad
holes. Attach the second molding adjacent to the

first, and use the same method for fitting in place. Continue with each successive piece until the panel is complete. Finish up the panels with a first sanding of 180-grit sandpaper. Sand with the grain on the stiles to make the joints flush, then with the grain on the rails to remove the scratches from sanding the stiles.

BUILDING THE HEADBOARD AND FOOTBOARD

The construction of the end boards is the same as that of the side panels except for cutting some additional angles (see Figures 3 and 4). Begin by ripping the stiles ⑥ and ⑫, bottom rails ④, and top rails ⑤ and ⑦ to width. Because the ends of the pieces are all 10 degrees, you can quickly crosscut the parts to length with one setup on your radial arm saw or table saw (add ½ inch to the length of the stiles for tongues). Finish the top rails by making the 45-degree cuts on the outside corners, and then do the inside cuts with a band saw. Complete the parts by cutting the panel halves ⑮ and ⑯, and then glue and clamp.

Trial-fit the stile and rail parts for both assemblies and clamp in place. When you're satisfied with the fit, mark each joint so that you can reassemble later in the same order. Now cut the tongue and groove joints and the panel grooves using the same procedure as for the side panels. Once cut, dry-clamp the parts together and verify that the joints are flush and tight. If the surfaces aren't flush, correct as described for the side panels, and then finish up with glue and clamps.

Although the attachment of the moldings is the same as for the side panels, cutting the angles takes a different approach. Make a poster board template of each corner, and then divide the angle in two. This gives you a gauge for setting up each cut on the radial arm saw or table saw. As before, cut the moldings on the long side and fit into position.

Now add the hand holes and the edge molding on the top rail as shown in Figure 4. Finish up by tracing the template for the double ogee shape on the front and bottom of the end boards. Chisel the concave part of the ogee with the bevel facing

down, then do the convex part with the bevel up. Always go with the grain. Give the headboard and footboard a first sanding with 180-grit sandpaper.

MAKING THE ROCKERS AND POSTS

Band saw the two rockers ① to shape and rout the edges of everything but the top surface with a 3/16-inch-radius roundover bit. Trace the double ogee on the top and front faces and then carve to the lines. Next, cut the posts ② and ③ to length and trace the finial pattern on one face of each post. Use a band saw to cut the waste from each side of the finial. Marking the finial for the second set of cuts is easily done by using several layers of double-sided tape to reattach the waste. This creates a flat surface for tracing the pattern and makes sawing to the line an easier task. Once cut, smooth out the curves with files and sandpaper blocks.

Move to the other end of the post and lay out the rocker slot on both sides and the bottom. Cut the sides of the slot with a band saw, keeping the blade to the inside of the line, then continue the cut with a handsaw to reach the end of the 10-degree bottom. Rough-cut the waste from the slot and make the 10-degree bottom with a mallet and chisel.

HEADBOARD AND FOOTBOARD ASSEMBLY

Test-fit the rocker, posts, and panel for one of the headboard or footboard assemblies shown in Figures 3 and 4. Make the outside surfaces of the panel and rocker flush, then clamp everything in place. Now mark the position where the panel contacts the posts, then disassemble and cut the biscuit pockets in the posts. To assure correct panel alignment, cut the biscuit pockets in a ¾-inch thick test piece; if the fit is acceptable, cut the pockets in the panel. Complete the biscuit joinery by cutting the pockets for the posts and side panels using the same procedure described for the end assemblies.

Test-fit the headboard and footboard assemblies one more time, then disassemble and redo with glue and clamps. Cut ¼-inch-square pegs from scrap and apply them to the bottom of the posts for an authentic look. Finish up by joining the end and side assemblies with glue and clamps.

FINISHING TOUCHES

Cut the side ears ⑬ from ½-inch stock using a band saw or scroll saw. Once cut, hold the ear in place and mark the contact area on the post, then cut pockets for a biscuit. Check for fit and glue in place.

Next, make four tie-down buttons, shown in Figure 2, from ¾-inch waste stock. Cut the stock to ⅝ inch square by 12 inches long, then lay out a button with the ⅜-inch diameter at the end of the piece. Cut the shoulder of the ⅜-inch diameter with a finetoothed handsaw, and chisel the diameter to shape. Do the remaining features with a half-round file, then cut from the stock. When the buttons are complete, mark their positions on the side panels, drill the mounting holes, and glue the buttons in place.

Now cut out, glue, and clamp the two floorboard pieces ⑲ as shown in Figure 10. The floorboard simply rests on a set of cleats ⑰ and ⑱ without fasteners. The two end cleats ⑰ are cut from ¾-by-1-inch stock and the side cleats ⑱ from the same material ripped with a 10-degree angle as shown in Figure 5. When cut, attach with glue and #8-by-1¼-inch flathead screws.

APPLYING THE FINISH

Give everything a nice rubdown with 280-grit sandpaper on the flat surfaces and #0000 steel wool on the moldings. If you used walnut, consider giving the cradle a coat of medium walnut stain to even up the color. The finish from here is your choice, but be sure to keep everything nontoxic. On my cradle, I wanted the finish to have an authentic antique look, or patina. I started with a medium walnut stain followed by two thin coats of shellac, rubbed down with #0000 steel wool.

Now apply the six-pointed star as shown in Figure 11. Step 1 shows the layout method for the design. Draw the star on poster board, cut out, then trace on the end panel with a pencil. Use an oil-based enamel and highliner brush to apply the lines, then fill in the segments.

To give the finish depth, I added a darker color to the recesses of the moldings, inside corners, and other logical places where dirt may collect. The color was applied as a glaze made by adding raw umber (Master Color by Behlen) to Watco Danish Oil. I brushed the glaze into the desired areas, then partially removed it with a rag to create a shadowed effect. When thoroughly dry, I sprayed on two thin coats of lacquer and rubbed it to a satin gloss with #0000 steel wool.

MILITARY DRUM TOY BOX

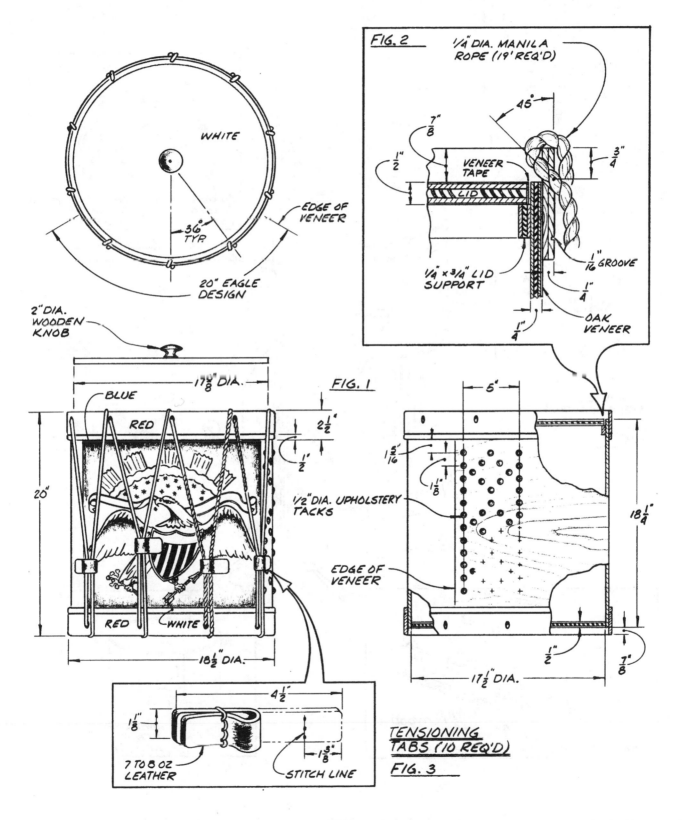

WHITE

EDGE OF VENEER

36° TYP.

20" EAGLE DESIGN

2" DIA. WOODEN KNOB

FIG. 2

1/4" DIA. MANILA ROPE (19' REQ'D)

45°

7/8"

1/2"

VENEER TAPE

LID

1/4" x 3/4" LID SUPPORT

3/4"

1/16" GROOVE

1/4"

1/4"

OAK VENEER

BLUE

RED

17 7/8" DIA.

FIG. 1

2 1/2"

1/2"

1/2" DIA. UPHOLSTERY TACKS

20"

5"

1 5/16"

1 1/8"

18 1/4"

EDGE OF VENEER

RED

WHITE

18 1/2" DIA.

1/2"

17 1/2" DIA.

7/8"

4 1/2"

1 1/8"

1 3/8"

7 TO 8 OZ LEATHER

STITCH LINE

TENSIONING TABS (10 REQ'D)

FIG. 3

135

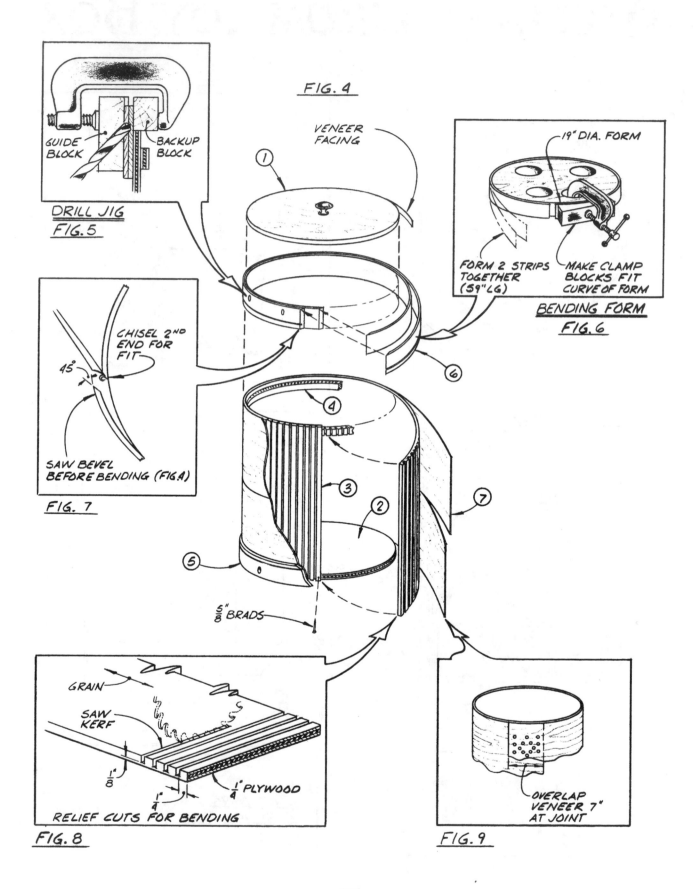

FIG. 4

DRILL JIG
FIG.5

GUIDE BLOCK

BACKUP BLOCK

VENEER FACING

①

19" DIA. FORM

FORM 2 STRIPS TOGETHER (59" LG)

MAKE CLAMP BLOCKS FIT CURVE OF FORM

BENDING FORM
FIG. 6

CHISEL 2ND END FOR FIT

45°

SAW BEVEL BEFORE BENDING (FIG.A)

FIG. 7

⑥

④

③

②

⑦

⑤

$\frac{5}{8}$" BRADS

GRAIN

SAW KERF

$\frac{1}{8}$"

$\frac{1}{4}$"

$\frac{1}{4}$" PLYWOOD

RELIEF CUTS FOR BENDING

FIG. 8

OVERLAP VENEER 7" AT JOINT

FIG. 9

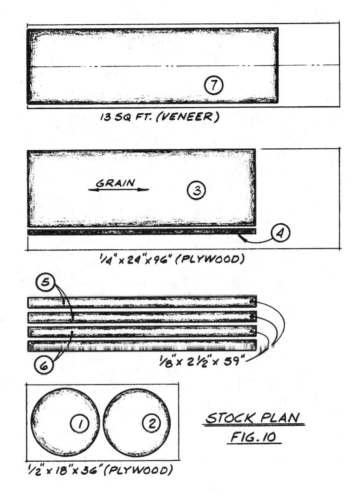

13 SQ FT. (VENEER)

GRAIN

¼" x 24" x 96" (PLYWOOD)

⅛" x 2½" x 59"

STOCK PLAN
FIG. 10

½" x 18" x 36" (PLYWOOD)

FIG. II

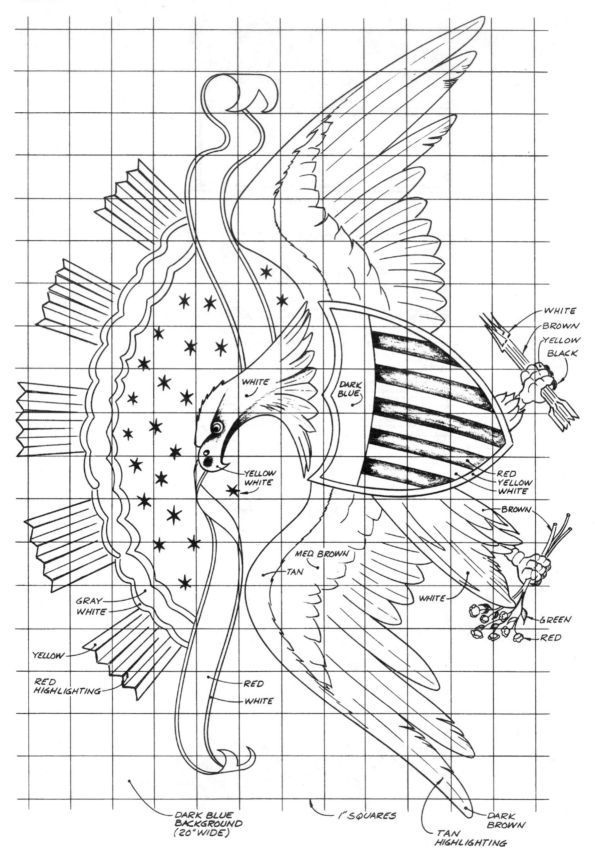

138

Fig. 12

BILL OF MATERIALS

Stock (inches)	Quantity	Item	Part
½ × 18 × 36 birch plywood	1	①	lid (one)
		②	base (one)
¼ × 24 × 96 birch plywood	1	③	body (one)
		④	lid stop (one)
⅛ × 2½ × 59 poplar	4	⑤	lower head band (one)
		⑥	upper head band (one)
18½ × 63½ oak veneer	1	⑦	body facing (one)

Hardware and Supplies	Quantity	Description
manila rope	1	1/4" dia., 19' long
veneer tape	1	¾" wide, 5'
upholstery tacks	50	½" dia.
wooden knobs	1	2" dia.
leather	1	1¼" × 60"
brown thread	1	25 yds.

MILITARY DRUM TOY BOX

This is the only project in this book where the subject is being used for something other than its original purpose. But what better use could a handsome early American drum serve today than as the theme for a piece of children's furniture. This project combines the best features of several early American drums to create an authentic-looking replica. And although this drum was conceived as a toy box, it would also make a perfect bedside stand or place for books and magazines. If you think you would like to build it but you're a bit intimidated by the thought of painting the eagle, you can purchase a decal that will give similar results.

The drummer boy and his instrument played an important role in military life during the American Revolution and the Civil War. On the field of battle, the beat of the drum was used to set the pace of marching troops and communicate orders to assemble, charge, and retreat. In camp, the drummer sounded daily calls and at nightfall tapped out his final message, which is the origin of "Taps."

Many of these drums were graced with a bald eagle with outspread wings and legs to symbolize freedom and power. This motif was particularly popular after 1782, when Congress approved this pose of the distinguished bird for the Great Seal of the United States. When the drum maker applied the decoration, the banderole behind the eagle's head was left blank for the regimental name and number.

Things to Know

Before you begin this project, you'll need to learn or review the techniques discussed in the following sections:
Drawing Your Patterns
Steam-Bending Wood
Decorating Your Projects

PLANNING THE PROJECT

Making a round cylinder can often be difficult, but the unique construction used for this drum makes the task easy. This technique uses grooved ¼-inch plywood as shown in Figure 8 to provide flexibility for forming the drum, topped by a layer of oak veneer to regain the rigidity. You may have difficulty locating a source for the veneer because of its size (18½ by 63½ inches, or 8 square feet). A line of oversize veneers called Monarch, which run 9 inches and wider by 7 feet, is available from Constantine's, telephone (800) 223-8087. You'll need to order two widths (about 13 square feet total) to cover the drum. For this project, I highly recommend a ratchet action band clamp. When clamping up the cylinder and head bands, a pair of these clamps will take the place of a dozen C-clamps and do a better job because they provide more even pressure.

BUILDING THE BODY

The body for the drum ③ is cut from a half sheet of ¼-inch birch plywood. The actual size required is 18¼ by 55⅛ inches, but the length should be cut to 55½ inches to allow for fitting later. When cut, measure and mark the positions of the relief cuts for bending, and saw as shown in Figure 8. Next, cut the lid ① and base ② to a diameter of 17½ inches. The lid will be cut down to 17⅜ inches later, but for now it will be used with the base to form the body. Now is a good time to mount the wooden knob, because it provides a convenient handle for positioning the lid.

Start the body assembly by placing the grooved side of the plywood down on the workbench. Have an assistant roll the plywood around the lid or base, while you do likewise from the other end. Slip a band clamp over each end of the body and lightly tighten. You should have an overlap at the joint. Mark the amount of material that has to be removed, then disassemble and trim. When you have a good fit, redo with just enough glue at the base and joint (you won't be able to get to any excess for cleaning). Use a brad at the beginning of the wrap at the base to prevent movement, and then roll up the body and clamp.

Apply the oak veneer facing next. If you ordered the Monarch veneer from Constantine, two strips will have to be edge-joined before gluing to the drum body. The easiest way to do this is with 2-inch transparent packaging tape. Before taping, the joining edges must be cut straight. To do so, use 2-inch packaging tape to stick the edge to be cut to an old sheet of plywood. Then cut through the tape and veneer using a hand-held circular saw with a fine blade. When the two edges are cut, join them together with a continuous strip of tape. Square up one end of the veneer with a razor knife, and then measure and cut a piece 63½ inches long, which will give you a 7-inch overlap as shown in Figure 9. This may seem like an unusual way to end the veneer, but it stimulates the scarf joint used on the old drums. Apply the veneer using contact cement; don't use water-based glue, which would create welts in the veneer. Have an assistant hold one end of the veneer while you progressively apply the other end with a roller to work out blisters along the way. To do the overlap, mark where the veneer ends, then lift to cement the dry surface.

HEAD BANDS

On the early drums, each head band was actually two hoops. The first hoop (marked white on the drawing) had the head skin wrapped around it while the second hoop (marked red) was used to apply force against the first hoop to tighten the head. On our drum this isn't required so the band is one piece.

The bands are made from two layers of ⅛-by-2½-by-59-inch stock that are preformed by steam bending as shown in Figure 6. This may seem like an unnecessary step, but the time spent on prebending will be returned many times during fitting and attaching to the drum body. First make the bending form by gluing up pieces of 2-by-4-inch stock. When dry, cut the 19-inch diameter, clamp holes, and clamp blocks to complete the form. Before forming the bands, cut a 45-degree angle on one end of each of the strips as shown in Figure 7 and add the 1/16-inch decorative groove on two pieces as shown in Figure 2.

To form the bands, steam a pair of strips about thirty minutes. Then, making sure that the end bevel and decorative groove are facing the correct direction, quickly clamp and wrap both pieces around the form. Be well prepared and move rapidly, because pieces this thin will start to lose their pliability after about thirty seconds. Leave the pieces on the form overnight, then remove and overlap the ends to join temporarily with a C-clamp. Put these pieces in a warm place to dry thoroughly and repeat the steaming process for the remaining two strips.

The band strips are made extralong and are held in place on the drum body by a band clamp. With a strip clamped in place, mark the cut line on the unbeveled end of the strip, then remove and cut. Use a sharp chisel to apply the bevel as shown in Figure 7, then reclamp to the drum. When the fit looks okay, redo with glue. Use the same procedure for the remaining bands, staggering the joints for strength.

LID AND SUPPORT

Now that the head bands are attached, support from the lid is no longer needed. Remove the lid from the drum and cut the diameter down to 17⅜ inches. Apply birch veneering tape to the lid's periphery using contact cement, then trim flush. The lid support ④ is a piece of ¼-by-¾-by-55-inch plywood that's grooved for bending (see exploded view drawing). The length is slightly oversize, so place the piece in position and mark the required length. Cut to size, then glue and clamp in place as shown in Figure 2. Finish up by filling the grooves on top of the support with wood filler.

ROPE HOLE JIG

The tensioning ropes require ten holes drilled at a 45-degree angle in each head band as shown in Figure 2. The quickest way to get accurate holes is to use a drill jig as shown in Figure 5. When making the jig blocks, cut the clamping faces on an arc that matches the head band to prevent distortion when clamping. Make the guide block from a hardwood so that it will last for the twenty holes. Drill a $^9/_{32}$-inch hole at approximately 45 degrees, then test-fit the ¼-inch rope to check for sufficient clearance. Mark the top band for the rope hole locations using 5 $^{13}/_{16}$ inches between center lines. Now mark the bottom band but note that the holes are shifted one half pitch to make the rope angles equal, as shown in Figure 1. Drill, then deburr both sides of the holes with sandpaper.

FINISHING THE DRUM

Sand everything down with 180-grit sandpaper, then progressively work to 320-grit. To capture the original appearance, stain the veneer on the body with a medium brown stain. When dry, give the entire piece several coats of shellac that's diluted 50 percent, rubbing out with #000 steel wool between coats. The background area for the eagle begins at the edge of the veneer and is 20 inches wide. Paint the colored areas now using an enamel, and leave the inside of the drum natural so that the inevitable scratches won't show.

Now add the ½-inch diameter upholstery tacks that simulate the decorative rivet joints on the body (see side view drawing). On original drums, the body was made from very thin steam-bent stock that had a scarf joint fastened with dozens of rivets. Rather than hide them, they were arranged in decorative designs. Lay out the tack locations, then drill pilot holes for the tacks.

Trim the tack length so that they won't protrude through the body, then glue in place with epoxy.

APPLYING THE EAGLE

There are two choices for applying the eagle design. You can hand-paint the design as shown in the pattern layout, or you can use a decal. An appropriate eagle decal (see Figure 12) is available from Decorcal, Inc. telephone (800) 645-9868. You can use the decal as is or paint in the banderole, star field, and wheat shocks for background. To hand-paint the eagle, you can do a full-size drawing on poster board using the pattern layout, then progressively cut the design apart to trace the major detail. If you have access to a photocopier that enlarges, that's even better. Once you have applied the eagle, give the entire drum a final top coat of semigloss varnish so that everything has a uniform sheen.

ROPING UP THE DRUM

All that remains is making the tensioning tabs and installing the rope. Figure 3 shows the details for making the tensioners. You can order the leather (#4493) and thread (#1210) from Tandy Leather Company, telephone (800) 821-0801, or buy them at a local leather-craft store. Cut the leather tensioners to size, then mark the stitch line on both ends. Use an awl or sharpened nail to make the holes for stitching, then sew up as shown. When stringing the rope, you can avoid having a visible joining knot by starting with a knot on the inside of the bottom flange and attaching the final end on the bottom with a glue block. Tighten up the tensioning tabs, and the toy box is ready for service.

PLAY WAGON

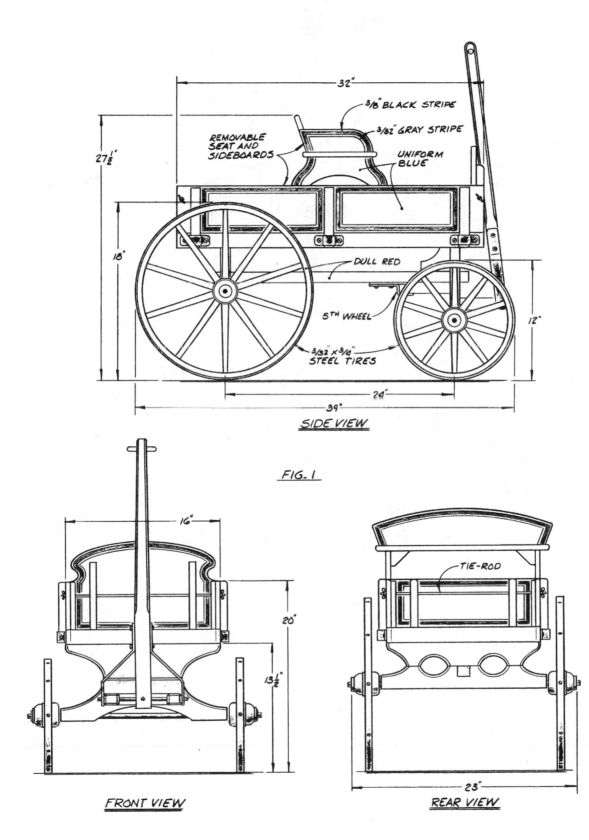

27½"

32"

3/8" BLACK STRIPE

3/32" GRAY STRIPE

REMOVABLE SEAT AND SIDEBOARDS

UNIFORM BLUE

18"

DULL RED

5TH WHEEL

12"

3/32" x 3/4" STEEL TIRES

24"

39"

SIDE VIEW

FIG. 1

16"

20"

13½"

FRONT VIEW

TIE-ROD

23"

REAR VIEW

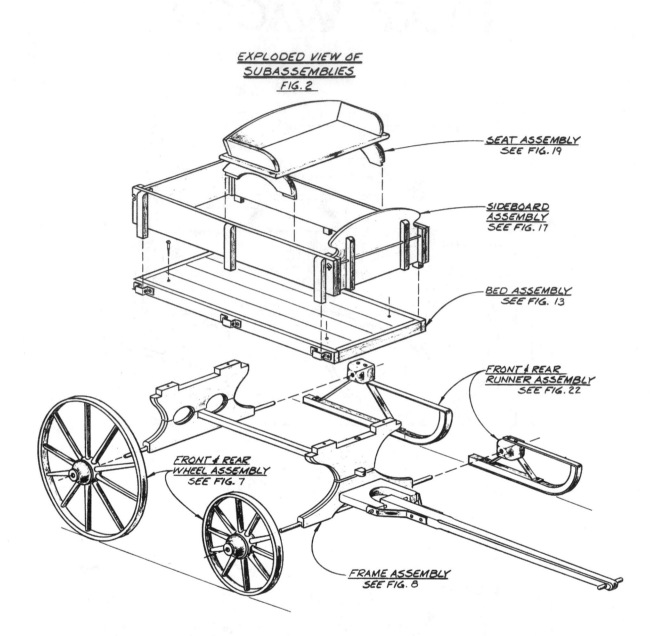

EXPLODED VIEW OF
SUBASSEMBLIES
FIG. 2

SEAT ASSEMBLY
SEE FIG. 19

SIDEBOARD
ASSEMBLY
SEE FIG. 17

BED ASSEMBLY
SEE FIG. 13

FRONT & REAR
RUNNER ASSEMBLY
SEE FIG. 22

FRONT & REAR
WHEEL ASSEMBLY
SEE FIG. 7

FRAME ASSEMBLY
SEE FIG. 8

STOCK PLAN
FIG. 3

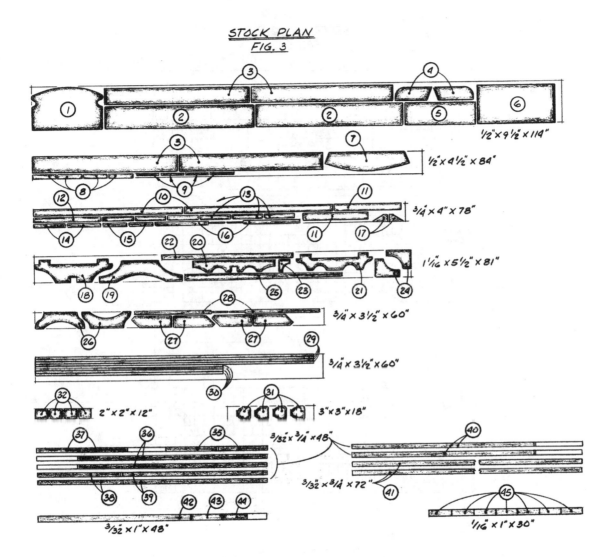

½" × 9½" × 114"

½" × 4½" × 84"

¾" × 4" × 78"

1 1/16" × 5½" × 81"

¾" × 3½" × 60"

¾" × 3½" × 60"

2" × 2" × 12"

3" × 3" × 18"

3/32" × ¾" × 48"

3/32" × ¾" × 72"

3/32" × 1" × 48"

1/16" × 1" × 30"

PATTERN LAYOUTS
FIG. 4

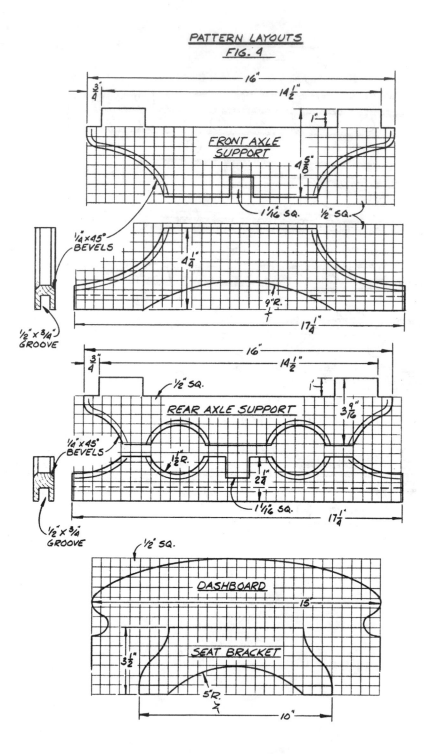

148

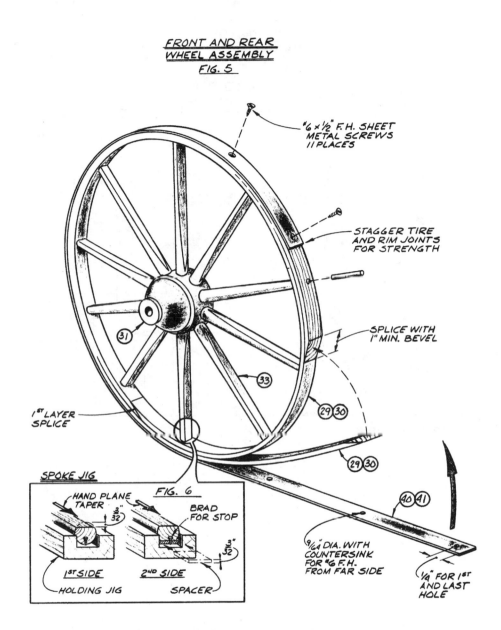

FRONT AND REAR
WHEEL ASSEMBLY
FIG. 5

#6 × 1/2" F.H. SHEET
METAL SCREWS
11 PLACES

STAGGER TIRE
AND RIM JOINTS
FOR STRENGTH

SPLICE WITH
1" MIN. BEVEL

31

33

29 30

1ST LAYER
SPLICE

29 30

40 41

SPOKE JIG

FIG. 6

HAND PLANE
TAPER

3/32"

BRAD
FOR STOP

1ST SIDE

3/32"

2ND SIDE

HOLDING JIG

SPACER

9/64" DIA. WITH
COUNTERSINK
FOR #6 F.H.
FROM FAR SIDE

1/4" FOR 1ST
AND LAST
HOLE

FRONT AND REAR
WHEEL DETAIL
FIG. 7

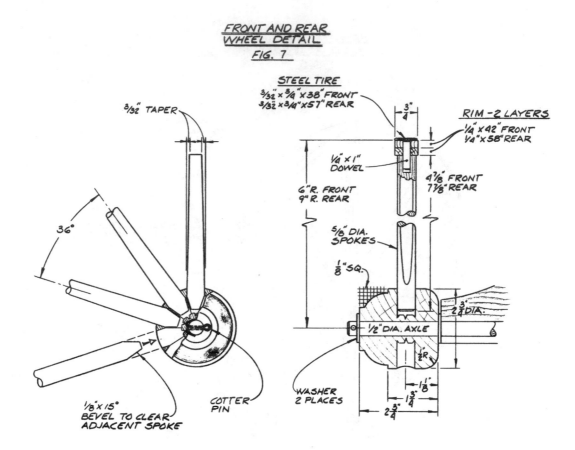

STEEL TIRE
3/32" × 3/4" × 38" FRONT
3/32" × 3/4" × 57" REAR

RIM – 2 LAYERS
1/4" × 42" FRONT
1/4" × 58" REAR

3/32" TAPER

1/4" × 1" DOWEL

6" R. FRONT
9" R. REAR

4 7/8" FRONT
7 7/8" REAR

5/8" DIA. SPOKES

1/8" SQ.

36°

1/8" × 15° BEVEL TO CLEAR ADJACENT SPOKE

COTTER PIN

2 1/4" DIA.

1/2" DIA. AXLE

WASHER 2 PLACES

3" / 4

1/2" R

1 1/8"

1 3/4"

2 3/4"

150

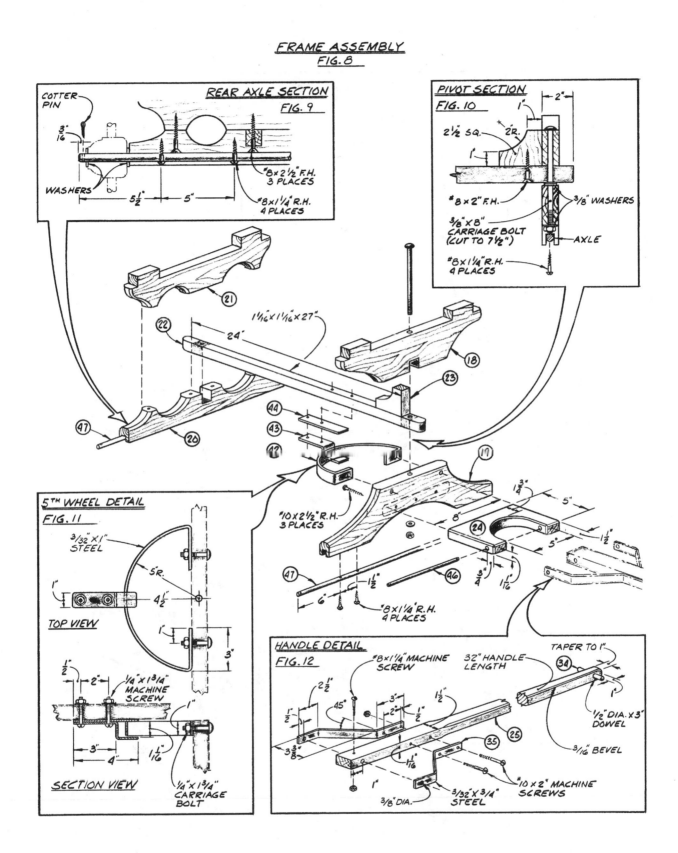

FRAME ASSEMBLY
FIG.8

REAR AXLE SECTION
FIG. 9

COTTER PIN

3/16

WASHERS

5 1/2"   5"

#8×2 1/2" F.H.
3 PLACES

#8×1 1/4" R.H.
4 PLACES

PIVOT SECTION
FIG. 10

2"
1"
2 1/2" SQ.
2"R.
1"

#8×2" F.H.

3/8" WASHERS

3/8"×8"
CARRIAGE BOLT
(CUT TO 7 1/2")

AXLE

#8×1 1/4" R.H.
4 PLACES

21

22
1 1/16"×1 1/16"×27"
24"

18

23

44
43
42

47
20

17

47

5TH WHEEL DETAIL
FIG. 11

3/32"×1"
STEEL

5"R.

1"

4 1/2"

1"

TOP VIEW

1/2"
2"
1/4"×1 3/4"
MACHINE
SCREW

1"

3"
4"

1 1/16"

3"

1"

SECTION VIEW

1/4"×1 3/4"
CARRIAGE
BOLT

#10×2 1/2" R.H.
3 PLACES

24

46

8"

1 3/4"
5"

5"

1 1/2"

1 1/16"

3/8"

1 1/2"

6"

#8×1 1/4" R.H.
4 PLACES

HANDLE DETAIL
FIG. 12

#8×1 1/4" MACHINE
SCREW

32" HANDLE
LENGTH

TAPER TO 1"

34

2 1/2"
1/2"
45°
3"
2"
1 1/2"
1 1/2"
1"

3 3/8"

1 1/16"

35

25

1/2" DIA.×3"
DOWEL

3/16" BEVEL

#10×2" MACHINE
SCREWS

1"

3/8" DIA.

3/32"×3/4"
STEEL

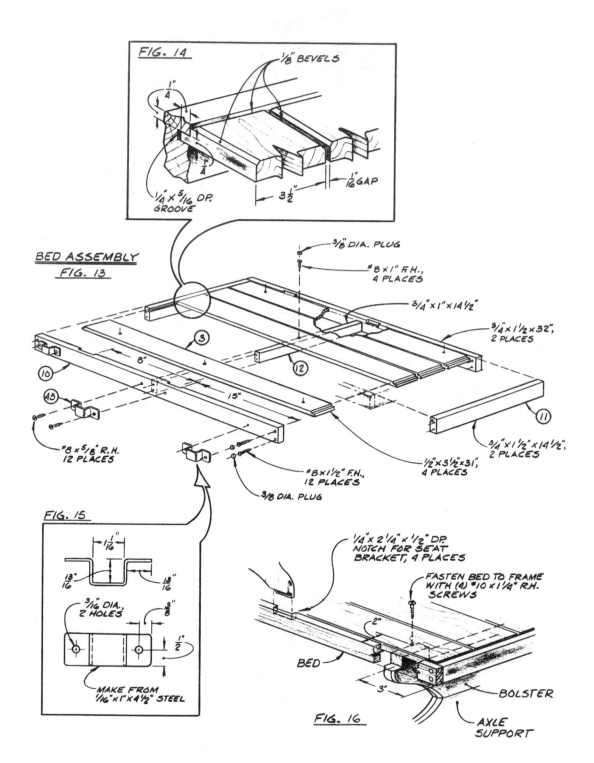

FIG. 14

$\frac{1}{8}$" BEVELS

$\frac{1}{4}$"

1"

$\frac{1}{16}$" GAP

$3\frac{1}{2}$"

$\frac{1}{4}$" × $\frac{5}{16}$" DP.
GROOVE

$\frac{3}{8}$" DIA. PLUG

#8 × 1" F.H.,
4 PLACES

BED ASSEMBLY
FIG. 13

$\frac{3}{4}$" × 1" × $14\frac{1}{2}$"

$\frac{3}{4}$" × $1\frac{1}{2}$" × 32",
2 PLACES

3

8"

12

10

15"

11

45

#8 × $\frac{5}{8}$" R.H.
12 PLACES

#8 × $1\frac{1}{2}$" F.H.,
12 PLACES

$\frac{1}{2}$" × $3\frac{1}{2}$" × 31",
4 PLACES

$\frac{3}{4}$" × $1\frac{1}{2}$" × $14\frac{1}{2}$",
2 PLACES

$\frac{3}{8}$" DIA. PLUG

FIG. 15

$1\frac{1}{16}$"

$\frac{13}{16}$"

$\frac{13}{16}$"

$\frac{3}{16}$" DIA.,
2 HOLES

$\frac{3}{8}$"

$\frac{1}{2}$"

MAKE FROM
$\frac{1}{16}$" × 1" × $4\frac{1}{2}$" STEEL

$\frac{1}{4}$" × $2\frac{1}{4}$" × $\frac{1}{2}$" DP.
NOTCH FOR SEAT
BRACKET, 4 PLACES

FASTEN BED TO FRAME
WITH (4) #10 × $1\frac{1}{4}$" R.H.
SCREWS

2"

BED

3"

BOLSTER

AXLE
SUPPORT

FIG. 16

152

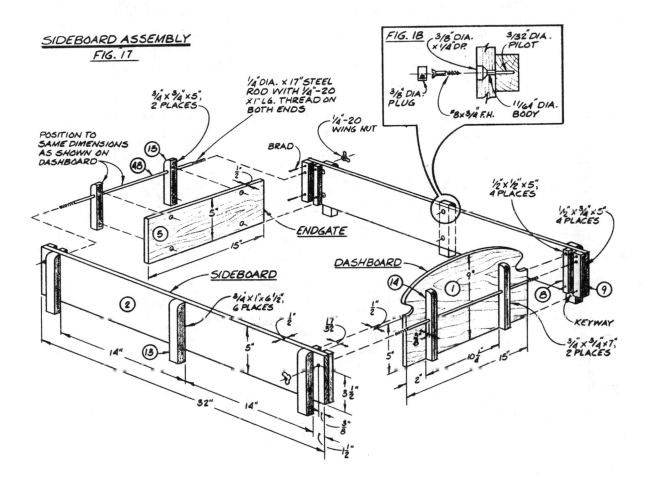

SIDEBOARD ASSEMBLY
FIG. 17

FIG. 18

3/8" DIA. x 1/4 DP.   3/32" DIA. PILOT

3/8" DIA. PLUG

#8 x 3/4 F.H.   11/64" DIA. BODY

3/4" x 3/4" x 5", 2 PLACES

1/4" DIA. x 17" STEEL ROD WITH 1/4"-20 x 1" LG. THREAD ON BOTH ENDS

1/4"-20 WING NUT

BRAD

POSITION TO SAME DIMENSIONS AS SHOWN ON DASHBOARD

13

48

1/2"

5"

5

15"

ENDGATE

SIDEBOARD

DASHBOARD

1/2" x 1/2" x 5", 4 PLACES

1/2" x 3/4" x 5", 4 PLACES

2

3/4" x 1" x 6 1/2", 6 PLACES

14

1

9"

8

9

KEYWAY

14"

13

1/2"

17/32"

1/2"

5"

5"

3/4" x 3/4" x 7", 2 PLACES

32"

14"

3 1/2"

5/8"

1 1/2"

2"

10 1/2"

15"

153

SEAT ASSEMBLY
FIG. 19

EDGE DETAIL
FIG. 20

"A" SCREWS, 8 PLACES
FIG. 21

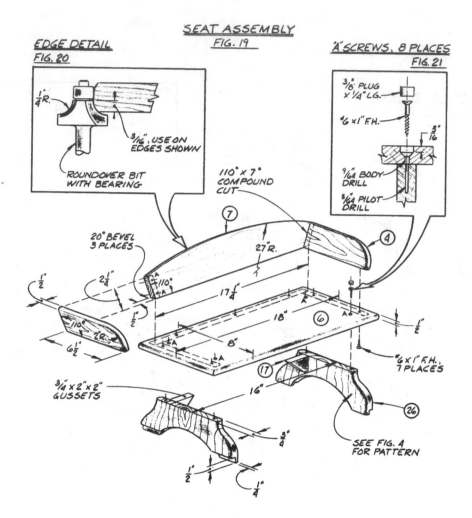

$\frac{1}{4}$ R.

$\frac{3}{16}$", USE ON EDGES SHOWN

ROUNDOVER BIT WITH BEARING

$\frac{3}{8}$" PLUG X $\frac{1}{4}$" LG.

#6 X 1" F.H.

$\frac{3}{16}$

$\frac{9}{64}$" BODY DRILL

$\frac{5}{64}$" PILOT DRILL

110° X 7° COMPOUND CUT

20° BEVEL 3 PLACES

27" R.

110°

$\frac{1}{2}$"

$2\frac{1}{4}$"

$\frac{1}{2}$"

110° 7 R.

$6\frac{1}{2}$

$17\frac{1}{4}$"

18"

8"

$\frac{1}{2}$"

$\frac{3}{4}$" X 2" X 2" GUSSETS

16"

#6 X 1" F.H., 7 PLACES

$\frac{3}{4}$"

$\frac{1}{2}$"

$\frac{1}{4}$"

SEE FIG. 4 FOR PATTERN

154

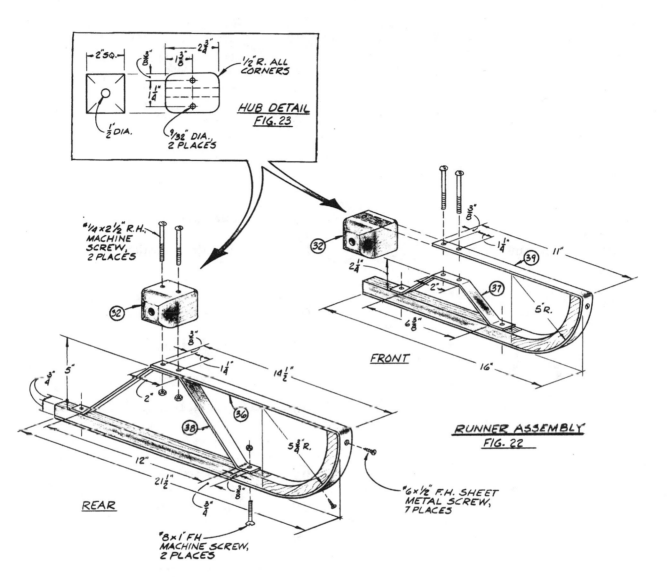

2" SQ.

¾" DIA.

2¾"

1⅜"

1½" R. ALL CORNERS

1¼"

HUB DETAIL
FIG. 23

½" DIA.

⁹⁄₃₂" DIA., 2 PLACES

#¼ x 2½" R.H. MACHINE SCREW, 2 PLACES

32

32

¾"

1¼"

11"

39

2¼"

2"

37

5" R.

6⅜"

16"

FRONT

5"

¾"

1¼"

14½"

¾"

36

2"

38

5¾" R.

12"

21½"

¾"

⅜"

RUNNER ASSEMBLY
FIG. 22

#6 x ½" F.H. SHEET METAL SCREW, 7 PLACES

REAR

#8 x 1" FH MACHINE SCREW, 2 PLACES

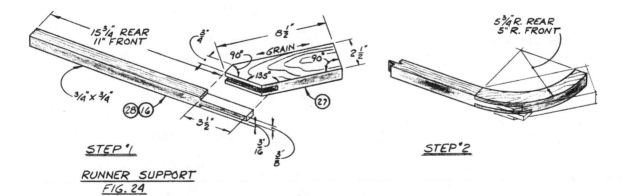

15¾" REAR
11" FRONT

¾"

8½"

90°

GRAIN

90°

2½"

135°

27

¾" x ¾"

28 16

3½"

³⁄₁₆"

DIA.

STEP #1

RUNNER SUPPORT
FIG. 24

5¾" R. REAR
5" R. FRONT

STEP #2

Bill of Materials

Stock (inches)	Quantity	Item	Part
½ × 9½ × 114 hard maple	1	①	dashboard (one)
		②	side boards (two)
		③	floorboards (four)
		④	arms (two)
		⑤	endgate (one)
		⑥	seat (one)
½ × 4½ × 84 hard maple	1	③	floorboards (two)
		⑦	back (one)
		⑧	inside strips (four)
		⑨	outside strip (four)
¾ × 4 × 78 hard maple	1	⑩	side rails (two)
		⑪	end rails (two)
		⑫	support (one)
		⑬	posts (six)
		⑭	stiffeners (two)
		⑮	stiffeners (two)
		⑯	front runners (two)
		⑰	gussets (two)
1¹⁄₁₆ × 5½ × 81 hard maple	1	⑱	front bolster (one)
		⑲	front axle support (one)
		⑳	rear axle support (one)
		㉑	rear bolster (one)
		㉒	coupling pole (one)
		㉓	gusset (one)
		㉔	handle mount (one)
		㉕	handle (one)

Stock (inches)	Quantity	Item	Part
¾ × 3½ × 60 hard maple	1	(26)	seat brackets (two)
		(27)	runner nosepieces (four)
		(28)	rear runners (two)
¾ × 3½ × 60 straight-grained oak	1	(29)	rear rim strips (four)
		(30)	front rim strips (four)
3 × 3 × 18 maple	1	(31)	wheel hubs (four)
2 × 2 × 12 maple	1	(32)	runner hubs (four)
⅝ dia. × 36 maple or birch dowel	8	(33)	spokes (forty)
½ dia. × 36 maple or birch dowel	1	(34)	hand grip (one)
⅜ dia. × 36 maple or birch dowel	1	–	screw plugs (forty-five)
¼ dia. × 36 maple or birch dowel	2	–	wheel rim dowels (forty)
³⁄₃₂ × ¾ × 48 steel	7	(35)	handle brackets (two)
		(36)	rear soles (two)
		(37)	front gussets (two)
		(38)	rear gussets (two)
		(39)	front soles (two)
		(40)	front tires (two)
³⁄₃₂ × ¾ × 72	2	(41)	rear tires (two)
³⁄₃₂ × 1 × 48 steel	1	(42)	fifth wheel (one)
		(43)	retainer (one)
		(44)	wear plate (one)
¹⁄₁₆ × 1 × 30 steel	1	(45)	brackets (six)
⅜ dia. × 9 steel	1	(46)	pivot shaft (one)
½ dia. × 48 steel	1	(47)	axles (two)
¼ dia. × 34 steel	1	(48)	tie-rods (two)

Hardware and Supplies	Quantity	Description
wood screws	45	#6 × ½" F.H
	20	#8 × ¾" F.H.
	12	#8 × 1½" F.H.
	12	#8 × ⅝" R.H.
	5	#8 × 2½" F.H.
	1	#8 × 2" F.H.
	8	#8 × 1¼" R.H.
	4	#10 × 1¼" R.H.
	3	#10 × 2½" R.H.
sheet metal screws	70	#6 × ½" F.H.
machine screws	8	#8 × 1" F.H.
	1	#8 × 1¼" R.H.
	2	#10 × 2" R.H.
	8	¼" × 2½" R.H.
	2	¼" × 1¾" R.H.
carriage bolts	1	⅜" × 8"
	2	¼" × 1¾"
nuts	9	#8
	2	#10
	12	¼"
	1	⅜"
wing nuts	4	¼"–20
washers	2	¼"
	3	⅜"
	8	½"
cotter pins	6	3/32" × ¾"

PLAY WAGON

Most of us can fondly remember our first wagon. It was probably red, made of sheet metal—and a prized possession. On one of my frequent antiques market visits, I discovered a nice nineteenth century play wagon, and a question immediately came to mind: Why don't they make them this way today? My old standby never would have measured up to this beauty. This classic was very sturdy and built entirely of wood. The wheels were large for easy rolling through grass and hopping curbs, the seat and side boards were removable, and there was a set of sled runners that replaced the wheels for use in the winter. It was perfect, and I knew I had to build it.

Like many early toys, these wagons were an attempt to create the adult world in miniature. Early manufacturers were eager to boast that they produced the best reproduction of the full-size farm wagon. By 1890, catalog retailers like Montgomery Ward and Sears, Roebuck were offering these wagons in several sizes and styles. Their main selling feature was their ability to be assembled in different combinations, and if you had the need, there was even an option to replace the handle with a single-tree for harnessing the family dog or goat!

Things to Know

Before you begin this project, you'll need to learn or review the techniques discussed in the following sections:
  Drawing Your Patterns
  Steam-bending Wood
  How to Make a Spoked Wheel
  Decorating Your Projects

The wagon presented here varies slightly from the original to keep the assembly as straightforward as possible. All of the details are provided for the complete wagon and its accessories so that you can build any combination. There are a lot of parts to cut out if you decide to make everything, but the joinery is simple, so the assembly moves along quickly. The only unusual part of the project is building the spoked wheels. At first glance they may seem a bit intimidating, but with the aid of an assembly jig, you can get first-class results.

PLANNING THE PROJECT

Referring to the exploded view drawing (Figure 2), decide what combination you want to build. The assemblies shown are treated as individual projects, so you only work with the drawings and construction details you need. The simplest version possible is the frame and bed assembly with either wheels or runners. From there you can add assemblies to create many interesting variations, as shown in the beginning photographs.

The stock plan in Figure 3 shows how to position the parts for correct grain direction and good utilization of the material. All of the parts for the complete wagon are included in the stock plan and the bill of materials, so if you decide to eliminate any of the assemblies, delete the associated parts from your list before heading to the lumberyard.

Wagons see a lot of hard use over their lifetime, so use good-quality hardwood. My preference is hard maple for all of the parts except the wheel rims. It is one of the more difficult woods to work with, so good, sharp tools are a must. This wood resists dents, is very strong, and sands glass smooth for a painted finish. If you prefer to use a natural finish, oak or ash would be a good alternative. And since wagons spend most of their time outside, put everything together with a weatherproof glue, such as Titebond II, Weldwood plastic resin, or G2 epoxy.

PATTERNS

Before you start cutting, take the time to lay out everything on your stock as shown in Figure 3. Start by drawing patterns of the irregularly shaped pieces (Figure 4) on poster board. Cut out the pat-

The wagon can be transformed into a sled by making runners to replace the wheels. Removable seat and side boards are other options.

terns then position them on the stock so that there is generous space between pieces for the saw cuts. When the arrangement looks okay, trace the pattens, draw the straight pieces, and number everything. Do not precut the parts before you need them. If you want to reduce the bulk of the boards, cut the parts oversize so that there is material left for final fitting.

WHEEL ASSEMBLY

The construction of the wheel (Figure 5) has been simplified considerably from the original. The hub is shown as a turning, but if you don't have a lathe, you can achieve the same results by cutting out a cylinder and rounding the edges with a chisel and file. The spokes are dowels that have been tapered to reduce the amount of surface contacting the rim and to add to the appearance. The rims on the original were made from a single piece of ½-inch thick oak that was steam bent and joined with a long scarf (bevel) joint. Divide the rim into two ¼-inch layers and stagger the splice joints. The thinner pieces make steam-bending easy to do, and the laminate construction eliminates the influence of grain direction in the individual strips, resulting in a near-perfect round wheel. The finishing touch on the wheel is the 3/32-inch thick steel tire. You could consider omitting the tires if your wagon is going to be used for decorative purposes only, but if it is going to be used, the tires are necessary for strength and protection.

To make the wheels, you first need to construct a steamer and jigs as directed in Steam-Bending Wood and How to Make a Spoked Wheel. You'll need two jigs, one for each size wheel. Use the dimensions in Figure 7 for determining the size of the features on the jigs.

Once you've made the steamer and the jigs, the next step is to make the parts for the wheels (Figures 5 and 7). Start by making four identical hubs ㉛ from 3-by-3-inch stock. If you don't have a lathe, you can make the hubs from a lamination of three disks cut out with a scroll saw, as described in How to Make a Spoked Wheel (page 15). Do not drill the spoke holes at this time; the layout and drilling will be done later on the assembly jig. Complete the hubs by drilling the ½-inch axle hole. Carefully mark off the center of the hub and use a drill press to assure squareness.

Next, make the spokes from ⅝-inch dowel stock. Cut twenty 4⅞-inch-long pieces for the front wheels and twenty 7⅞-inch-long pieces for the rear wheels. Figure 6 shows a holding jig that will allow you to apply the taper quickly and accurately on the spokes. To make this jig, use a 10-by-1½-by-¾-inch piece of hardwood and cut a ⅜-inch-deep groove to a width that creates a snug fit with the dowel stock. Then put a brad at the end of the groove to back up the dowel when cutting the taper. Mount the jig in a vise, then, using a small hand plane, cut the taper so that it starts about ⅞ inch from one end of the dowel and removes 3/32 inch from the other end (see Figure 6). Do all of the dowels on one side, and then go back and taper the other sides. When doing the second side, you will need to use a 3/32-inch spacer under the tapered end of the dowel to prevent rocking during hand planing. Finish up the spokes by adding clearance bevels on the hub end, using a radial arm saw or a handsaw to cut two ⅛-inch-by-15-degree bevels as shown in Figure 7.

Next, make the rim strips ㉙ and ㉚. Use a wood that has good steam-bending characteristics, such as oak, ash, or hickory. The grain must be straight and free of flaws so that tight, smooth curves can be made without breaking. Cut out the rim strips to size, and as a precaution, cut an extra piece of each size in case one breaks during bending. Steam-bend the rim pieces as described in Steam-Bending Wood (page 13).

Now assemble the wheel parts, again referring to How to Make a Spoked Wheel. The jigs are used in every step of the assembly and consequently become a bottleneck in the process. Making more jigs would help, but I've found it convenient to move on to other parts of the wagon and come back to the wheels when the jig becomes available.

The final step in building the wheels is making and attaching the metal tires ㊵ and ㊶. The tire material is $^3/_{32}$-by-$^3/_4$-inch mild steel and is available in the required 4- and 6—foot lengths at hardware stores and home-improvement centers. Start by bending the tire to shape, and then add the holes for the mounting screws. Don't be tempted to drill the holes first, because they create weak spots and make bending a smooth curve very difficult. When bending the metal, the goal is to gently form the stock by using your hands to avoid kinks. First, draw a pattern of each tire size on a piece of cardboard. Then clamp the tip of the stock (about $^3/_8$ inch) in a metal vise so that the bending can be done parallel to the floor. Grip the free end of the stock with one hand and apply a pulling force while using the palm of your other hand to push on the point where you want the bend to occur. Go to the vise end of the stock and massage the curve into shape with this hand technique. Do about half of the tire, then remove it from the vise and check it against the pattern. Use a grease pencil to mark where the part strays from the curve, and return the piece to the vise. When the tire is completely formed, there will be an extra length of stock to remove. Temporarily attach the tire on the rim of the wheel with several C-clamps and check for fit. If everything looks okay, mark the joint on the excess end of the stock and cut with a hacksaw. Remove the tire from the wheel and drill the holes for the #6-by-$^1/_2$-inch flathead sheet metal screws as shown in Figure 5. Finish up by mounting the tire on the rim in a position that creates a good stagger between the joints.

FRAME ASSEMBLY

The frame of this wagon shares many features with that of its big brother, the farm wagon. The most noteworthy is the way the front axle assembly gains it strength through the use of a part called a fifth wheel. It's not really a wheel, but a member that resists the rearward forces created by the wheels going over rough ground (see Figure 11).

Begin construction by cutting the coupling pole ㉒ and gusset ㉓ to size as shown in Figures 8 and 10. Measure and mark the position of the gusset and rear axle support ⑳ onto the coupling pole. Join the gusset to the pole with glue and one #8-by-2-inch flathead screw. Finish up by rounding the ends of the pole with a rasp and sanding block.

Cut the parts for the front and rear axle supports ⑱, ⑲, ⑳ and ㉑. Use a table saw for the straight cuts and follow up with a band saw or jigsaw for the curved surfaces. Accurately cut the 14$^1/_2$-inch dimension on top of the front and rear bolsters ⑱ and ㉑ because these must engage with the bed assembly . Also, when doing the 1$^1/_{16}$-by-1$^1/_{16}$-inch cutout in the axle support and front bolster, test-fit with the coupling pole as you cut to ensure a snug joint and a sturdy frame. The next step is to cut the $^1/_2$-by-$^3/_4$-inch deep axle grooves into the supports ⑲ and ⑳ with a table saw and a dado blade. Then smooth out the curves with a spokeshave and do a first sanding with 180-grit paper. Add the $^1/_4$-inch bevels as shown with a router and 45-degree chamfer bit.

Start the assembly by dry-clamping the axle support ⑳, rear bolster ㉑, and coupling pole ㉒ together. When you're satisfied with the fit, drill and countersink for the three #8-by-2$^1/_2$-inch flathead screws required to join the assembly (see Figure 9). Disassemble, then redo the assembly with glue and screws and verify that the coupling pole is perpendicular to the support. When dry, continue this assembly by dry-clamping the front bolster onto the coupling pole. Check frame straightness by setting the assembly on a level surface. Block up the front of the assembly until the coupler pole is level, then take a level reading on top of each bolster. If the readings don't match, loosen the clamps on the front bolster and adjust. Use the gusset edge to mark the correct position of the front bolster and disassemble. Redo the joint with glue and recheck the alignment.

Metal Parts. Lay the frame aside for now and move on to making the metal parts; or, as our ancestors would have said, "ironing the wagon." The front and rear axles ㊼ are the same size (½ inch diameter by 24 inches) but have different mounting screw locations as shown in Figures 8 and 9. Cut the axles to length, and while you have the hacksaw handy, cut the ⅜-inch diameter-by-9-inch pivot shaft ㊻. Measure and center-punch the positions of the ³⁄₁₆-inch mounting holes and the ⁷⁄₆₄-inch cotter pin holes. Drill all of the shaft holes, and follow up with a countersink tool to deburr both sides of the holes.

Next, start making the fifth wheel ㊷ by laying out a pattern for bending. Use the dimensions in Figure 11 to draw the shape of the part on a piece of cardboard. Then mark the first bend position 3 inches from the end of a piece of ³⁄₃₂-by-1-by-48-inch steel stock. Clamp to the bend line in a metal vise and make a sharp bend by carefully striking the stock at the bend point with a heavy (2-pound) hammer. Remove from the vise and reclamp across the width of the stock. Now bend the curved portion of the part with your hands to avoid kinking. Remove the part from the vise and check it against the pattern. When the shape matches the pattern, make the second sharp bend, and cut the part from the stock. Finish the part by drilling ⁹⁄₃₂-inch holes for the ¼-by-1¾-inch mounting bolts. The fifth wheel engages with a retainer ㊸ and wear plate ㊹ that is bolted to the frame. Use ³⁄₃₂-by-1-inch steel to make these parts to the dimensions shown in Figure 11. Complete by drilling ⁹⁄₃₂-inch holes for the ¼-by-1¾-inch roundhead mounting screws.

The last two parts to make are the handle brackets ㉟ shown in Figure 12. Draw the shape of the part on a piece of poster board. Then mark the first bend position 3 inches from the end of a piece of ³⁄₃₂-by-¾-inch steel stock. Place the stock in a vise and make a sharp 45-degree bend. Lay your work on the pattern, and if the first bend looks good, mark the position of the second bend. Return to the vise and do another sharp 45-degree bend. Check your work against the pattern, and if you have a good match, cut the part to length and repeat the process for the second bracket. Finish the brackets

by drilling the ⅜-inch pivot holes. Then test-fit with the handle shaft. If the fit is a bit tight, use a round file to increase the size of the hole. Skip the #10 mounting screw holes for now; they will be done later as an assembly with the handle.

Front Axle Assembly. Draw the handle mount ㉔ onto the stock in two halves as shown in the stock plan (Figure 3). Cut out the pieces with about a ¼-inch allowance on all sides for final cuts. Match the two halves together so that the wood grain runs in the same direction as the handle, then glue and clamp. When dry, cut to size and rout ³⁄₁₆-inch bevels on all edges except at the mounting surface. The ⅜-inch pivot shaft hole must be drilled from both sides of the part because of the distance. Measure and mark the positions carefully, and use a drill press for accuracy. Test-fit the shaft for alignment; if there is a bind, use a ⅜-inch round file that can bridge the distance between the two holes to correct the problem. On the front axle support ⑲ that you made earlier, mark the position of the handle mount as shown in Figure 8. Dry-clamp the two parts together. Drill pilot holes for the three #10-by-2½-inch roundhead wood screws, and then disassemble. Redo the assembly with glue and screws.

Now drill the holes for the front axle assembly as shown in Figure 10. Use a ⅜-inch spade bit or a long bradpoint drill bit and a drill press for accuracy. Carefully square up and clamp the axle support in the drill press. To ensure an accurate hole, retract the bit frequently while drilling to clear the chips so that the bit will not bind and wander. While you have the ⅜-inch bit in the drill press, retrieve the frame assembly and add the pivot hole in the front bolster ⑱ using the same procedure described for the axle assembly. Test-fit the pivot joint assembly with the carriage bolt and all its hardware.

Retrieve the fifth wheel parts that you made earlier. Remove the front axle support from the frame, and position the fifth wheel on the support as shown in Figure 11. Mark the positions of the two mounting bolts, and drill the clearance holes with a ¼-inch bit. Join the two parts together with two

¼-by-1¾-inch carriage bolts, and then remount this assembly onto the frame. Position and clamp the retainer ㊸ and wear plate ㊹ as shown in the section view of Figure 11. Check the fifth wheel for alignment by rotating the axle support from side to side. If there is a problem, try more or fewer washers on the pivot bolt. Mark the positions of the two mounting screws, and drill the clearance holes with a ¼-inch bit. Join the plates to the frame with two ¼-by-1¾-inch machine screws. Complete the frame by attaching the two axles ㊼ with #8-by-1¼-inch roundhead wood screws.

Handle. The handle (Figure 12) is the last part to make for the frame assembly. Cut the handle ㉕ to a starting size of 1¹⁄₁₆ by 1½ by 32 inches. Then mark the positions and drill the holes for the ⅜-inch pivot shaft and the ½-inch dowel. On the 1½-inch face, measure 10 inches from the pivot end and mark an equal-sided taper down to 1 inch. Cut the taper with a band saw, and smooth the surface with a jointer or hand plane. Round the end of the taper and then cut ³⁄₁₆-inch bevels with a spokeshave or router table and chamfer bit.

The next step is to assemble the handle and brackets ㉟ that you made earlier. Align the ⅜-inch handle and bracket holes for the pivot shaft ㊻ as follows: Mark and center-punch the positions of the mounting holes on one bracket only, and drill with a ⁷⁄₃₂-inch bit. Then join the handle, pivot shaft, and brackets together with a clamp positioned between the mounting holes. Finally, with the existing mounting holes as pilots, use a hand drill to drill through the handle and remaining bracket. Remove the clamp and permanently join the assembly with two #10-by-2-inch roundhead machine screws. The last piece of hardware to apply is the #8-by-1¼-inch roundhead machine screw that locks the pivot shaft and handle together. Make sure the shaft is centered in the handle, then drill a ³⁄₁₆-inch hole through both parts at one time. Complete the handle with the addition of the hand grip ㉞, a 3-inch piece of ½-inch dowel stock. Round both ends and glue in place.

BED

The bed is a basic part of the wagon to which several optional features can be attached. Each side has three metal brackets for quickly mounting the side boards. And if you like the idea of using the wagon with just the seat, the side rails are notched for just that purpose.

Begin the construction by cutting out the four floorboards ③ to size. Then refer to Figure 13 for dimensions on the tongue and groove joint that's used to fasten the floorboards to the end rail. Cut the floorboard tongues on a router table, if you have one, or use a dado blade and table saw. Finish up by adding a ⅛-inch bevel on all of the top edges. A router and chamfer bit will quickly do the side bevels but not the ends, because the floorboard tongues will interfere with the bearing guide on the bit, so cut the end bevels on a radial arm saw with a 45-degree blade setup.

Start the outer framework by cutting the side rails ⑩, end rails ⑪ and support ⑫ to size. Each side rail has a pair of notches used to key the seat into the bed. Mark the positions of the notches, and cut them on a router table with a straight bit. Once cut, use a chisel to make sharp corners on the inside of the notches. Finish the parts by cutting a ¼-by-⁵⁄₁₆-inch deep groove in the end rails.

Bed Assembly. Dry-clamp the framework and floorboards together. Adjust the position of the floorboards so that there are equal gaps (about ¹⁄₁₆ inch) on each side of the boards and mark their positions on the end rails. Turn the assembly over and check the alignment of the support ⑫, then mark its position. When you're satisfied with the fit, drill the counterbore and pilot holes for the #8-by-1½-inch flathead wood screws in the side rails and floorboards. Disassemble, then redo the assembly with glue and clamps adjacent to the screw holes. Check the corners with a square and make sure the top is warpfree. If you need to improve the squareness, quickly place a bar clamp diagonally across the top, ease up on the holding clamps, and pull the corner into square. Then add the screws and scrub off any glue seepage from the joints. When dry, glue the ³⁄₈-inch plugs into the screw counterbores on the frame and floorboards. Use a chisel to trim the plugs flush with the surface, then finish-sand the whole assembly.

The side board brackets ④⑤ shown in Figure 13, are the last parts to make for the bed. Cut six 4¹⁄₂-inch pieces from ¹⁄₁₆-by-1-inch steel stock. Measure ¹³⁄₁₆ inch from the end of the stock and mark the first bend position. Then clamp to the bend line in a metal vise and make a sharp bend by striking the stock close to bend point with a heavy (2-pound) hammer. Measure from the first bend to locate the second bend, and so on until the bracket is finished. The stock length was slightly longer than needed to make the part, so trim the last mounting leg formed to match the first. Now that you have the touch, make the remaining five brackets and drill the ³⁄₁₆-inch holes. Don't attach the brackets now, however. Wait until the side board assembly is built, and then use the side board mounting posts to position the brackets to ensure proper alignment.

Complete the assembly by mounting the bed onto the frame bolsters as shown in Figure 16. Position the front of the bed 3 inches from the center of the front axle support. Then use a #10-by-1¹⁄₄-inch roundhead wood screw to attach the bed to each side of the front and rear bolsters.

SIDE BOARDS

Although the side board assembly (Figure 17) is optional, it's easy to make and will enable you to do a lot more with the wagon. The side and end boards are held together with two tie-rods ④⑧ and wing nuts so that a child can easily build different combinations without tools. Use the side boards alone by placing them in the wagon bed brackets ④⑤, or attach the endgate or dashboard for a different look.

Retrieve the stock with the side board assembly part layouts ①, ②, ⑤, ⑧, ⑨, ⑬, ⑭ and ⑮ drawn earlier. Cutting out these parts is easy because everything but the dashboard is made with straight cuts on the table saw. Once cut, put a half-round on the top edges of the side boards ②, endgate ⑤, and dashboard ① using a router and ¹⁄₄-inch-radius roundover bit as shown in Figure 20. Follow up with 180-grit sandpaper to smooth out the half-round surfaces and at the same time maintain the distinct edge at the faces of the board. This treatment creates a nice, soft look and increases the durability of the edges. Finish with a first sanding on the flat surfaces using 180-grit sandpaper.

Next, band saw a ¹⁄₂-inch radius on one end of each of the six posts ⑬ and the four stiffeners ⑭ and ⑮; then smooth out the curves with a file and sanding block. The next step is adding the holes for the ¹⁄₄-inch tie-rods. This can be tricky, because the holes in the side boards and stiffeners must be in good alignment so that the tie-rods can pass through these parts without binding. This problem can be solved by match drilling, a technique in which a hole in one part is used as a guide to drill holes in other parts. Mark the rod position on one of the stiffeners, and drill a ⁹⁄₃₂-inch hole. This part becomes a temporary drill jig for the remaining seven holes. Match up the jig with one of the side board ends so that the bottom and end surfaces are flush, then clamp in place. Run the bit through the jig hole to drill the side board hole, and you end up with a perfect match. Then repeat the process for the remaining holes.

The two tie-rods ④⑧ are ¹⁄₄-inch-diameter-by-17-inch steel with ¹⁄₄-20 threads that need to be cut on each end. If you don't have access to a ¹⁄₄-20 threading die, you can buy a small tap and die set at the hardware store. If you would like to avoid the threading operation, use continuous-threaded rod, which is available at most hardware stores.

Side-Board Assembly. Start with the mounting of the stiffeners ⑭ onto the dashboard ①. Mark the positions of the stiffeners and dry-clamp in place. Test the assembly by using the tie-rod to mate the dashboard to one of the side boards. When you're satisfied with the alignment, drill the counterbore and pilot holes for the four #8-by-³⁄₄-inch flathead wood screws mounting the stiffeners. Disassemble, then redo the assembly with glue, screws, and ³/₈-inch plugs. When dry, use a chisel to trim down the plugs, and then sand flush. Lay the dashboard aside for now and repeat the above process for the endgate ⑤.

Next, mark the positions of the posts ⑬ on the side boards and dry-clamp in place. Apply the screws for the posts as described for the dashboard. Each end of the side board has a keyway, formed by an inside strip ⑧ and an outside strip ⑨, to contain the end boards. Position the outside strips flush with the ends of the side board, and attach using glue and several ⁷/₈-inch brads. Then position the inside strips using a piece of ¹/₂-inch stock plus a layer of thin poster board to create a keyway with extra space for easy assembly. Dry-clamp the strips in place and test-fit the end boards in the keyways. When you're satisfied with the positions, mark the locations of the strips. Disassemble, then redo with glue and brads. Finish up by drilling the tie-rod holes in the outside keyway strips using the existing holes in the side boards as pilots.

To mount the side board assembly onto the wagon bed, first line up the side board assembly with the bed so that the outside surfaces are flush on all sides, then clamp in place. Position the side board brackets ㊺ you made earlier over the posts ⑬ so that there is equal clearance, then mark the mounting hole positions. Drill the pilot holes and fasten the brackets with #8-by-⁵/₈-inch roundhead wood screws to complete the assembly.

SEAT ASSEMBLY

The removable seat (Figure 19) adds flexibility to the wagon and makes riding more comfortable. It can be used on top of the side boards or placed directly on the wagon bed. If you plan to build the seat later, include the seat bracket notches on the bed at this time anyway; they're easier to do before assembly, and you won't have to cut into your paint job.

Retrieve the stock with the seat assembly part layouts ④, ⑥, ⑦, ⑰ and ㉖ drawn earlier. Start by ripping the two arms ④ and back ⑦ to width.

These parts have a series of angular cuts that must be done carefully to avoid error, so spend some extra time studying the exploded view drawing. First rip a 20-degree bevel on one edge of the back and arm parts using a table saw or radial arm saw. Then mark the 110-degree angles on each end of the back piece and cut to size. Band saw the curve on top of the back and lay the part aside for now.

The next step is to make the left and right arm parts. Lay the arm stock on the bench with the sharp edge of the bevel on top (this will be the inside of the arms). Mark the 110-degree angle on one part and a mirror-image angle on the remaining part. For the arms to fit correctly with the back, a 7-degree cut is added to the 110-degree cut to create a compound angle. Start at the inside corner of the arm and mark the 7-degree angle. As a final check, hold the arms up to the back and verify the direction of the angle lines. If correct, make the cuts with a table saw. Finish cutting the parts by band sawing the 2-inch radius on the ends of the arms. Smooth out the curves with a hand plane and put a half-round on the top edges of the parts using a router and ¹/₄-inch-radius roundover bit as shown in Figure 20. Follow up with 180-grit sandpaper to smooth out the half-round surfaces and at the same time maintain the distinct edge at the faces of the board.

Now fasten the arms to the back. Mark the positions for the two A screws at each end of the back (see Figure 21). To keep the joint in alignment during assembly, drill a close-fitting hole for a 1-inch brad between the two screws. Begin the assembly by clamping one of the arms in your bench vise with the joint face up. Glue, then align the back to the arm and tack in place with a brad driven partway home. Have a helper hold the free end of the back while you drill and counterbore for the #6-by-1-inch flathead wood screws. Apply the screws and ³/₈-inch plugs, and remove the brad. Then repeat the process for the other arm. When dry, trim the plugs flush with a chisel.

Lay the back assembly aside for now and cut the seat ⑥, seat brackets ㉖, and gussets ⑰ from the stock. Smooth out the curves on the brackets and rout a half-round on the seat and bracket edges as shown in the exploded view drawing. Finish the parts by cutting a ½-inch rabbet on the bottom of the brackets and do a first sanding with 180-grit sandpaper.

Mark the bracket positions onto the seat and dry-clamp them in place. Then test-fit the brackets for engagement with the notches on the wagon bed and the sideboard assembly. Adjust the brackets if necessary, then drill and counterbore for the four #6-by-1-inch flathead mounting screws. Disassemble, then redo with glue and screws. Glue the gussets ⑰ in position and the ⅜-inch plugs in the screw counterbores.

All that remains is mounting the back assembly onto the seat. To ensure accurate positioning of the mounting screws, center the back assembly on the seat, then trace the assembly's periphery with a sharp pencil to create a "footprint" (see dashed outline on seat in Figure 19). It's now an easy task to mark the positions of the #6 screws onto the "footprint" and drill the pilot holes into the seat. Once drilled, use the "footprint" to match the seat and the back, then dry-clamp in place. Turn the seat over and redrill the pilots and add the countersinks for the #6-by-1-inch flathead wood screws. Disassemble, then redo with glue and screws. When dry, finish-sand the whole assembly with 240-grit sandpaper.

RUNNERS

Sled runners were a popular accessory on the old wagons, but inevitably, being loose pieces they went their separate ways as the years passed, and today it's rare to find a wagon complete with seat and runners. Fortunately you can have this option so that your wagon can be enjoyed all year long.

To build the runner assembly (Figure 22), start with the construction of the front and rear runner supports as shown in Figure 24. Cut the four front and rear runner pieces ⑯ and ㉘ as shown in step 1. Then cut four identical nosepieces ㉗ and rout the ⅜-by-¾-inch deep grooves. Once cut, glue and

clamp the nosepieces to the runners. Now make posterboard patterns for the front and rear nosepieces (step 2) and identify. Be certain you have the nosepiece patterns correctly matched with the runner lengths, and then trace the shapes onto the blanks. Band saw to shape, then smooth out the curves with a file and sandpaper block.

The hubs ㉜ in Figure 23 are identical for the front and rear runner assemblies. Cut the four hubs to length, then carefully mark and center-punch the positions of the pivot and mounting holes. Note that the mounting holes must match up with holes in the runners, so for accuracy, drill with a ⁹⁄₃₂-inch bradpoint bit. You can get similar results by drilling a ³⁄₃₂-inch starter hole and then the ⁹⁄₃₂-inch hole with a standard bit. Use the same procedure for the ½-inch pivot holes, retracting the bit often to clear the chips so that the bit will not bind and wander. Finish up the hubs with ½-inch roundovers on each end of the part. Mark the start and finish lines for the roundovers and then rough in the curves on a bench-mounted belt sander. Alternatively, draw the radiuses on the corners and cut with a band saw. Then clean up with a file and sandpaper block.

Metal Parts. Draw a pattern for bending the gussets ㊲ and ㊳ and runner soles ㊱ and ㊴. Starting with the front runner sole, mark the first bend 11 inches from the end of a piece of ³⁄₃₂-by-¾-by-48-inch steel stock. Clamp to the bend line in a metal vise and make a sharp bend by carefully striking the stock at the bend point with a heavy (2-pound) hammer. Remove from the vise and reclamp across the width of the stock. Now, bend the 5-inch radius with your hands to avoid kinking. Check the shape against the pattern, and when you have a match, cut to length. Repeat the process for the remaining front and rear runner soles.

The gussets are the last parts to be made. Starting with the front runner gusset, mark the first bend ¾-inch from the end of a piece of ³⁄₃₂-by-¾-inch steel stock. Clamp to the line in a vise and make a sharp, roughly 45-degree bend. Lay your work on the pattern, and if acceptable, mark the second bend. Repeat for bends three and four, and cut to length. Then make the remaining gussets using the same procedure.

Mark and center-punch all of the hole positions on the gussets and the runner soles. Start with a $\frac{9}{32}$-inch bit and drill the hub mounting holes in the gussets and runner soles. Skip the holes in the gusset feet for now; they will be done during assembly. Complete the drilling by adding the clearance holes and countersinks for the seven #6-by-$\frac{1}{2}$-inch flathead sheet metal screws in each runner sole.

Runner Assembly. With either a front or rear runner assembly, test-fit a runner support with a sole, and if necessary, make corrections by bending the sole. Clamp the parts in several places, then pilot-drill and join with #6-by-$\frac{1}{2}$-inch flathead sheet metal screws. Next, join the gusset, runner sole, and hub in place with two $\frac{1}{4}$-by-2$\frac{1}{2}$-inch roundhead machine screws.

All that remains is fastening the two gusset legs to the runners. First, check the alignment of the parts and the overall height of the assembly. Make any necessary adjustments, and clamp the front leg to the runner. Then align the rear leg with the runner by placing a clamp across its width. Drill the $\frac{3}{16}$-inch mounting hole through all of the parts and countersink the sole. Unclamp and fasten the rear leg with a #8-by-1-inch flathead machine screw. Go to the front leg and mark and center-punch the hole position on the sole. Secure the leg by placing a clamp across the runner, then drill, countersink, and add the screw. Repeat the process for the remaining runners.

APPLYING THE FINISH

Detach the metal parts where practical and spray with a metal primer. Finish-sand the wooden parts, then apply a coat of sandable primer and lightly sand. Apply an enamel top coat in the color of your choice. The original wagons usually had a dark green or slate blue body, complemented by black striping and filigree, and red wheels, sled runners, and frame.

CHILD'S SLED

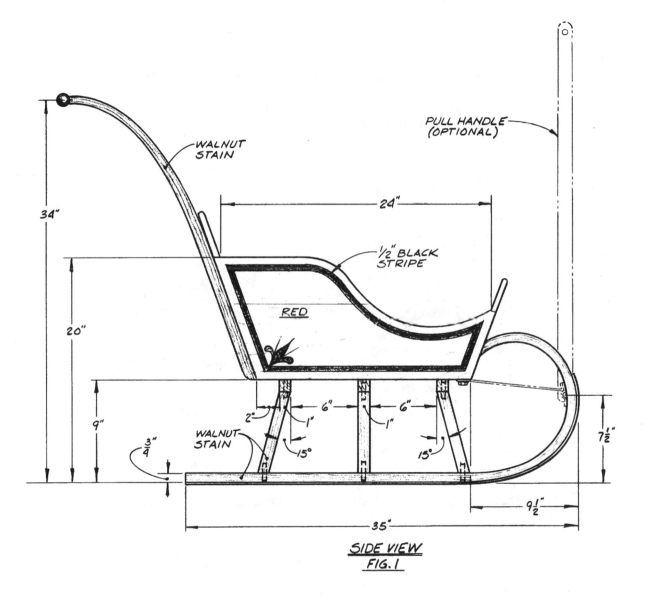

WALNUT STAIN

PULL HANDLE
(OPTIONAL)

24"

½" BLACK
STRIPE

RED

34"

20"

9"

¾"

WALNUT
STAIN

2"

1"

6"

6"

1"

15°

15°

7½"

9½"

35"

SIDE VIEW
FIG. 1

FRONT VIEW
FIG. 2

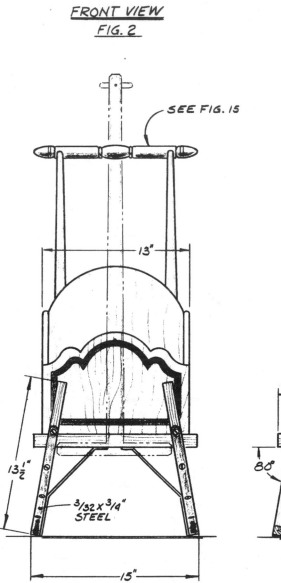

SEE FIG. 15

13"

13½"

³/₃₂ x ³/₄"
STEEL

15"

CENTER STRUT
FIG. 3

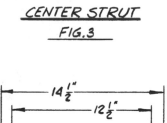

14½"

12½"

80°

¹/₁₆" x ³/₄"
STEEL

1" SQ.

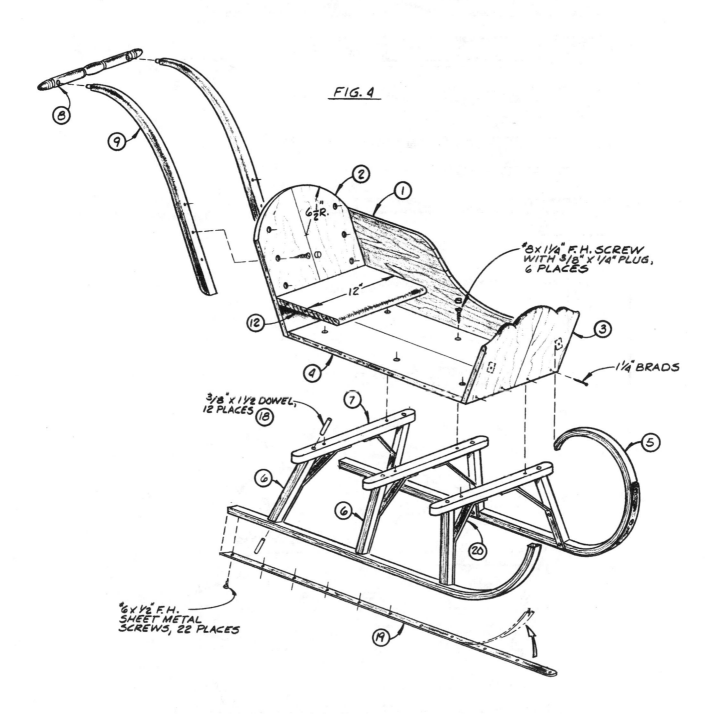

FIG. 4

⑧

⑨

2

6½" R.

①

#8 X 1¼" F.H. SCREW
WITH ⅜" X ¼" PLUG,
6 PLACES

12"

⑫

③

1¼" BRADS

④

⅜" X 1½ DOWEL,
12 PLACES ⑱

⑦

⑤

⑥

⑥

⑳

#6 X ½" F.H.
SHEET METAL
SCREWS, 22 PLACES

⑲

171

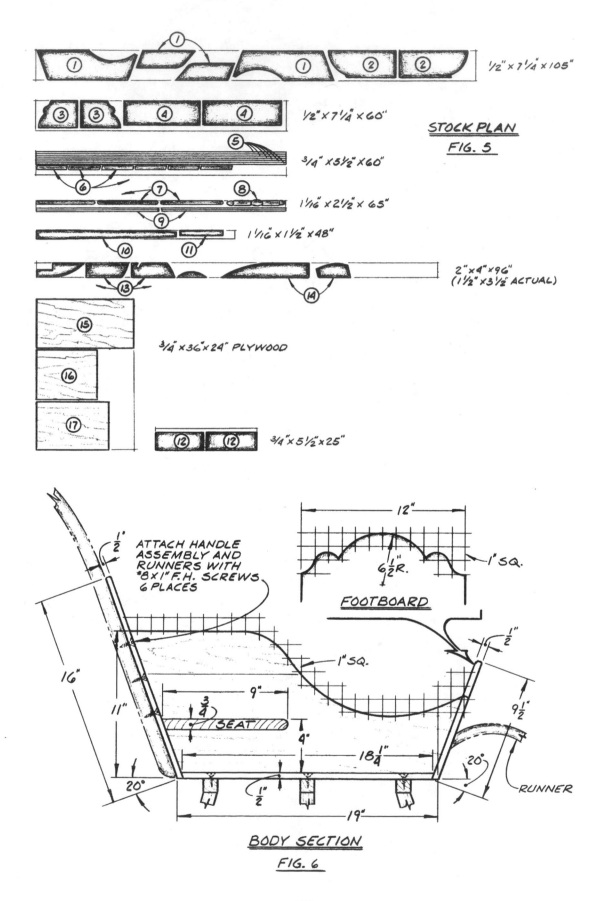

① ① ① ② ②   ½" × 7¼" × 105"

③ ③ ④ ④   ½" × 7¼" × 60"

⑤   ¾" × 5½" × 60"

⑥ ⑦ ⑧ ⑨   1 1/16" × 2½" × 65"

⑩ ⑪   1 1/16" × 1½" × 48"

⑬ ⑭   2" × 4" × 96"
(1½" × 3½" ACTUAL)

⑮ ⑯ ⑰   ¾" × 36" × 24" PLYWOOD

⑫ ⑫   ¾" × 5½" × 25"

STOCK PLAN
FIG. 5

ATTACH HANDLE
ASSEMBLY AND
RUNNERS WITH
#8 × 1" F.H. SCREWS
6 PLACES

½"

16"

11"

20"

½"

9"

¾"

SEAT

4"

18¼"

19"

12"

6½" R.

1" SQ.

FOOTBOARD

1" SQ.

½"

9½"

20"

RUNNER

BODY SECTION
FIG. 6

172

RUNNER BENDNG FORM
FIG. 7

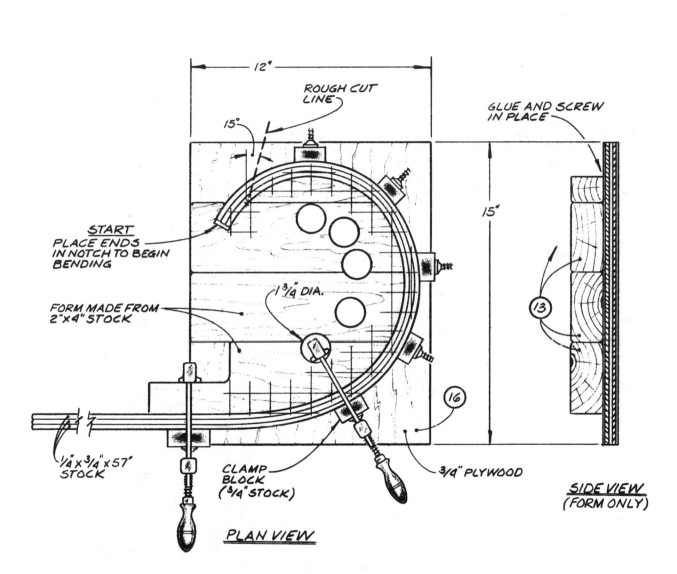

12"

ROUGH CUT LINE

15°

GLUE AND SCREW IN PLACE

15"

START
PLACE ENDS IN NOTCH TO BEGIN BENDING

1 3/4" DIA.

FORM MADE FROM 2"x4" STOCK

13

16

3/4" PLYWOOD

1/4 x 3/4" x 57" STOCK

CLAMP BLOCK (3/4" STOCK)

SIDE VIEW
(FORM ONLY)

PLAN VIEW

RUNNER STRUT ASSEMBLY JIG

FIG. 8

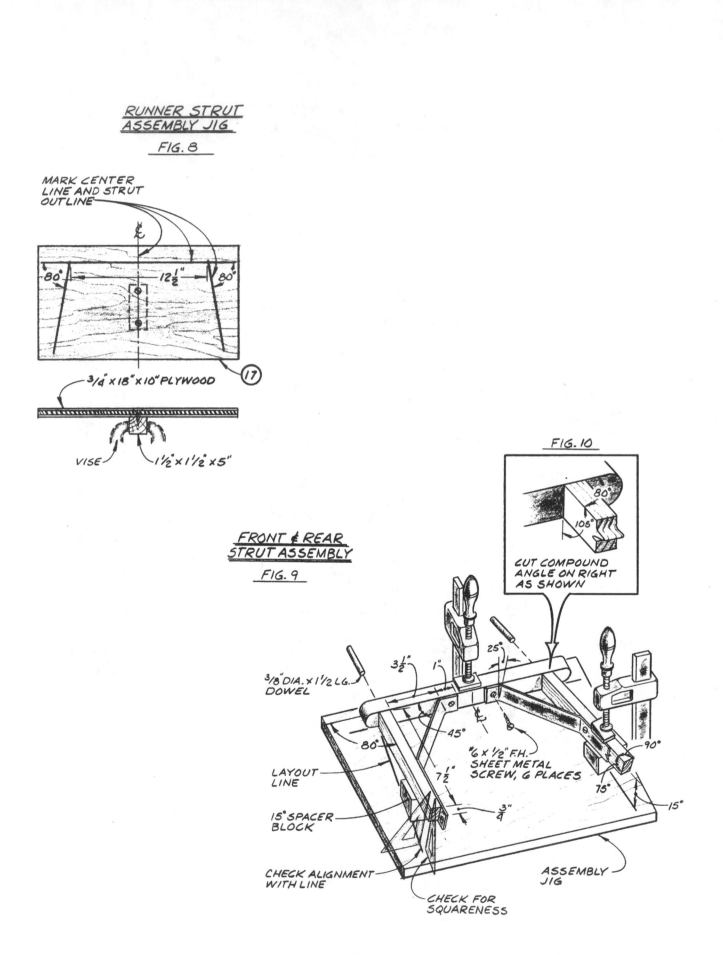

MARK CENTER LINE AND STRUT OUTLINE

℄

80°   12½"   80°

3/4" x 18" x 10" PLYWOOD

(17)

VISE   1½" x 1½" x 5"

FRONT & REAR STRUT ASSEMBLY

FIG. 9

FIG. 10

80°
105°
CUT COMPOUND ANGLE ON RIGHT AS SHOWN

3/8" DIA. x 1½" LG. DOWEL

3½"   1"   25°

45°

80°

90°

#6 x ½" F.H. SHEET METAL SCREW, 6 PLACES

LAYOUT LINE

7½"   1"

75°

15° SPACER BLOCK

3/4"

15°

CHECK ALIGNMENT WITH LINE

CHECK FOR SQUARENESS

ASSEMBLY JIG

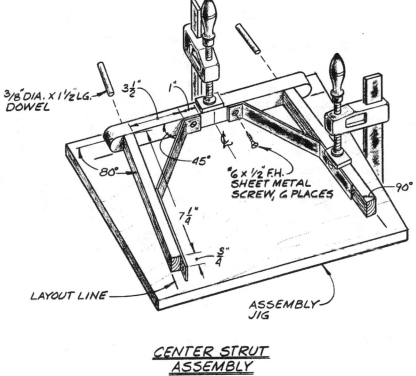

3/8"DIA. X 1½"LG.
DOWEL

3½"

1"

80°

45°

"6 x ½" F.H.
SHEET METAL
SCREW, 6 PLACES

90°

7¼"

3"
4

LAYOUT LINE

ASSEMBLY
JIG

CENTER STRUT
ASSEMBLY
FIG. 11

175

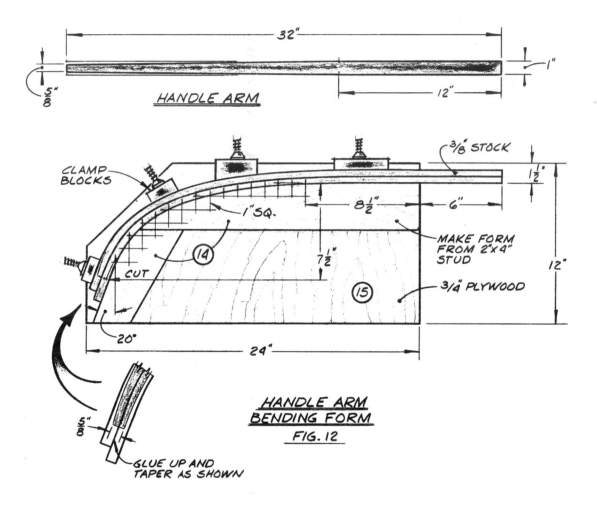

32"

1"

5/8"

HANDLE ARM

12"

CLAMP
BLOCKS

3/8" STOCK

1 1/2"

1" SQ.

8 1/2"

6"

14

7 1/2"

MAKE FORM
FROM 2"x 4"
STUD

12"

CUT

15

3/4" PLYWOOD

20"

24"

HANDLE ARM
BENDING FORM
FIG. 12

5/8"

GLUE UP AND
TAPER AS SHOWN

PULL HANDLE AND
BRACE ASSEMBLY
FIG. 13

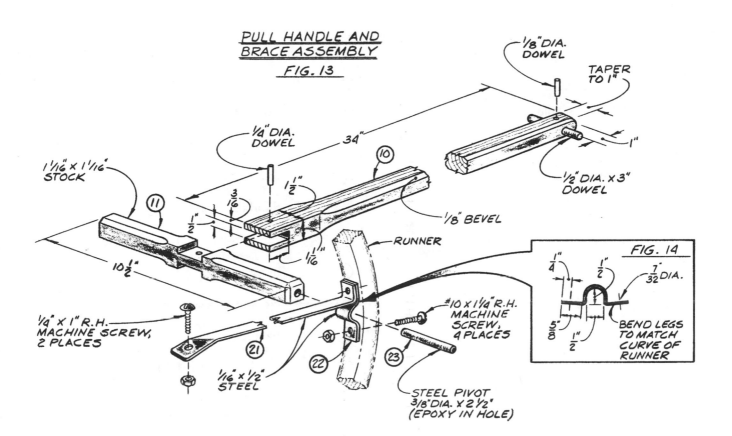

1/8" DIA. DOWEL

TAPER TO 1"

1/4" DIA. DOWEL

34"

⑩

1 1/16" X 1 1/16" STOCK

1 1/2"

3/16

1/2"

⑪

1/8" BEVEL

1/2" DIA. X 3" DOWEL

1"

1 1/16"

RUNNER

10 1/2"

1/4" X 1" R.H. MACHINE SCREW, 2 PLACES

#10 X 1 1/4" R.H. MACHINE SCREW, 4 PLACES

㉑

1/16" X 1/2" STEEL

㉒

㉓

STEEL PIVOT 3/8" DIA. X 2 1/2" (EPOXY IN HOLE)

FIG. 14

1/4"

1/2"

7/32 DIA.

5/8"

1/2"

BEND LEGS TO MATCH CURVE OF RUNNER

PUSH HANDLE
FIG. 15

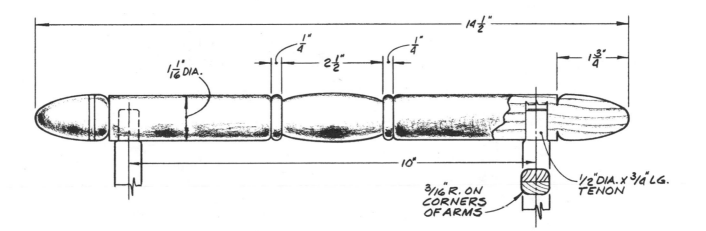

14 1/2"

1/4"

2 1/2"

1/4"

1 3/4"

1 1/16" DIA.

10"

3/16" R. ON CORNERS OF ARMS

1/2" DIA. X 3/4" LG. TENON

177

BILL OF MATERIALS

Stock (inches)	Quantity	Item	Part
$\frac{1}{2} \times 7\frac{1}{4} \times 105$ hard maple	1	①	sides (two)
		②	headboard (one)
$\frac{1}{2} \times 7\frac{1}{4} \times 60$ hard maple	1	③	footboard (one)
		④	floorboard (one)
$\frac{3}{4} \times 5\frac{1}{2} \times 60$ oak	1	⑤	runner strips (six)
		⑥	uprights (six)
$1\frac{1}{16} \times 2\frac{1}{2} \times 65$ oak	1	⑦	cross members (three)
		⑧	handle (one)
		⑨	handle arm strips (four)
$1\frac{1}{16} \times 1\frac{1}{2} \times 48$ oak	1	⑩	pull handle arm (one)
		⑪	pull handle crosspiece (one)
$\frac{3}{4} \times 5\frac{1}{2} \times 25$ hard maple	1	⑫	seat (one)
$1\frac{1}{2} \times 3\frac{1}{2} \times 96$ construction lumber	1	⑬	runner form pieces (four)
		⑭	arm form pieces (two)
$\frac{3}{4} \times 36 \times 24$ plywood	1	⑮	bending form base (one)
		⑯	runner form base (one)
		⑰	strut jig base (one)
$\frac{3}{8}$ dia. $\times 36$ maple dowel	1	⑱	strut dowels (twelve)
		–	screw plugs (twelve)
$\frac{1}{2}$ dia. $\times 36$ maple dowel	1	–	handle pull

Stock (inches)	Quantity	Item	Part
¼ dia. × 36 maple dowel	1	–	handle dowel (one)
⅛ dia. × 36 maple dowel	1	–	handle dowel (one)
³⁄₃₂ × ¾ × 48 steel	2	⑲	runner shoes (two)
¹⁄₁₆ × ¾ × 24 steel	3	⑳	strut gusset (six)
¹⁄₁₆ × ½ × 24 steel	1	㉑	handle braces (two)
		㉒	pivot brackets (two)
⅜ dia. × 12 steel	1	㉓	handle pivots (two)

Hardware and Supplies	Quantity	Description
wood screws	6	#8 × 1" F.H.
	6	#8 × 1¼" F.H.
	2	#8 × 1¼" R.H.
machine screws	4	#10 × 1¼" R.H.
	2	¼" × 1" R.H.
	4	¼" × 1¼" R.H.
nuts	4	#10
	6	¼"
washers	4	#10
	10	¼"
sheet metal screws	60	#6 × ½" F.H.

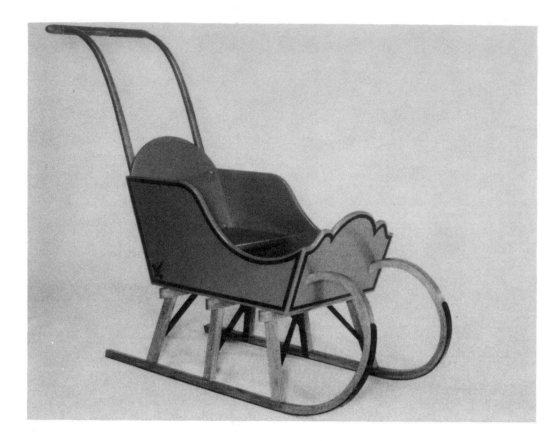

CHILD'S SLED

If you live in snow country and have small children who like the outdoors, get this project under way before the snow flies. This graceful bow runner sled is a delightful example of superior design. It can be built with a push handle for cruising roads and sidewalks or a front handle for pulling through more adventurous terrain. And it's built tough. The oak undercarriage is braced with steel brackets, and the runners have metal shoes to take on those dry patches in the snow. The 24-inch-long body can comfortably hold a four- or five-year-old child, and when he or she outgrows it, put this classic on the patio or front porch with a couple of potted plants to make a great decorative piece.

This is a reproduction of a piece that was made around the turn of the century. What makes it so attractive are the bent wood parts, which are made by steaming. This infrequently used technique is

easy to master. By making a couple of bending forms and a simple steamer, you can achieve results that will match the original sled.

Things to Know

Before you begin this project, you'll need to learn or review the techniques discussed in the following sections:
    Drawing Your Patterns
    Steam-Bending Wood
    Decorating Your Projects

PLANNING THE PROJECT
Before heading to the lumberyard, determine which handle version you want to build. All of the handle parts are included in the bill of materials, so delete

180

the stock for the version you won't be making. If you wish, you can make both handles for extra flexibility. In this case, change the mounting method for the push handle from six screws to four through bolts so that the assembly can be easily removed.

Sleds take a lot of punishment, so use good-quality hardwoods. My first choice for the body is hard maple, followed by poplar. For the under-carriage, the wood must be tough, steam-bendable, and straight-grained. Oak, ash, and hickory are equally suited to the task.

A good waterproof glue is a must for your sled, as it will be used in a wet environment. Dap phenol resorcinol glue and G-2 epoxy, both two-part mixes, are excellent choices.

PATTERNS

The first step in the project is making the patterns for the irregularly shaped pieces. Lay out the body panels and bending forms on poster board as shown in Figures 2, 6, 7, and 12. With the board widths shown in the stock plan (Figure 5), the body parts ①, ②, ③ and ④ each have to be made by joining two pieces. Cut out the patterns, then mark the board width on pattern 1 and cut in two. Cut patterns 2 and 3 in two equal pieces. Position the patterns on the stock so that there is generous space between pieces for the saw cuts. When you're satisfied with the arrangement, trace the patterns, draw the straight pieces, and number everything.

MAKING THE BODY

Cut the pieces for parts ① through ④ from the stock, ignoring the 20-degree cuts on the floorboard and end boards for now. Glue and clamp the two halves of each of the body parts. Clean off excess glue with the appropriate solvent. When dry, cross-cut the 20-degree angle on the ends of the floor-board and end boards. Smooth out the curved surfaces with a spokeshave and sandpaper block, then round over the edges with a router and 3/16-inch-radius bit. Stop the roundover 1/2-inch from each end of the side boards because of the glue joint. Give the parts a first sanding with 180-grit sandpaper.

Now test-clamp all of the body parts in posi-tion using a helper to work the clamps. If the fit looks okay, drill pilot holes for the brads using the spacing shown in the exploded view drawing. Dis-assemble, then redo with glue, clamps, and brads. Ignore the seat ⑫ for now; it can't be installed until the body has been joined to the undercarriage.

BENDING THE RUNNERS

The original sled runners were made from a single piece of 3/4-inch square stock that was steam-bent to shape. Today, high-performance glues allow the use of laminations to make bending easier without reducing strength.

First build the bending form shown in Figure 7. Start by cutting the base ⑯ to size. Use the run-ner pattern made earlier to trace the form segment pieces ⑬ onto a 2-by-4-inch construction stud (see Figure 5). Cut the segments to size, then glue and clamp to the base. Complete the form assembly by drilling the clearance holes for the clamps you intend to use. I used lightweight bar clamps, which slip nicely into a 1 3/4-inch hole. Have about ten clamps and fifteen clamp blocks available to do the job.

Now make a steamer as described under Steam-Bending Wood. Bring the steamer up to full tem-perature and insert three runner strips. It will take about thirty to forty-five minutes for the 1/4-inch-thick strips to reach their best bending condition. Use this time to prepare for the bending operation; when the strips are removed from the steamer, you will only have about fifteen seconds before they begin to lose their pliability. Have the form clamped to your benchtop, the clamps set to the correct gap, and the clamp blocks in a reachable place. Use an assistant, and discuss each move now, while the wood is steaming. When the strips are ready, remove them from the steamer and insert the ends in the starting notch. Bend the strips to the first clamp point and wait for your helper to apply a clamp, then complete the bend around the form in one steady motion. Hold in position while your helper catches up with the clamps.

Allow at least two days drying time before removing the strips from the form. If the stock appears damp between the laminations, separate the strips and run a cord between the beginning and end of the bend to hold its shape during additional drying. In preparation for gluing up the laminations, cover the contact surfaces of the form with waxed paper. Apply the glue to the mating surfaces of the strips and clamp in place. Once dry, mark the 15-degree rough cut line and remove from the form. Complete the runner by making the 15-degree rough cut (this surface will be fitted at assembly) and doing a first sanding with 180-grit sandpaper. Repeat the forming procedure for the other runner.

MAKING THE STRUTS

Strut Assembly Jig. The undercarriage has two types of strut assemblies: the center strut (Figure 11) and the front and rear struts (Figure 9), which have an additional 15-degree angle on the upright members for strength. These assemblies must be identical, so a jig is used for the construction.

Begin by cutting out the jig base ⑰ as shown in Figure 8. Attach a 1½-by-1½-by-5-inch piece of scrap wood on the bottom of the jig for mounting in a vise. Draw lines for the center of the assembly, the outside of the uprights, and the underside of the cross member. Both strut types are built to these lines to ensure a straight undercarriage.

Center Strut. Start with the construction of the center strut assembly. Cut the cross member ⑦ to 1-by-1-by-14½ inches and round over the ends. Next, cut the two uprights ⑥ to ¾-by-1-by-7¼ inches, and then add the 80-degree angle on the ¾-inch face. Mark the center of the cross member, then align on the jig as shown in Figure 9 and clamp in place. Clamp the two uprights in place and drill for the ⅜-inch-diameter-by-1½-inch dowels. Disassemble, then redo over waxed paper with glue, clamps, and dowels. Clean up excess glue with the appropriate solvent.

The steel gussets ⑳ are the last parts to make on the strut. First draw a full-size pattern of the gusset as shown in Figure 11. Note the ¾-inch gus-set dimension at the bottom of the upright. This extension is used to attach onto the runners later in the assembly. Starting with a piece of ¹⁄₁₆-by-¾-by-12-inch steel, form crisp bends with a hammer and a metal working vise. When the shape is right, remove the excess stock, then drill and countersink for the three #6×½" flathead sheet metal screws. Finish the gussets with a metal primer followed by a coat of black enamel. Lay the pair aside for mounting at final assembly.

Front and Rear Struts. First cut the two cross members ⑦ to 1 by 1 by 14½ inches, mark the center of the parts, and round over the ends. Now cut the four uprights ⑥ to ¾ by 1 by 7½ inches, and then add the 75-degree angle on the 1-inch face of each piece (see Figure 9). The other end of the upright requires a left and right compound angle on each strut. Figure 10 illustrates the angles for the right; for the left, simply reverse the 80-degree cut. Test the setup on your saw by cutting a piece of scrap; when the angles are correct, cut the final parts. Next, cut a pair of 15-degree-by-3-inch long spacer blocks to go between the jig base and the uprights. Dry-clamp the parts to the jig and check the alignment of the uprights to the layout lines. Carefully drill the ⅜-inch-diameter dowel holes in line with the uprights to avoid breaking out through the edge of the part. Disassemble, then redo over waxed paper with glue, clamps, and dowels. Clean up any excess glue.

Now make the steel gussets using the same procedure described for the center strut. The only difference in the gussets is the 1-inch bend, which is made at a 25-degree angle to align with the uprights.

MOUNTING THE RUNNERS

Put the body assembly on your bench with the bottom facing up. Draw a center line lengthwise on the floorboard and mark the positions of each strut assembly as shown in Figure 1. Locate the positions of the strut mounting screws and drill the pilot holes. Starting with one strut, align to the positioning lines and clamp in place. Flip the assembly over and drill the pilots in the strut from the top side using the previously drilled holes as a guide. Attach the strut with glue and #8-by-1¼-inch flathead screws. Repeat these steps for the second and third struts.

To fit the runners to the undercarriage, put the body on your bench with the struts facing up. Place one of the runners in position and clamp in place. Note the fit between the end of the bow and the headboard. Mark the material to be removed, then disassemble and pare to shape with a sharp chisel. After the second runner is fitted, clamp both in place and compare the symmetry of the runners from the front of the sled; the angles should be equal and the contact points on the footboard balanced. When the runners are properly in place, trace the contact area of the runners on the footboard using a sharp pencil. Remove the runners and drill a pilot hole in the top of each contact area for the #8-by-1¼-inch roundhead attachment screws. Reclamp the runners in position and drill the pilots into the runners from the inside of the footboard using the previously drilled holes as a guide. Also drill the six ⅜-inch dowel holes for attaching the runners to the uprights. Disassemble, then redo with glue, dowels, and screws at the footboard.

Now that the undercarriage is mounted to the body, the seat ⑫ can be installed. Glue up the two pieces required for the seat, and when dry, cut to size. Round over the front edge and sand the exposed surfaces with 180-grit sandpaper. Mark its location in the body, then join with glue and brads.

SHOEING THE RUNNERS

As with horses, steel shoes on a sled are an absolute necessity for durability. The shoes for these runners are made from ³⁄₃₂-by-¾-inch steel cut to a length of 42 inches. To get a snug fit with the runners, prebend the shoes before mounting. First clamp the tip of the stock (about ⅜ inch) in a metal vise so that the bending can be done parallel to the floor. Grip the free end of the stock with one hand and apply a pulling force while using the palm of your other hand to push on the point where you want

the bend to occur. For the gentle bend required, do not use a hammer. Test-fit on the runner when you think you're close. Use a grease pencil to mark any spots needing correction, and go back to the vise. When the runner fits properly, locate, drill, and countersink for the #6-by-½-inch flathead mounting screws. Finish the shoes with a metal primer followed by a coat of black enamel. Lay aside for final assembly.

PUSH HANDLE

If you decided to go with the steam bent push handle, start with the bending form shown in Figure 12. Cut the 12-by-24-by-18-inch base ⑮ from the ¾-inch plywood stock. Then cut the form pieces ⑭ from the stock and glue and screw in position. Make the handle arm parts ⑨ by ripping four pieces ⅜ by 1 by 32 inches. Measure and mark the taper on the 1-inch face, then cut to size with a band saw. Fire up the steamer, and steam one pair of arms for about forty-five minutes to an hour. Again, think everything out beforehand and use a helper. When the wood is ready, have your helper apply the first clamp at the tip. Then complete the bend and hold in position while your helper follows with the clamps. When dry, cover the form with waxed paper and glue up the parts. Mark the 7½-inch cut line at the tip of the arm, then remove from the form and trim to length.

A final shaping needs to be done on the thickness of the arms so that the handle end is ⅝-inch square at the tip. Use a hand plane for the outside of the arm and a spokeshave for the inside to create a taper through the length of the curve.

Again, using a hand plane and spokeshave, add a ³⁄₁₆-inch roundover on all of the edges except at the mounting surface. Complete the arms by filing a ½-inch-diameter-by-¾-inch tenon on the tips of the arms (see Figure 15).

The handle design in Figure 15 will be easy if you have a lathe. Alternatively, you can start with 1⅛-inch-diameter dowel stock cut to the same length and use a chisel and file to apply a simple half sphere on the ends or duplicate the design shown.

Early craftsmen used this technique to make simple turnings without a lathe. Drill the two, $1/2$-inch-diameter-by-$13/16$-inch holes for the arm tenons. Mark the hole depth on the bit using tape to prevent overdrilling. Give the pieces a first sanding with 180-grit sandpaper.

Dry-assemble the handle on the arms and clamp onto the body. To permanently mount the handle assembly, drill and countersink for the six #8-by-1-inch flathead screws. Glue the handle onto the arms and install the #8 screws with plugs. To make the handle removable, use four, 10-by-$1/4$-inch round-head machine screws with washers and nuts.

PULL HANDLE

The optional pull handle (Figure 13) is great for off-road traveling in deep snow. To take the pulling load, braces are added between the body and handle pivot. Make the pivot brackets ㉒ first, using $1/16$-by-$1/2$-inch steel as shown in Figure 14. Do the bend for the $1/2$-inch-pivot hole first, then insert a spacer block, clamp in the vise, and bend the two legs. Cut the legs to length and drill the $7/32$-inch mounting holes. Position the pivot hole of the bracket $7\,1/2$ inches from the bottom of the runners and clamp in place (see Figure 1). Mark the screw locations and drill the runners (the shoes can be drilled later).

The handle braces ㉑ are also made from $1/16$-by-$1/2$-inch stock. Start at the runner end of the part and bend a $9/16$-inch foot on the stock. Next, mount the pivot bracket on the runner with the lower screw. Set the brace foot on top of the bracket and locate the mounting hole. Drill the mounting hole with a $7/32$-inch bit, then join with the bracket using the upper screw. With the brace in place, mark the bend point and length needed at the sled body. Cut to length and make the bend at a slight skew to compensate for the runner angle. Drill a $9/32$-inch hole in the bracket and body and test-fit with the screws. Remove the brackets and braces and finish with a coat of metal primer followed by black enamel. Lay the parts aside for final assembly.

Cut the pull handle arm ⑩ and crosspiece ⑪ to their basic size. Mark the taper on each side of the handle arm and cut with a band saw. Follow up with a hand plane to smooth down the taper. Measure and mark the cut lines for the double dado joint on the handle arm and the crosspiece. Make the cutout in the handle arm first. You can use a band saw with an $1/8$-inch blade or a table saw with a tenoning jig. Cut the notches in the crosspiece and test-fit the joint. Before gluing the joint, cut the $1/8$-inch bevels on a table router or use a spokeshave and files. Glue up the joint and add the $1/4$-inch peg if you want an authentic look. Next, make the handle pull by cutting a piece of $1/2$-inch dowel stock 3 inches long. Drill the hole for the pull, then glue and peg in place. Now use a drill press to drill a $3/8$-inch hole, $1\,1/2$ inches deep on each end of the crosspiece. Cut two pivot shafts from $3/8$-inch steel rod and install into the crosspiece using epoxy.

FINISHING TOUCHES

The original sled had natural runners and push handle, and red paint on the body. Whatever color scheme you use, the finishes must be suitable for outdoor use. For my sled, I used a medium walnut stain on the runners and handle, followed by several coats of spar varnish, and painted the body with a red enamel decorated with black striping and filigree.

After the finish is thoroughly dry, attach the runner shoes, strut gussets, and pull handle brackets. If there's snow on the ground, this beauty is ready for a test run.

SUPPLIERS

The following list of suppliers can be used to help you find the tools, materials or hardware for your projects. Each company provides a mail-order service and catalog or price list for its products.

LEATHER

Tandy Leather Co.
4406 A Menaul Blvd. N.E.
Albuquerque, NM 87110
(800)821-0801

The Leather Factory
1435-E Henry Brennan Dr.
P.O. Box 26825
El Paso, TX 79926
(800)200-2499

HARDWOOD LUMBER AND VENEER

Albert Constantine and Son, Inc.
2050 Eastchester Rd.
Bronx, NY 10461
(800)223-8087

The Woodworkers' Store
4365 Willow Dr.
Medina, MN 55340-9701
(800)279-4441

Certainly Wood
11753 Big Tree Rd.
Rt. 20A
East Aurora, NY 14052
(716)655-0206

Steve Wall Lumber Co.
P.O. Box 287
Mayodan, NC 27027
(800)633-4062

SCREWS, SCREW PLUGS AND DOWELS

McFeely's
1620 Wythe Rd.
P.O. Box 11169
Lynchburg, VA 24506
(800)443-7937

TOY PARTS AND MARBLES

Misel Hardware Specialties
P.O. Box 70
Mound, MN 55364-0070
(800)441-9870

STEEL STOCK

Enco Manufacturing Co.
5000 W. Bloomingdale Ave.
Chicago, IL 60639
(800)860-3400

WOOD AND BRASS HARDWARE

Whitechapel Ltd.
3650 West Highway 22
P.O. Box 136
Wilson, WY 83014
(800)468-5534

ROUTER TABLES, ACCESSORIES AND BISCUITS

Eagle America
P.O. Box 1099
Chardon, OH 44024-1099
(800)872-2511

MLCS
P.O. Box 4053
C-19
Rydal, PA 19046
(800)533-9298

R B Industries, Inc.
1801 Vine St., P.O. Box 369
Harrisonville, MD 64701
(800)487-2623

Woodsmith Shop
2200 Grand Ave.
Des Moines IA 50312
(800)444-7002

GENERAL WOODWORKING

Garrett Wade Company, Inc.
161 Avenue of Americas
New York, NY 10013
(800)221-2942

Lee Valley Tools Ltd.
1080 Morrison Dr.
Ottawa, Ontario, Canada K2H8K7
(613)596-0350

Woodcraft
210 Wood Country Industral Park
P.O. Box 1686
Parkersburg, WV 26102-1686
(800)225-1153

Woodworker's Supply
1108 North Glenn Rd.
Casper, WY 82601
(800)645-9292